ST CHARLES OF SEZZE

ST. CHARLES OF SEZZE

AUTOBIOGRAPHY

Translated and edited by
FATHER LEONARD PEROTTI, O.F.M.

With an Introduction and Postscript by
FATHER SEVERINO GORI, O.F.M.
Editor of the Italian edition

Reproduced exactly from the Original by:

MEDIATRIX PRESS

MMXVII

ISBN: 978-1-953746-13-9

©Mediatrix Press, 2017, 2019.

Typesetting ©Mediatrix Press. All rights reserved. No part of this work may be reproduced in electronic or physical format except for quotations in journals, blogs, and classroom use.

Cum permissu Superiorum

Nihil Obstat:
JOANNES M. T. BARTON, S.T.D., L.S.S.
CENSOR DEPUTATUS

Imprimatur:
✠ E. Morrogh Bernard
VICARIUS GENERALIS
WESTMONASTERII: DIE 8a SEPTEMBRIS 1962

The Nihil obstat *and* Imprimatur *are a declaration that a book or pamphlet is considered to be free from doctrinal or moral error. It is not implied that those who have granted the* Nihil obstat *and* Imprimatur *agree with the contents, opinions or statements expressed.*

Mediatrix Press
607 E. 6th Ave
Post Falls, ID 83854

TABLE OF CONTENTS

INTRODUCTION................................ xiii

Chapter 1
    Why St. Charles Wrote the Account of His Life.... 1

Chapter 2
    His Parents 3

Chapter 3
    His Birth to Good Parents andTheir Care for Him
    5

Chapter 4
    Vocation to the Religious Life.................... 9

Chapter 5
    Restoration of Health Through Work on the Farm
    15

Chapter 6
    Fervent Spirit from God: Vow of Chastity 17

Chapter 7
    Prayer of Interior Recollection 21

Chapter 8
    Discussion of Prayer of Recollection 23

Chapter 9
    Means God Employed to Keep HimMindful of His Vocation....................................... 29

Chapter 10
    Manifestation of Intention of becoming a Lay-brother; Obstacles to Realizing this 33

Chapter 11
    OTHER OBSTACLES; THE APPEARANCE OF ST. FRANCIS AND ST. ANTHONY OF PADUA 37

Chapter 12
    Two Journeys to Rome to Be Received into the Franciscan Order 41

Chapter 13
    Difficulties Preceding His Admission 45

Chapter 14
    Departure from Rome for Nazzano 49

Chapter 15
    Clothed in the Habit of St. Francis.............. 55

Chapter 16
    Manual Work 59

Chapter 17
    Penitential Exercises 63

Chapter 18
    Interior Desolation During The Entire Year of Novitiate................... 67

Chapter 19
    Some Temptations and Illusions from the Devil .. 71

Chapter 20
    Temptation to Vainglory...................... 75

Chapter 21
    Profession of Vows............................. 77

Chapter 22
    Assignment to the Morlupo Monastery............ 83

Chapter 23
    The Cook..................................... 89

Chapter 24
    Further Points about the Time He Was Cook...... 95

Chapter 25
    Determination to Practise Rigorous Penances 99

Chapter 26
    New Guardian and Master 103

Chapter 27
    New Spiritual Director........................ 107

Chapter 28
    A Command from the Spiritual Director......... 111

Chapter 29
    Monastery at Ponticelli: Gardener 113

Chapter 30
    Cook Again: Trouble in the Kitchen 117

Chapter 31
    Renewed Temptation to Vainglory 121

Chapter 32
    Increase in the Desire for Penance............. 123

Chapter 33
Rome, Palestrina 127

Chapter 34
    Beginning of Ecstasies: Their Causes 131

Chapter 35
    Many Contests with the Demons 135

Chapter 36
    Porter: Charity to the Poor 139

Chapter 37
    Transfer to Carpineto 145

Chapter 38
    Strict Spiritual Director 149

Chapter 39
    New Confessor-office of Sacristan 153

Chapter 40
    Desire for Martyrdom 157

Chapter 41
    Spirit of Fornication 161

Chapter 42
    Appearance of the Devil in the Form
    of Our Saviour 165

Chapter 43
    Exercise of Carrying a Cross 169

Chapter 44
    Epidemic Around Carptneto 171

Chapter 45
    Devotion to St. Salvator of Horta 177

Chapter 46
    First Attempt at Writing 181

Chapter 47
    Transfer to Rome 185

Chapter 48
    Freedom from Two Serious Trials 189

Chapter 49
    Considerations on Discerning the Spirit of God and Avoiding a False Spirit 193

Chapter 50
    Printing of a Small Book of Meditations 199

Chapter 51
    Desire to Possess the Love of God 203

Chapter 52
    Appearance of St. Teresa; The Three Ways of Meditation 211

Chapter 53
    Assignment to the Monastery of St. Francis a Ripa
    215

Chapter 54
    Daily Holy Communion 219

Chapter 55
    Cure of Illness Through the Intercession of the Blessed Virgin and St. Ann 221

Chapter 56
> Revelations and Visions:
> The Holy Ghost Is His Teacher 225

Chapter 57
> Understanding of Sacred Scripture 229

Chapter 58
> The Interior Journey 233

Chapter 59
> Some Trials and Graces from Our Lord 237

Chapter 60
> Relation of Obedience and Charity to Prayer 241

Chapter 61
> Mortification of the Bodily Senses............ 249

Chapter 62
> Stay at Nocera for the Cure 255

Chapter 63
> Final Degree of Prayer:
> State of the Love of God 261

Chapter 64
> Elevations of Spirit and Interior Locutions...... 265

Chapter 65
> Further Spiritual Elevations and Interior Locutions Enjoyed in Prayer............................ 271

Chapter 66
> Special Favours Received Through the Mystery of the Nativity 277

Chapter 67
> Still Further Spiritual Elevations Dueto the Appearing of Several Saints 281

Chapter 68
> The Particular Virtues and Exercisesthe Saint Practised
> 283

Epilogue 289

POSTSCRIPT
> BY FR SEVERINO GORI, O.F.M. 291

Appendix II
> Works Written by St. Charles of Sezze 296

Appendix III
> Personages Who Had a Great Esteem for St. Charles and Sought His Help 298

APPENDIX IV
> SAINTS CONTEMPORARY WITH ST. CHARLES 299

BIBLIOGRAPHY 300

INTRODUCTION

HE author of this autobiography was not a man of letters, not a student, not of the nobility. He was a child of the country from the village of Sezze in Italy. Located on a spur of the Apennines, this little town looks out over the rich countryside and the Tyrrhenian Sea as it stretches from Anzio and Nettuno to Circeo, even as far as the mountains of Terracina.[1] He was born on 19 October 1613, of Ruggero Marchionni or Melchiori [2] and Antonia Maccioni.[3]

At school he learned "to read a little and to write poorly", as he admitted himself;[4] then he gave up elementary school to strengthen his very poor health as a shepherd in the pure air of the mountains. Later he gave his time to farming. He had a preference for the plough because he liked oxen very much, "having learned that these animals, along with donkeys, were part of so great a mystery in the cave of Bethlehem".[5]

At twenty-two he became a religious in the Order of Friars

---

[1] Sezze is well known for its Passion Plays promoted by the association of that name.

[2] In his Autobiography the Saint wrote Marchionni; Marchionni or Marchionne or Marchionno simply repeat the official register of reception of candidates into the Franciscan Order, as those think who knew the family well. On the other hand, the parish baptismal register gives the name Melchiori for the Saint and his brothers. It is a matter of two spellings of the same family name, one official (as found in the parish register), and the other popular.

[3] Antonia Maccioni or Maccione was the second wife of Ruggero; the first was Virginia di Nicola, who bore him two children, Francis and Mary. Seven were born of Antonia: John Charles (the Saint), John Baptist, John, Margaret, Joseph, Anthony, and Mary Valenza.

[4] Autobiography, 1 lr (that is, from the autograph, as are the following citations entitled Autobiography).

[5] Ibidem.

Minor and in it chose the humble state of a lay-brother, against the will of all his relatives. This meant that once he had made his year of novitiate (1653-1636), his life was given to the modest tasks that pertain to a cook, gardener, quester of alms, and sacristan. With all these duties it is clear that he had enough on his hands from morning till night without getting into books. "Brother Charles never did any studying", very emphatically declared Brother Anthony of Sezze, one of his brethren, in the process of canonization. This brother had known him intimately as a boy.[6]

The author had no background for the task of writing. Besides, in his rule, St. Francis exhorts "those who do not know letters not to be anxious to learn them but to pay attention to that which above all they are to desire and possess, which is the spirit of the Lord and his holy operation".

Nor was the mentality of his brethren at that time any more sympathetic in this matter. How, then, could this lay-brother be a writer? How could he leave behind works such as were not left us by famous writers of his and other Orders, writers who spent their lives between library and church?

It was God himself who wanted this. The Saint's more important works were willed by God, either directly or through his superiors. This is made clearer when we point out that at first the superiors were decisively against him. At least three times they forbade him to write and inflicted severe public penances on him.

Because God willed it he wrote the following: *Trattato delle tre vie della meditazione e stati della santa contemplazione*[7] ("Treatise on the Three Ways of Meditation and States of Holy

---

[6] *Summary of the Processes*, 123.

[7] Since St. Charles wrote in Italian, the titles of his works are given in that language. However, the English translation of those titles as found in parentheses will be used hereafter in this introduction, in the text itself, and in the table of contents.

Contemplation"), of which there have been three editions (Rome, 1654, 1664, 1742); *Cammino interno dell'anima* ("Interior Journey of the Soul"), (Rome, 1664); *Settinari Sacri* ("Sacred Septenaries"), (Rome, 1666); *Le grandezze delle misericordie di Dio* ("The Grandeurs of the Mercies of God"), which is his Autobiography[8] herewith published in English for the first time; *L'Esemplare del cristiano* ("The Model of the Christian"), still unedited; and *Discorsi sulla Passione di Gesù Cristo* ("Discourses on the Passion of Jesus Christ"); not to mention other smaller works.

In his *Treatise on the Three Ways*, etc., after speaking of ordinary meditation adapted to everyone, he masterfully describes—since he had personally experienced them—the different degrees of infused contemplation.

When, in the *Interior Journey of the Soul*, he comments on eighteen spiritual songs he had composed, he launches out into the highest mysticism in a manner still more detailed and original than in the *Treatise*. Here his writing reminds us of the classical works of St. Teresa of Avila and St. John of the Cross.

The *Sacred Septenaries* are a series of meditations on the seven days of creation, the three theological and four cardinal virtues, seven principal moral virtues, the seven journeys of Jesus in his Passion, the seven petitions of the Our Father, and the seven gifts of the Holy Spirit.

The Model of the Christian is the life of our Lord Jesus Christ. In his considered opinion on this work, the well-known Father Jerome of Montefortino, one of the censors, wrote: "In reading this book I must admit that my greatest wonder did not come from seeing that one who was not at all versed in the humanities could gather in his heart so great a treasure of heavenly doctrine that like examples are simply not found, however rare; but rather my wonder arises from

---

[8] This translation is made from an abridgement of "The Grandeurs of the Mercies of God".

the way the intrinsic value of this doctrine is presented. It is this, I have to confess, which surprised and deeply moved me."

The Discourses on the Passion of Jesus Christ treat of the subject preferred by the Saint, if we may so speak. It is to this subject that he gladly returns often in his other works. Devotion to the sufferings of Christ is certainly one of the more characteristic marks of his spirituality.

St. Charles of Sezze is a writer eminently ascetical, seraphically mystical; and his spiritual theology was lived—a point which increases its importance and efficacy. He teaches and comments on the principles of the interior life with examples from his own life.

This is particularly evident in this *Autobiography*, written at the order of his confessor.

He gives examples of every virtue. Fraternal love, humility, obedience, patience, purity, penance, the spirit of prayer and devotion to a heroic degree, in the midst of struggles and vicissitudes of every sort. In recounting his life it seems he set out to show us that whatever happens to us within or without, even to the smallest details, is permitted or willed by the providence of God for our good, for our sanctification.

The liveliness with which he describes the trials which strike him one after the other surprises us. Interior and exterior storms alternate, and at times they unite to form a general frontal attack to annihilate him, if possible, justifying the candid outburst coming from him spontaneously in the fifty-ninth chapter: "How strange it is! When tribulations start raining down on the servants of God, one would think that heaven's cataracts have burst forth, for like a flood they come down to drown them!" One could really use as a title for the account of his life the saying: War without quarter!, so uninterrupted is the series of battles engaged in and won by him.

For this reason the *Autobiography* stands as a very strong

refutation of the opinion, quite common among religious people, that saints are born saints, that they are privileged right from their first appearance on this earth. This is not so. Saints become saints in the usual way, due to the generous fidelity of their correspondence to divine grace. They had to fight just as we do, and more so, against their passions, the world and the devil.

Consequently we can say with St. Augustine: "If they, why not I?—If these men and women could become saints, why cannot I with the help of him who is omnipotent?"

What has been said thus far shows why this book has the style and interest of a romance, just because of its genuinely historical content and its very pure spirituality. It is not limited to mystical phenomena, like the *Autobiography* of St. Veronica Giuliani,[9] nor is it presented as a running chronicle like that of Salimbene,[10] though it has got variety and sprightliness. The Saint's whole life is treated in a lively way, as are all the religious and earthly surroundings in which he lived and worked, right to the eve of his death (1670). His Autobiography is similar to that of St. Teresa of Avila, but it deals more than hers with external events.

What pleases and edifies above all in these pages is the Spirit of God pervading and moving the Saints always. It never decreases, not even when the counterweights of tribulation, as he likes to call them, make us think of the story of Job. In every circumstance all he wants "is to let himself be carried by God".[11] That is why, strengthened by grace, he sees and masters all events in the divine light, and though the storm seems to overpower him it is just then he writes the

---

[9] Scritti di S. Veronica Giuliani, Città di Castello, 1883-5, in 3 vol., cf. vol. 1.

[10] Salimbene, *Cronaca*, edited by G. Pochettino, San Casciano, Val di Pesa, 1926.

[11] *Autobiography*, 176r, 219v, 355v, etc.

chapter on "Cheerfulness of Heart"[12] which, though a few centuries later, faithfully translates the "perfect joy" of St. Francis.

Of particular importance and interest is his description of the mystical states.[13] It is clearly apparent from this, as indeed from the whole book, that God who "playing in the world"[14] usually chooses the meanest instruments for accomplishing the masterpieces of his grace, has truly been liberal and munificent in repaying the generosity of his servant. And so, "to a flood of tribulations and temptations" he counters marvellously with a "flood" of heavenly gifts: ecstasies, visions, divine locutions, miracles, infused knowledge, discernment of hearts, spirit of prophecy, wound of love, certitude about the remission of sins, confirmation in grace!

This humble brother who "had never been a student" writes works that excite the admiration of the greatest theologians of his day. If at times "he is vilified by everyone", still his counsel is sought by the highest prelates in the Church and he is ordered by cardinals and by the Supreme Pontiff himself, Clement XI, to test the lives of outstanding persons. If he is frightfully beset by demons and by men, still he confidently asks our Lord one day in a vision, and obtains it, to be "a saint like Saint Charles Borromeo"![15]

We can, then, justly repeat with the Psalmist: "God is wonderful in his saints",[16] and with our Lord himself: "I confess to thee, O Father, Lord of heaven and earth, because thou hast hid these things from the wise and prudent, and

---

[12] *Treatise on the Three Ways, etc.*, Part III, Ch. 5.

[13] The description of these has been omitted for the most part in this abridged edition.

[14] Proverbs 8. 31.

[15] *Autobiography*, Appendix, n. 9.

[16] Psalm 67. 36.

hast revealed them to little ones."[17] With greater reason would St. Francis de Sales have passed the same judgment on the mystical doctrine of this Saint of Sezze as he did on St. Teresa of Avila: "Against her untaught wisdom the knowledge of many intellectuals appears ignorance: for all their long laborious study, they are put to the blush, so brilliantly does she describe the practice of charity. In this way, God, who presents his sovereign power on the stage of our weakness, has chosen what the world holds foolish, so as to abash the wise. (I Cor. i. 27)."[18]

A complete and critical edition of this Autobiography is in preparation. The present one is an abridgement published on the occasion of the author's canonization. The critical edition will constitute the first volume of the Opera Omnia of St. Charles of Sezze, to be edited by scholars of the Roman Province of the Friars Minor in the monastery of St. Bonaventure on the Palatine, Rome.

In this abridgement anything that would not be of interest to the readers for whom it is meant has been omitted. It is a work of selection. I have therefore omitted whole chapters, or a part of a chapter, or the secondary circumstances of some event, and sometimes even a sentence has been shortened. But what I have selected is what the Saint said in his own words, except for the correction of some evident slips of the pen,[19] or of purely grammatical errors. Thus I have followed the criterion he fixed for those to whom he gave his works for

---

[17] Matt. 11:25.

[18] This passage from St. Francis de Sales is found in his *The Love of God*, trans. Vincent Kerns, M.S.F.S., London, 1962, pp. xxix-xxx.

[19] These are frequent and at times serious because Brother Charles, as can clearly be seen from the autograph, recopied his work whenever he had a minute. This was almost always at night when he was tired and sleepy. With the exception of rare passages he did not read over again what he had recopied (cf. Introduction to the critical edition).

revision, before sending them to the printer:[20] correct grammatical mistakes without at all changing the words.[21]

Thanks, especially, to its author, the reading of this book will doubtless attain the purpose he had in mind in writing it: to manifest "the grandeur of the mercies of God in pitiable man when helped by his grace"; to show forth the grace of that God who, "looking with a sad and humble heart on us turned away from him, once more embraces and caresses us, treating us with a familiarity and love so great that never has an earthly father given the like to his children".[22]

FR SEVERINO GORI, O.F.M.
Rome, Monastery of St. Bonaventure on the Palatine,
Feast of the Visitation of the Virgin Mary, 2 July 1958.

---

[20] *Summary of the Processes*, 58. Among the revisers of the Saint's works are mentioned Don John Francis Topini, a Roman, Rector of S. Salvatore delle Coppelle, Rome, who revised the *Interior Journey* (*Summary of the Processes*, 58 and 126) and Don Nicholas Grappelli of Frosinone (Father Angelus of Naro, *Memorie intorno a fra Carlo da Sezze*, I, 55b).

[21] Father Angelus of Naro, op. cit., I, 55a; 103a-b. His corrections, however, mostly concern orthography, punctuation and word endings, rarely the tense and mood of verbs.

[22] *Autobiography*, lv.

TRANSLATOR'S FOREWORD

IT is not enough that a translation present in substance what the author had to say. There is a completeness needed, a completeness that takes into view the author's every thought, phrase and expression. The translation needs to say what he said, with—as closely as words will permit—the same candour, the same warmth, the same colour, the same simplicity, where these are found; no attempt should be made to invent them where they are lacking.

St. Charles of Sezze belonged to the seventeenth century. We ought not try to remake his manner of expression and the channel of his thought into those of the twentieth. Any such effort will surely result in hiding his personality and simple charm.

The Italian editor did well in subtitling the autobiography the Fioretti of Brother Charles. The Saint has made the story of his life read like a new chapter, as it really is, in the account of the first Franciscans as told by the ancient chroniclers.

Chapter 1
Why St. Charles Wrote the Account of His Life

Come and hear, all ye that fear God; and I will tell you what great things he hath done for my soul. Ps. 65:16.
The mercies of the Lord I will sing forever. Ps. 88: 2.

ECAUSE God and my Father confessor have commanded me to write the pitiable account of my life, it will be enough to say, and thereby include everything, that since I have been a great sinner and have received a sea of graces from His Divine Majesty,[1] everyone will clearly see the grandeur of his unlimited mercy. This will be acknowledged all the more when I am allowed later to write specifically about all my sins.

In doing what I have been commanded under holy obedience, I will stress only what is most essential from the beginning of my life to the present moment.[2] I will tell how I regained the state of grace after many falls, how our Lord gave me a religious vocation with its graces and favours, and how I made my way to perfection through it under many forms and degrees of prayer.

Our Lord who wills everything for his glory began making me experience a very powerful impulse in my soul. This urgently prompted me to write the story of my life as a source of great profit to my neighbour, and the more I advanced, the greater this desire grew.

During this time I had the chance of going outside Rome

---

[1] Consistently in his *Autobiography* St. Charles uses this expression when he speaks of God.

[2] The Saint began writing his life sometime in 1661 and completed it on 15 August 1665.

to beg for alms and to talk to a Poor Clare who had the reputation of being a great servant of God. I discussed my secret with her, so that she would pray in a special way to our Lord, asking him to show us what his will was. She told me that four months previously, not only had our Lord in a vision revealed to her my whole life and this particular prompting, but had directed her to tell me to write this autobiography since it would be a great light to the faithful.

Even with this I was not entirely satisfied, and so I did not take any action. First I wanted to place myself under obedience. When this is done, a mistake cannot be made and diabolical promptings are silenced. Sometimes the demons put these ambitions in our hearts to make us stumble and fall headlong into pride.

At this tune Father John of Sezze was a penitentiary[3] at St. John Lateran and was like a spiritual father to me. I quickly related what I had in mind and what the Poor Clare nun had said, for he knew her. After carefully thinking it over in his orderly way, he warmly ordered me to do it. Once I had this advice, I sought the opinion of my confessor, Father Anthony of Aquila. He not only commanded me to write the life, but, what is more, he gave me the merit of holy obedience.

---

[3] This term is applied to the priests who are officially appointed to hear confessions in St. Peter's Basilica, St. John Lateran, St. Mary Major and St. Paul outside-the-walls, the four Major Basilicas. For centuries priests of the Order of Friars Minor have been the penitentiaries at St. John Lateran.

Chapter 2
His Parents

Y father's name was Ruggero Marchionni, and my mother's, Antonia Maccioni. Both came from old families of Sezze, a city where respected members of the Apostolic Household lived.[1] My parents had a marvellous fear of God.

Goodness made my father like that saint, the elder Tobias, of whom Sacred Scripture says that he observed the divine law while wearing himself out in acts of worship and works of piety. Seeing myself in him I learned to acquire the devotion that was his. Very often the rosary could be seen in his hands when he was at home, away from his work, and he frequented the sacraments especially on feast days.

My father was an honest man; there was truth in his heart and on his lips as he treated everyone fairly and sincerely. That is why when conversation turned on the topic or when the occasion presented itself, he often reminded me of what is written in the two commandments of the natural law: First, "Do not do to others what you would not want done to you"; second, "Do to others what you would want done to you". To help me avoid bickering and keep a clear peace of soul he gave me this short and very useful advice: "Have eyes that do not see, ears that do not hear, and a mouth that does not talk."

From my father I learned the virtue of patience and the way to train myself in it, for he was one who seldom thought of trouble; changing events left him quite undisturbed. Not only was he calm in his dealings with those at home but still more with his neighbours. When trying situations developed

---

[1] This means that it had a part in the administration of the Papal States. In ancient times Sezze was a flourishing Latin city in the territory of the Volscians. Its fourteenth-century cathedral of Gothic-Cistercian style is artistically noteworthy.

he used to say: "God will take care of us." He had confidence in God in everything.

I cannot recount everything, but I also learned charity from my father, since he did not hold back from giving help to the unfortunate, as far as his means allowed. Among the talents His Divine Majesty had given him was a skill in setting broken and dislocated bones. Crippled people were constantly at our home, not only from Sezze itself but from other places too. For the love of God who had given him this gift, he cared for all of them.

My mother did not take a second place to my father in goodness of life and ways. She was very dedicated to prayer and devotion. She, too, received the sacraments often and visited the churches of the city. She was especially devoted to St. Francis and recited the hours which his lay-brothers say, that is the *Our Fathers*.[2] Among her virtues charity in relieving the needs of her neighbours stood forth. When she could not go alone she accompanied other good women in approaching wealthy and God-fearing people to ask alms for the poor. For a long time she tended a young man of wealth and of good family who had been wounded by an arrow, from which he finally died.

My mother took a lot of care in bringing up her children in the fear of God and in good habits, educating them more for heaven than for the perishable things of earth. After the death of my father she suffered many trials in her last years, but then her life ended peacefully.

---

[2] In the Order of Friars Minor the Rule written by St. Francis says in the third chapter: "Let the lay-brother say twenty-four Our Fathers for Matins, five for Lauds; for Prime, Terce, Sext and None, for each of these, seven; twelve for Vespers, seven for Compline." Thus, like the priests with their breviary, the brothers follow the "hours".

Chapter 3
His Birth to Good Parents and Their Care for Him

T pleased our Lord to have me first see the light of day through such good parents, and his mercy towards me started at that moment. I mention this because in line with what Jesus Christ left us in his Gospel, in the parable of the good tree bearing good fruit, it is a special grace to have parents who fear God when one considers the good education that flows from this. There are many fine examples of this in the Old and the New Testament.

According to what is found in the baptismal register, I was born on 19 October 1613, and on the 22nd of the same month was baptized and given the name John Charles.

I cannot give any account of what happened during the time I was an infant, except what my mother told me when I had grown up. When I began to walk—always a big occasion not only to parents but to everyone in the house—they used to dress me in a gray frock habit with cord and hood, out of devotion to St. Francis and St. Anthony of Padua. Then my mother kept this habit for me till I was older. And because I was always quiet and did not say much she used to remark as she looked at me standing so still, dressed in the habit: "Look at little Friar John who is now making his novitiate and does not speak!" Jokingly she called me by that name until I was three or four years old. All the while I grew up on the milk of love.

At this age, my grandmother on my mother's side, whose name was Valenza Pilorci, was very affectionate to me and wanted me to stay with her. She was then old and a very exemplary lady. Those who knew her thought very much of her rare Christian virtues as well as of her family origin. She always kept her door open to the poor; she sent no one away empty-handed who asked her for an alms. So as not to embarrass those who were ashamed of their poverty, she used to send me at night with alms for them. And because her love for me was even more tender than that of my own mother, she took very good care of me, helping and instructing me to be devout and to avoid sins.

When my years of childhood were over and I entered boyhood I went to school to learn good manners along with school subjects, and in time considered myself a man of great learning. To further this my parents sent me to different teachers since at that time there were some good ones. But I did not profit much from them since my thoughts were on games; and once I learned to read, most of my time was spent reading books about wars and battles. It was my great delight to know what heroes had done and the impressive deeds of the paladins. Even though a Jesuit Father scolded me I still did not change my ways.

Only God knows the falls I had in spite of having such a good education and being naturally inclined to devotion. All this evil came from the companions with whom I surrounded myself and from the freedom I had. As a result I am able to warn others how wrong it is to give freedom to young persons; with it they follow dangerous paths and entangle themselves in sin.

As I hurried along like a person on the way to perdition, the devil plotted a very wicked deception on me. He appeared to me in the form of our Saviour. I do not remember if I was asleep or awake, but this I can say for certain, that he had a very troubled face and showed great indignation as he told me very angrily that there was no point in my going to confession any more, for I was damned.

I believed the vision, for I was sure it had been our Lord and that out of great anger he had cancelled me from the book of eternal life because I had committed such great sins. Since my judgment was not yet mature, nor at all versed in matters like this, I did not quickly go to my confessor as I should have, but went on believing the vision for a long time. At last our Lord willed to help me and I took the matter to my mother. She told me that this vision was not really genuine but a deception of the devil to hold me tightly bound so that I would commit greater evils. This is what he aims at getting from us.

Not long after this success of the devil, our Lord willed to bring a very serious sickness upon me. The doctors gave up hope and my family wept as for one already dead. They consoled themselves by doing what they could to help me recover my health and they gave me whatever I asked for, to please me.

One day the whole family was in the room with some other persons. They put money on the bed for me, along with a few trinkets. When they noticed I was not really interested in these things they asked me if I wanted something else. I said I wanted a cross. My father heard this. Since he was also a carpenter by trade, he immediately went and made a cross about eight inches long. When he brought it in I took it with great devotion, held it tight and kissed it many times as the object I considered the most precious of all. Then it was our Lord showed how merciful he is. In virtue of his cross he gave back my health, for from then on the sickness began to leave me.

CHAPTER 4
VOCATION TO THE RELIGIOUS LIFE

THOUGH it was true that, as I said, I had wandered away from the path of the divine law at this time of my life, still I always felt called to the religious life and kept saying that I wanted to belong to the Order of Friars Minor. Besides the monastery of the Conventuals and that of the Capuchins, in my city there is a Franciscan monastery by the name of St. Mary of Grace,[1] an isolated place inspiring devotion, about a mile away from any habitation, very well suited for prayerful and mortified persons.

My parents thoroughly approved of this desire of mine and, to enable me to put it into effect, sent me to a very good school.

My father's desire was that in the religious life there would bud forth a man of letters and an excellent preacher who would sow the seed of God's word for the faithful; and my mother's longing was for me to be a priest, celebrating Mass, so that after her death I would help her to leave Purgatory through these Masses.

Though they had the very best intentions, our Lord who is the absolute master of our hearts permitted everything to turn out just the opposite. I made greater efforts to learn; still, it happened that because of something I did, my teachers gave me such a whipping and left my whole body so beaten with

---

[1] The monastery of St. Mary of Grace, built in 1567 by the Capuchins, was ceded to the Friars Minor in 1614. It was a *ritiro*, that is, a place of special seclusion and recollection. In the church one may admire the painting by Lanfranc above the main altar and the crucifix carved from wood by Fra Paolo of Val di Noto (sixteenth century). The Venerable Brother Boniface of Sezze (d. 1799) is buried there. After suppression by the Italian Government the church and monastery became used as a city cemetery.

lashes that for a time I was beside myself, like one who is out of his mind. Because of this strange turn of events all at home were very sad. They thought I would die. From that moment on I made use of this occurrence to have them take me back home, to take better care of me.

Once I had returned to my father's house like another prodigal son of the Gospel, my good parents used every means to distract me from the melancholy caused by the beating just mentioned. But I remained very depressed. Nothing gave me any pleasure though everyone did a lot for me.

There were two other younger brothers of mine who had no desire to go to school for fear of its discipline. They worked the land which we leased for vineyards and grain. My parents thought that by my joining them and seeing the countryside I would become somewhat happy; and that is how it was, for in being with my brothers I began bit by bit to get my mind off myself, partly due to their talk—very enjoyable, for we were all young—and partly at seeing the open country which I liked very much.

When the season for sowing came I felt a surge of devotion on seeing the oxen, as I recalled how these animals along with donkeys were part of the wonderful mystery of Bethlehem's cave, when Jesus Christ was born of the Virgin Mary; they kept him warm with their breath as he lay on the straw of the manger. I took very good care of them and was unusually happy at seeing them, while my contentment grew so rapidly that in a short time everything gave me joy.

Though I had forgotten all except a little that I had learned at school—for I did remember to read and write a bit, although poorly—all this was as nothing compared to my restored health.

Just as the morning-star arises, so a holy vocation began to appear in my soul. Up to that time it was hidden. Now it more ardently stirred up my love for the holy Order of St. Francis and his followers whom I considered angels from heaven. That is how they appeared to me.

At times I experienced coming from them, as it were, a most pleasant scent that was refreshing and left a holy and reverential fear as a spur to my devotion. I was even more strengthened on listening to them sing the divine praises to our Lord in the canonical hours. When they were in procession they called out the most tender names of Jesus and Mary to signal a start or a stop,[2] and when I heard their church bells ringing I stood still as though deprived of my senses.

My vocation was very sincere but I did not know the difference between the religious who are priests and say Mass, and the others who stay in the humble state and perform the lowly tasks of lay-brothers.[3] When I went to the monastery church to say my prayers I often read a small book there on the life and miracles of Blessed Salvator of Horta;[4] and besides, there was a picture of Blessed Paschal Baylon.[5] Both were outstanding for their holiness and miracles; and they were lay-brothers, who did not say Mass. On reading the life of the one and admiring the picture of the other, a great desire to imitate them in their holy actions was inflamed in me. Many

---

[2] The custom is still very strong in Sezze, and continues to exist in other villages, of calling out the most Holy Names of Jesus and Mary during processions to signal a halt or a going ahead.

[3] The brothers are engaged in manual work while the priests apply themselves to studies and the sacred ministry.

[4] Salvator of Horta in Spain (1520-67) was famous for many miracles worked in life and after death. He was beatified by Pope Paul V in 1606 and was canonized by Pope Pius XI, 17 April 1938.

[5] Paschal Baylon (1540-92) was distinguished by his devotion to Jesus in the Holy Eucharist. He was beatified by Pope Paul V in 1618 and canonized by Pope Alexander VIII on 16 October 1690. Under Leo XIII he was named the Patron of Eucharistic Associations and Congresses, 28 November 1897.

times I said to myself: "If I become a brother I want to be like these saints; I want to stay in church all night and perform very austere penances!"

Once I knew the difference between the lay-brothers and the clerics, our Lord put in my heart a determination to become a lay-brother with a great desire to be poor and to beg alms for his love.

I urged a companion of mine, Peter de Vecchi, to embrace this humble state. He had made a vow to become a Capuchin. Peter had taken an interest in me and had got me to join the Sodality[6] established by the Jesuits in their college. As a member I learned the Christian virtues, frequented the sacraments and carried out specific exercises of penance. Whenever he and I were together our thoughts about the religious life and lay-brothers and saints were of these as found in the Franciscan Order.

So that no one would bother us we used to go outside the city with others to secluded places. Peter had read a good deal and had mature judgment. He told us several stories; one of them highly praised the humility of St. Francis and the heroic reason the saint had for not wanting to say Mass. Though he was the founder of a religious Order he fell into serious doubt as to whether or not he should seek the privilege of saying Mass. While he was praying over this problem an angel appeared holding a pitcher of water as clear as crystal, and said to the saint: "Francis, as you see the water in this pitcher, so you have to be if you want to say Mass and be a priest". After hearing that, he took a lot of time and thought the vision over very well. Finally he decided that he was not worthy to say Mass.

I had determined to be a lay-brother in imitation of this

---

[6] This is the *Sodality of Mary* which the Jesuit Fathers usually erect in each of their institutions. The Jesuit college at Sezze was founded in 1590 and after a short time the church of St. Peter, consecrated in 1614, was built next to it.

saint. But I was not qualified for reception. To be a lay-brother one had to be at least twenty years old,[7] an age I had not yet reached. While I could not carry out my desire immediately, still I had no wish to go back to school and to studies for the time that still remained. I simply wanted to be in the fields with my brothers.

There was a divine plan in all this, for I got back some of my devotion through the talks and the guidance my good father gave me. He was always speaking of the things of God, as if preparing me more for the desert than for the world.

My grandmother died during this time and because she always kept her home open to the poor we may piously hope that our Lord has had mercy on her by opening the door of his pity to give her his kingdom.

Because it stirred my devotion to see oxen, as I said before, I gave them a lot of attention and I very badly wanted to have a pair for my own use. So I pressed my father very much for them. Against his own and my mother's will he gave in to me. They did not want the work I would perform with them to become a source of trial and suffering. Besides, my father would have been displeased if, in allowing this attachment to worldly goods, he had cooled my desires concerning a vocation; they would have been very upset at that, especially my mother.

So as not to be frightened by the penances performed in the religious life and by its rigours, I bolstered up my spirit by thinking of the great love that existed among the Friars, who were not foolish though the world thought they were. I also reflected that if a mother loves and cares for her children, they did this even more for each other because they had been born in Christ and united through love.

---

[7] This was prescribed by the *Constitutions* of that time. The age required for reception into the novitiate according to the present *Constitutions* is sixteen.

CHAPTER 5
RESTORATION OF HEALTH THROUGH WORK ON THE FARM

AS I said, the years of boyhood are very dangerous to the welfare of one's soul. Mine were now past and I entered the age of young manhood. Here one has a better knowledge and judgment of things and this showed in the way I went at my work of tilling the soil with the oxen. In time I became skilled at this; it was our Lord's way of letting me know that for the time being he had called me to this work, that through it I might be separated from the world, leave bad companions who are the start of ruin for young people, and begin to live a solitary life in the mountains and fields.

The wonderful happiness that came from this life as I gave myself to it was much greater than any merchant experiences in the market-place from his hankering after riches. Now I realized that I had become the richest man in the world in this humble life that held everything one could ever desire. With the help of grace a great change for the better took place in my way of living.

I liked spiritual books and so I brought some of them with me for reading. They are very useful and beneficial in every case, for helping those who have fallen to rise again, as well as for fanning into a bright flame the fire of devotion of those who want to love God in the midst of the world.

The books that helped me most were these four: *Spiritual Mirror*, written by a Franciscan, Father Angelus Elli of Milan, and treating of the beginning and the end of human life; *The Seven Trumpets Awakening the Sinner*, written also by a Franciscan, Father Bartholomew of Salutio; *The Lives of the Holy Fathers of the Desert*, by Saint Jerome and other authors; and *The Lives of the Virgins*.

Some companions of mine joined me in the same kind of

work. When we were together putting the oxen out to graze on feast days we strengthened our resolves by reading from good books. If we slept out in the open at night, as happened at certain of the busier seasons, we said the Litany of the Saints or of our Lady before going to sleep.

But what brought more joy to my heart than all else was my coming in contact with a priest of the Society of Jesus. Up till that time I had not had a regular confessor. I did not realize how necessary the direction of a spiritual father was for proceeding safely. To him we make known the stirrings of our evil inclinations and the sentiments of our heart, that he may provide us with a remedy for the one and, for the other, rules and ways of advancing. Part of the good advice he gave me was that I should become a brother in the Franciscan Order.

Although our Lord gave me very great help, such was the fickleness of my nature that every little wind of opposition still knocked me down. It was at this time that an awfully fierce temptation to impatience struck me. Farmers are usually bothered this way when the animals take a fancy and so stubbornly refuse to budge that sometimes they seem possessed. The result is that they become so impatient as to fall into the sin of blasphemy. Occasionally this temptation struck me so violently that it made me slip badly and then I felt a very great sorrow at these offences to my Lord.

Chapter 6
Fervent Spirit from God: Vow of Chastity

HEN I was about seventeen our Lord willed to grant me a very fervent resolve to abandon sin and myself entirely, and follow him who is really the way of truth and life eternal. This inflamed me completely with a love of him and with a longing to do great and generous things in his holy service.

May His Divine Majesty be pleased to give me the ability through grace to make him known, that he may become more widely hailed for his generosity since it reaches out to bestow grace even on sinners who have seriously offended him. This thought should be a great help to anyone to do penance over and over.

Here a comparison with new wine is very much to the point. Hardly is it pressed from the grapes when it begins to bubble and froth; then the force of fermentation bursts the hoops and blows the stoppers from the barrel and the wine begins to spill out on the ground; nor does this natural process end until the wine is entirely purified. Such was the first effect of my new determination. It worked within me and broke out, not in any ordinary, but in unusual and marvellous ways.

At night when I was in the fields, far away where no one could hear me, I began to pray so fervently that I marvelled at it. The Holy Spirit supplied words of love and sorrow through which my soul was greatly lifted above itself. With loving desires it yearned for the highest and infinite love of God its creator, sighing and crying for love, weeping at having offended him, awakening more than ever in my heart the call to the religions life.

To take me out of the Egypt of misery our Lord did not

will to grant me anything beyond the fervour of his Holy Spirit, something very necessary for beginners in the school of love. In the Canticle of Canticles the Holy Spirit points out this truth when the soul says to her divine Spouse: "Draw me. We will follow you eagerly."[1] So slothful is our human nature that if His Divine Majesty does not draw us to himself with the all-powerful hand of grace, in every instance we find that we are failing.

Favoured as I was by our Lord with his Spirit, my devotion to the most Blessed Virgin increased greatly. After her son I had always been devoted to her as my principal patron. Once for recreation my friends and I were with some farmers in the fields on a feast day when a book on the glories of our Lady was being read. It told of the number of people who had escaped actual danger due to different devotions they carried out in her honour. So all of us began the devotion of fasting on bread and water every Saturday—something I kept doing until I entered the religious life. But I did not stop there, for shortly afterwards I made a vow of chastity to the most Blessed Virgin which I promised to keep, with her help, for the rest of my life.

Now that I had consecrated my body and soul to our most holy Mother, a terribly great rebellion rose in me, and I found myself in a violent sea of impure and shameful temptations; so fierce and threatening were the waves of these vivid thoughts and imaginations that they well meant to swallow me alive, as the whale did poor Jonas.

For my part I did all I could, though it was little, to stand firm and not to consent to these wicked temptations. I hurried for help to the Blessed Virgin. When alone I used the discipline on myself very severely and I tried to distract these thoughts by singing praises to our Lord. Sometimes it even helped to sing popular songs, as I offered them up in my heart to the Creator.

---

[1] Cant. 1:3.

To these temptations was added the occasion of sin coming from an old woman whose home I had to pass sometimes at a very early hour in the morning and sometimes at night, always on certain errands of charity. Though this woman was very old and had no teeth so that she slurred her speech, still the devil put her in my heart so firmly that I could not find any peace day or night. He kept placing before me the occasion, place and ease of offending God; my life was very strained and unhappy because of this and I was unable to find a remedy.

But after some time had passed our Lord willed to free me from this clear-cut danger by using the means I will now relate. We can learn from it that temptations are overcome not so much through penance as through humility. Now, one of my fellow farmers was a very good-living person and I had great confidence in him. We were often in the fields together when it turned out that we had work to do in the same region.

One evening we found ourselves on top of a mountain at a kind of shelter under a rock shelf hollowed out like a grotto. We carried on a long discussion in there before dropping off to sleep. Now I do not know whether someone said, or perhaps I had read it in the *Lives of the Holy Fathers*, that discussing one's temptations is the most efficacious way of overcoming them, since this act of humility destroys the enemy's power and uncovers his lies. Just then I happened to remember this and I made up my mind to speak of the temptation to my friend as to my own confessor. I had hardly finished telling him of my problem—and he consoled me as well as he knew how—when the diabolical temptation left my heart and the evil images disappeared from my mind. From then on, seeing the woman gave me no further trouble but rather filled me with greater disgust.

From this I came to realize that the devil sometimes avails himself of any kind of object; by varying our desires he causes our bodily eyes to see what does not really exist. This teaches us, then, that we have to be on our guard always and must not trust ourselves when occasionally we need to speak to persons who are a temptation to us.

Chapter 7
Prayer of Interior Recollection

ITH the fervent spirit our Lord had generously given me I advanced greatly in the love of God. As holy King David says, it is our Lord who makes the soul run quickly in the observance of the divine law[1] and prepares it for a reform of habits. Sacred history tells of great sinners, grown old in their evil ways, who did penance and practised other virtues in such a way as to be the wonder and marvel of the people of every age, once their souls had been touched by the fire of the Holy Spirit.

So as to give me greater graces our Lord introduced me to another kind of prayer, more interior and heartfelt, in which the soul proceeds in a different way—a way in which it appears that the mystical new wine, mentioned earlier, becomes quite purified by the fervour of that prayer and reposes quietly in the vessel of the soul, giving it greater nourishment and better direction in the virtues through its clear light.

How much our Lord appreciated the mark of affection shown toward the most holy Virgin by the vow of chastity I made in her honour, will be seen in the heavenly gifts which he so graciously gave me during my lifetime. Though in my lower nature I felt a very strong rebellion, in the higher faculties I began to be more generous in letting myself experience a tasting of that inner spiritual recollection in him who lives in us. The result was that I sensed myself completely remade in a way very difficult to describe.

Our Lord started showing me his mercy in this manner when one day I was praying before a painting of the Madonna in the church of the Jesuit Fathers in Sezze, a Madonna like

---
[1] Psalm 118:32.

the one painted by St. Luke,[2] seen in St. Mary Major. The image became so fixed in my heart and mind that I was completely inflamed with love of it and well could I say with the divine Spouse in the Canticle of Canticles: "You have ravished my heart", O holy Virgin and my beloved, "with one glance of your eyes".[3]

When I went to pray before the Madonna I was changed into another person, losing thought and intellect in the divine light. Like one dazed I rested in my enjoyment and my soul was very content.

The change that came over me through this kind of prayer was very great. By the divine grace in it I was interiorly taught to do everything for God and I came to understand that without divine help our works are really nothing and have no value, even though performed with all possible exactness. When it was work-time in the fields and the oxen were hitched to the plough, I knelt down on the ground before starting, lifted my mind and my heart to God and said the *Our Father*, the *Hail Mary* and other prayers with joined hands; and in the name of God and of Jesus, as St. Paul teaches,[4] I began my work after first making the sign of the cross as I had been taught by my father.

Though I paid attention to what had to be done I took care to keep as much control over my mind as possible, and I sang praises to our Lord so as not to listen to the temptations the devil suggested.

---

[2] This is the Madonna of the Borghese Chapel in St. Mary Major at Rome, called Salus Populi Romani. It is commonly attributed to St. Luke, but artists judge it to belong to the thirteenth century.

[3] Cant. 4.:9.

[4] Col. 3:17.

Chapter 8
Discussion of Prayer of Recollection

EFORE going on to other points I will spend a little more time discussing the kind of prayer that grew in my soul with the reception of Holy Communion. Through that heavenly and super-substantial Bread which is the very life of the soul I came to conceive a devotion to the Passion of our Lord, along with other deep sentiments.

I went to confession more frequently than I had done at first, to the Jesuit Father whom I mentioned previously, and to the Franciscans. By frequenting this sacrament I sensed within me a great lightness that disposed my soul to run to God as to its centre. This made my confessions easier each time. As a result of the short time in between confessions, my faults were fewer, they were fresher to my memory, and I was more content than when I put off this sacrament because then it was more confusion than confession.

Though I had not yet been entirely stripped of my old defects—their roots had yet to be pulled out—still with its almighty power the goodness of God worked with the most efficacious means of his grace and lifted me entirely outside them as he had done with glorious St. Augustine. As I think of this now I cannot hold back the tears. In the meantime, His Divine Majesty increased this heavenly contemplation when I received him in the most Blessed Sacrament of the Eucharist from the hands of the priest. And it is not a matter of imagining wonders, for the heavenly King was there in my soul as on a throne. His name is a spreading perfume,[1] ravishing hearts with its scent and drawing to itself the interior and the exterior senses of the soul in a very sweet and gentle way. Its fragrance lifted me above myself and drew me

---
[1] Cant. 1:2.

away from everything created as it melted me in love. I seemed to be no longer on earth but in heaven.

I grew meek and quiet, patient in suffering, with a longing to suffer martyrdom for the love of that Lord who died for me and whom I had received into my soul. When I was urged by my friends and my brothers to join in some recreation, I told them after the usual time had been spent at it: "This is all I can do today, for I have received the most Holy Sacrament!"

We can now discuss what are the delights and experiences coming to one who worthily receives the most holy Body of our Lord. They are many; and among the more outstanding, one of them is the remembrance of our Lord's remarkable Passion. This is the life of the soul and the key for entering heaven to enjoy its imperishable fruit, the vision of God.

Out of an intense devotion to the Passion I began fasting and taking the discipline on Fridays, the day the price of our salvation had been paid. Whenever I was living outside in the fields with other farmers I used to get up at night during the best hours of sleep and go off where I could not be seen; there I scourged myself, all the while thinking of the terribly cruel lashes that were given Jesus Christ at the pillar, so many and so merciless that they covered his entire body and did not spare one spot. When this devotion was over I went back to my companions and as best I could tried to sleep and pass the rest of the night.

Any man who has ever been wounded by the Holy Spirit and felt the effects of his love, is ready for anything. Things he once found difficult become easy; what was once distasteful is soon made pleasant; and this flesh most of us are so prone to pamper, becomes for him a thing to be mortified by prayer, penance and discipline. In all things he praises God who continually works in us by his grace.

When I began to taste God in prayer and in the reception of the most Blessed Sacrament, my heart was set on fire more intensely and I was moved with pity and compassion towards the poor. I was kind toward everyone and I tried to take care of everyone's needs without considering that thereby I would have to do without something myself. Our Lord joined faith and hope to my charity and I firmly believed and trusted that he would be my sure provider. Among the favours I asked of him, one was that he would have me bring back as many provisions as were needed to support our home and to help the poor.

I never hid from the poor so as to keep from giving them something, and when I went outside in the morning they were waiting where I had to pass. One morning during a very bad year there were more than usual. They all stood round me, as the poor do when they think that they are going to fare pretty well. A woman happened to come along and when she saw so many people around me—the majority were children—she got angry and scolded them. She told them they were to let me go about my way and not bother me. I turned and said to her kindly: "Lady, one does not shout at the poor of Jesus Christ, nor send them off, for they represent the Lord himself who became poor for us!"

I once refused an act of charity to a poor man since I hated him for his detestable office of inspecting the fields, and because I believe that some time before he had displeased me—I do not remember just how. Perhaps he had made me very angry. Anyway, hardly had he gone away when such remorse of conscience came over me that I could not regain my peace of mind, because in this duty of being charitable for the love of God we are not to look to the quality of people. Poverty often causes a man out of necessity to lay aside his own self-respect, even though his relatives are thereby disgraced.

The charity I showed the poor began to cause those at home to have some suspicions about me. They thought that maybe I had been stealing things, especially because, before going out to the poor, I used to go to the principal church in

Sezze, St. Mary, at a very early hour for my devotions. I prayed there before a very old crucifix[2] in the first chapel on the left. When I returned home I sensed my mother looking at me. But when they were sure of what I was doing they finally left me in peace without ever again saying anything.

The virtue of obedience was highly ennobled by Christ our Saviour in his exercise of this virtue, and wishing to exalt it to the highest place the Holy Spirit in Sacred Scripture says that obedience is better than sacrifice.[3] To teach me to lose myself and to be entirely his, our good Lord got me to walk along the path of this virtue by the light of his grace.

As my teacher here, our Lord gave me my father who was very partial to this virtue and saw in it the perfection of every Christian. When I talked to him about it he would burst out in these words: "My son, I would rather see you truly obedient than apparently devout. You know, obedience is better than sacrifice, because obedience is the great sacrifice one makes of one's very self to God." When my father called for obedience he wanted me to carry it out with faith and hope, without any discussion or objection, though at times it would seem hard.

He explained this better by some examples: "Take this case: suppose I told you to sow seed on the bare rock. Though it would have no way of getting water and of striking root, still if you did this with faith and without any hesitation I would put my trust in God to send you a fine crop of grain, more than if you had put the seed in fertile and good ground. You would be like St. Isidore, another keeper of oxen, who struck a rock with the stick he was carrying and water came out of it for himself and his employer in the fields when they were parched with thirst." This is the way he went along, as he quoted examples from the saints.

---

[2] It is still venerated there.

[3] 1 Kings 15:22.

I enjoyed solitude very much. When I could go somewhere by myself and be able to carry out my devotions, then I was happy. For this reason I was given the name of being unsociable among the farmers who knew me. Sometimes the friendlier of them made a joke of it, especially when they saw me with a rosary in my hands. This was for old people who have one foot in the grave, they said; not for healthy and strong young people, like myself, in the prime of life.

On one occasion I tried in a kind way to correct one of these young men to make him fear God and give up his evil life. I made him think of the pains of hell and the terrible punishments the Divine Majesty metes out to sinners. His reply was an evil one, more heretical than Christian: "If the soul is a spirit, as you say, and the devil also is a spirit, then if at the moment of death he causes my soul to be taken, the damage will be his!" I answered that horrible blasphemy by saying that, because of his evil life, it would not be as he so wrongly thought; for, though the soul is a spirit, still it comes under the justice of God as its Creator and Lord; and though the devils have rebelled from God they still are the ministers of his justice. The soul that lives evilly and, worst of all, dies to grace, will be judged willingly or unwillingly by him, the Eternal Judge, according to his works. After this judgment, the body will also be judged.

Chapter 9
Means God Employed to Keep Him Mindful of His Vocation

N returning to a discussion of my vocation to the religious life, we will see as though in a painting the likeness of a true father who loves his son sincerely and knows how to deal with him, now with kindness, now with strictness.

As the time kept coming closer for me to become a religious of St. Francis, I think I was somewhat coolly neglectful of my original desire, at the very moment when I should have been more eager to answer the call of our Lord. But the hand of the Master, who sees everything, struck me with a long and very dangerous sickness. I suffered constant fever and very terrible stomach pains.

Our weakness is so great that, if our Lord leaves us even for a moment, we quickly return to our first undisciplined ways. This verifies what the Holy Spirit says, that if the Lord does not guard the city of our soul, in vain do we take care of it.[1]

Some months had already passed during which I lay in bed without strength and without any devotion, plagued by evil. One day death appeared to me in the form we usually see in paintings, a skeleton with a scythe in its hands. Without saying a word, with a dark and threatening face it came terribly near me. It seemed to come so close as to take away my life with a powerful stroke of the scythe it was holding; yet it did not touch me in the least.

I was terrified and I called out loudly for help, as anyone does who suddenly sees he is attacked by enemies. At that very moment my soul was pierced, in the same way as the

---

[1] Psalm 126. 1.

soul of St. Paul, by a light that enlightened me completely. I understood what His Divine Majesty wanted of me: I was to keep my promise. I began to pray: "Yes, O Lord, I do want to be a religious!" I repeated these words many times over. My sickness was cured.

I went back to my ordinary work, very withdrawn to myself, very favoured with special heavenly illuminations from God. But I still did not form any resolution. And yet our Lord did not stop knocking at the door of my heart; he wanted me for what he had created me and he would make me understand his divine will by human means.

As I said before, I had some oxen that I used in my work. My affection for them was very great, not only because of my devotion to the crib but also because to me they were wonderful and gentle. One of them was a young one which I had trained to the plough. In every way I liked him more than all the others and, as we say, he could do everything but talk. Sometimes it happened at night that he became separated from the others. All I had to do was call his name and as soon as he heard me he would come running to me, lowing. For me this was a great consolation and it made me praise God in his creatures.

Now one of these oxen was given a sudden fright. Since he was hitched to the plough with others they all ran off together in their fear and did themselves a lot of damage; their feet were badly injured. After this I sensed a change inside me, as if someone had spoken in my soul and said: "Our Lord does not want you in the world any longer!"

The next time the oxen ran away I was put in the greatest danger to my life. I was hitching them to the plough, and was in front of them putting the finishing touches when suddenly they took fright and ran off at a great speed. For about a stone's throw they dragged me away on my back, and then I lay there on the ground. When I saw the danger I was in, I loudly called out the names of Jesus and Mary. The iron plough, which must surely have hit and killed me, was miraculously raised and passed over me without even grazing me. I got up and kneeling on the ground thanked the Lord God and the most Blessed Virgin for having freed me from such evident danger and again I promised to enter religion.

I was twenty-one when this mishap occurred and, if I am not mistaken, it was the month of October. The months passed right up to February of the next year. I still had the desire to be a religious but took no steps towards carrying it out. I really did not know the reason for my being so irresolute; and I speak the truth that, the more negligent I was, the greater was the help from God and his Blessed Mother. That shows how anxious they are to help those who love them.

One morning when I reached a certain place called *Cona dell'unera*[2] as I was going to the fields with my oxen, saying my prayers, the Queen of Heaven appeared to me. She said: "My son, if you want to keep all your promises to me, then become a religious as soon as possible".

At this apparition I was as if out of myself for a long time, full of unspeakable consolation, burning with the love of God, and determined to leave the world.

---

[2] He is alluding to ruins of Roman arch construction which exist in many places around Sezze. Most likely he wishes to indicate the ruins at the foot of Mt Antoniano, at the right of which one goes towards Rome along the consular road, and which are called *Cona dell'uva nera* (bunches of dark grapes). Perhaps *Cona dell'unera* comes from that.

CHAPTER 10
MANIFESTATION OF INTENTION OF BECOMING A LAY-BROTHER; OBSTACLES TO REALIZING THIS

I OFTEN went to the monastery of the Franciscan Fathers; my mother would take me there to go to confession. She highly praised their goodness and their ability as confessors and wanted me to tell my sins to them.

One morning I was going to confession, along with other people, to Father Bonaventure of Rome, a very prudent man. I took the time on this occasion to tell him what I was thinking of doing, namely, becoming a religious, and that I wanted to be a lay-brother. This good Father showed how very wise and practical he was for he did not give me his approval for this right away; nor did he leave me very happy when he said that this was something I was to recommend to God, something I had to examine very closely so that later I would not have any regrets.

Afterwards I talked about this to one of the lay-brothers who used to go on the quest for alms, Brother Angelus of Sezze. He had guided many another young man into his Order.[1] After a short talk with him he told me that the time had not yet come for me, but that he would commend me to God.

I had no rest till I made the entire matter known to those at home, my father, my mother and my brothers. With all the affection that bound them closely together and that still ruled our home, they gave in to me with our Lord's help, since they did not want to keep me from this worthy goal. There was one exception, my brother John Baptist, whom I loved more than the others. I calmed him when I said that I had taken a

---

[1] The Order of Friars Minor.

vow and that is why I was not able to do less. He should be patient, then, since each of us has to search out his own path on which to save his soul. We are not born for this world but to reign with God.

Once I knew my parents had given in to my wishes I went back to school again, this time in charge of the curate of our parish of St. Lawrence. His name was Don Joseph Piacentino, a very serious man, theologian and preacher. He began an inquiry to see what I had in mind. I told him that it was my determination to become a religious of St. Francis, of the community of our Lady of Grace, but that I wanted to be a lay-brother, not a priest. He praised this resolution of mine very much and as if amazed and in wonderment at it, he broke out in these words which he said in Latin—words, I am told, of St. Augustine: "The ignorant and the unlettered come and carry off paradise, and we, with our learning, go off to hell!"[2] He said he was glad I was going to school but that I should learn only what is related to the life of a lay religious, such as about serving Mass, the works of mercy, the sacraments of the Church, along with other devotions and virtues that are practised in religion.

Once my purpose of being a lay-brother became known, I was the centre of some disturbance among my parents and the others at home for, as I said, my mother and father wanted me to be a priest. However, since my wonderful old father was very happy as long as he saw all his children busy in serving God, he gave in peacefully.

Those who gave me trouble on this point were my relatives; some of them were unyielding. They had no light guiding them except for seeing the vanities of the world. Poor people! They thought it a great degradation and of little honour to my kin for me to embrace the humble state of a lay religious. My answer to them was that there were lay-brothers of St. Francis from the better families of Sezze and

---

[2] Confessions, 8, 8.

that in the Order of the same St. Francis there were great saints who out of humility did not want to say Mass, in imitation of their holy Founder; besides, it was not necessary that all the members of a religious society be priests.

Really, what caused me even greater anxiety than this was that someone in the family made my resolve known to one of my uncles, my mother's brother, Don Francis Maccioni. He was a canon in the cathedral at Sezze, and at Rome was in the court of Anthony Cardinal Barberini.[3] He let it be known that he would not be happy at all at my becoming a religious.

That made me very worried when I heard it. I had put my hope in him as being the person who was in a position to help me more than anyone else. Now that I saw my way was cut off, there was no more peace in my heart. Most of my nights were spent in tears and sighs.

In order the better to shake my resolve this canon let it be made known through a very devout and influential person that he would sign his canonry over to me just as soon as I changed my mind. But our Lord God gave me such constancy and such a distaste for worldly things that I would not have allowed myself to give in if they had offered me a kingdom. I said to myself: "Tell me, John Charles, if the proposal were made to you, would you prefer being a Cardinal of Holy Church or a poor friar of St. Francis?" The answer was: "I would give up the cardinalate without any hesitation and willingly embrace the holy poverty of religion".

There was another less dangerous attack. It was this: at the same time as I was trying to put this inspiration from God into effect, one of my very close friends began talking one day very cleverly about marriage, right in the middle of a conversation about ordinary things. Actually he was bluntly suggesting that I should marry. I would not let him say another word. I was very upset and said: "Don't ever talk to

---

[3] Anthony Barberini, senior (1569-1646), Capuchin, was created a cardinal in 1624 by Pope Urban VIII, his brother.

me again about what you just mentioned!" The poor fellow became mute at what I had said and left without saying a word.

Chapter 11
Other Obstacles; the Appearance of St. Francis and St. Anthony of Padua

O sooner was one set of obstacles out of the way when others appeared without giving me a breathing-spell. On this sea of disturbances I was like a ship without rigging, without oars and sails, battered by the storm, guided only by the providence and counsel of God. When he wants us to accomplish great and important things, it is not his way to allow everything to go along very gently and smoothly; rather to ensure that we embrace these tasks with great determination, he permits difficulties to arise so that what we do will be well grounded on the rock of virtue.

With God's permission it happened that I fell sick again, together with my brother who was next to me in age. I thought much of this brother and he returned this esteem. As I said before, his name was John Baptist. He was nineteen years of age, very honest and of pleasing speech and manners.

My sickness did not amount to much but John Baptist kept getting worse all the time. The last sacraments, the most Holy Eucharist and Extreme Unction, were given to him. One day, when he was so sick that we thought he was surely going to die, I was with my grief-stricken mother in another room getting ready the clothes that would be needed for the deceased—there really was no longer any doubt that we would be burying him. In the midst of many tears my mother began speaking sadly to me: "My son, if your brother dies, you will not be able to become a religious since there is no one else to help at home. Your father is now an old man, your other three brothers and two sisters are very young; think how it would be without the two of you!" Though naturally I grieved at seeing my mother so sorrowful at the expected loss of a very dear son, what she had said to me did not sadden me very much. I answered her gently and urged her to have confidence in the most Blessed Virgin, for she would help us in this great trial just as she had done with our little brother who at birth was very ugly and after a few days became so pretty and lovable that we were all amazed. I went on like that consoling her, and then I asked her if I could not please leave the house for a while and I would come back right away.

She said I might and I went off to visit an image of the Madonna that is about half a mile outside the city, along the road just as it comes down the mountain and enters the valley, and is called *Cona dell'appoggio*. I had a special devotion to this image.[1] Whenever I passed it I said some prayers and saluted it with the *Ave Maria*, the *Salve Regina*, and the *Pater Noster* for the Infant Jesus our Lady held in her arms.

I knelt before the Madonna and with deep affection I pleaded for the health of my brother. With great faith I said: "Most Holy Mother, I will not leave here until you make him well for me so that I can keep my promise to you". With uplifted soul and peaceful mind I stayed there a long time until I understood interiorly that I had obtained the favour. I left the sacred image with great trust and went back home. There I found my brother very much better and in a short time he recovered his health with the help of our Lord.

One night during these difficulties I had a vision. It seemed that I found myself in a deep place. It was about two stones' throws in depth, its opening was round and as wide as the place was deep, but it narrowed at the bottom; it was full of brambles and of such interwoven thorn-bushes that I was unable to walk at all. There I was, right in the middle, even

---

[1] To the present day this image is called the *Madonna dell'appoggio* (The Madonna of Help), and is venerated in a little church—now sadly ruined by the war—situated along the old mule-road that goes from the town to the plain.

though I had tried hard to get out for a long time. There was no way for me to take even one step ahead.

I was covered with sweat due to my efforts and was terribly upset. I did not know what I was going to do. All of a sudden I saw coming towards me two Friars Minor of venerable appearance, wearing the habit and cord and the clerical tonsure, as the Friars do yet at St. Francis a Ripa in Rome. They spoke to me with very great gentleness and friendliness: "Son, what are you doing here, so out of breath?" I said: "Fathers, here I am trying to get out of this place, and I cannot!" Then, full of charity, they consoled me like loving fathers. At the same time they took me by the hand, one at my right and one at my left, and in the twinkling of an eye lifted me out of the pit and put me down on a wonderful plain.

Many times I told this to different spiritual directors and close friends of God. They all said that these two Friars were St. Francis and St. Anthony of Padua, and that this was a sign as to the Order I should enter.

Once I had to go from one piece of our land to another, both of which were near the road to Rome. After hitching up the oxen and plough I had hardly started to walk when two Franciscans overtook me. From what they told me they were going to Rome. According to their holy custom they greeted me with *"Deo gratias! "* and *"Praised be Jesus Christ! "* I returned their greeting and was very happy to see them. We walked along together and as they were full of love and zeal for the salvation of souls they began to converse very intimately with me about the kingdom of God.

When I saw their humility and detachment from the world I confided in them about my resolution to enter their Order, hoping they would give me some information on what I had to do. They gladly did so; they told me to go to the monastery of St. Francis a Ripa in Rome for the octave of Easter which was not very far off. The reception of novices would take place then, and I would surely be received.

We talked about other things in the short time that we walked along together. They gave me some saintly instructions as to how to live in a spiritual way. Everything they said I stored up in my heart, for to me I had found two angels from paradise. From the moment that I had seen them I knew within my very soul that it was not by chance that I met these religious, but by a special providence of God.

One thing made me very sure of this. The oxen that I had with me were very timid, as I have noted before, and would run away on seeing anything unusual. This time they went along in front of these friends of God quietly and meekly, as though they knew they were safe from any harm, until we reached where I had to stop. There my friends saluted me cordially and left me in peace, consoled with the blessing of God.

Chapter 12
Two Journeys to Rome to Be Received into the Franciscan Order

HE first time I went to Rome I did so with the consent of my whole family during the Holy Year of Urban VIII, of happy memory.[1] This time one of my elder brothers, who had to go to Nettuno, gladly accompanied me a good distance of the way. He stayed with me until we met a man from Sermoneta who was also going to Rome. After giving me some money my brother left me with him, begging him to see that I did not meet any harm during the journey and to instruct me in what I had to do.

This person graciously offered his services; he promised my brother to do this for me, especially when he learned that I was going into the religious life there. He was very Christian and pleasant in his ways, and once we were in Rome he took me to a hotel near St. Andrew della Valle, called The Paradise.[2] He introduced me to the manager whose name was Signor Bernardino. Then with marked cordiality towards me he left to see to his own affairs.

The first thing I did was to find out where my priest uncle lived. I went to see him, to tell him why I had come to Rome. He received me kindly and gave in easily to my becoming a religious, but a clerical religious. He emphasized the reasons why I should not enter the state of the lay-brothers, and said I would not be able to persevere in it because of the many difficulties concerning obedience.

Without settling anything on this he himself took me to St.

---

[1] This was the Holy Year of 1625.

[2] The hotel still stands between the Piazza del Paradiso and the Largo dei Chiavari.

Francis a Ripa[3] and spoke to the Fathers about my intentions. But, since the reception of novices was not taking place at that time, they dismissed me kindly and promised that when the next time for reception came around they would advise me by letter and would be glad to put me in the novitiate.

With this good news I went back to Sezze a very happy person. When some of the town loafers, including a few close friends, saw me, they laughed and made a joke of what I wanted to do.

I was back in Sezze only a short time when word reached me from Rome that I should come there immediately, as a reception of novices was to be held. I told this news to my family. Before she would let me go, my mother wanted me to stay home another day so that I could have a meal with my father, brothers and sisters on the morning of my departure. It was like an Easter Day for us!

While we were at table, towards the end of the meal my mother, good woman that she was, could not restrain her affection and began to show by what she said how much she felt my leave-taking. "Son, I think this will be the last time we will eat together and I do not know if I will see you again. So I beg you, for the love that I have always had for you, to leave something with me, something that you usually carry with you, to make me remember you on seeing it; in that way I will be consoled in my grief!"

---

[3] The monastery of St. Francis a Ripa was built at the place where St. Francis stayed on coming to Rome and where his cell is still preserved. Through a Bull of Pope Gregory IX in 1229, the monastery was given to the Order of Friars Minor. According to Father Luke Wadding, famous Franciscan historian, the Friars lived there from the year 1212.

In the church repose the bodies of St. Charles of Sezze, Blessed Ludovica Albertoni, and the Venerable Innocent of Chiusi, Bartholomew of Salutio, Francis of Cisterna, and others. Next to the cell of St. Francis there has been arranged an interesting *Museum of St. Charles of Sezze.*

The Minister Provincial to whom John Charles went for admission to the Franciscan Order lived there.

I controlled myself during this sad moment, with the help of God. I wanted to comfort her and so with a smile told her that I was going only to be admitted and that I would come back before being clothed in the habit. If I remember correctly, I took my rosary and gave it to her.

When the day came for leaving, a Thursday, it turned out that Peter de Vecchi also had to go to Rome to be received into the Capuchins, in fulfilment of a vow he had taken. Because we were very close companions we decided to go together. We left for Rome at a very early hour and there we stopped at the same hotel in the Piazza del Paradiso where I had stayed the first time.

After getting something to eat we went off anxiously to see my uncle, Don Francis Maccioni. We found him at home and he said he had settled everything with the Fathers at St. Francis a Ripa. I was to be received; I should certainly go there confidently and was to inform him at once if any difficulty arose. Then he took us to the hotel where we were staying and spoke to the manager, Signor Bernardino, a good friend of his. He asked him to look after me and deposited with him as much money as I needed. Then he left me there, once again telling me to go to St. Francis in the morning.

Who does not wonder at the profound judgments of God and at the way he manages all things? The one person who, perhaps out of natural love, had been so against my choice as to make me weep many times, was now completely changed and was taking care of my affairs as though they were his own! What the Holy Spirit says in Sacred Scripture is certainly true, that the man who trusts in God will not be confounded.[4]

---

[4] Romans 10:11.

Chapter 13
Difficulties Preceding His Admission

HE following morning my friend and I went to St. Francis a Ripa. After greeting the Minister Provincial who at that time was Father John Baptist of San Marcello, some of the religious later took me to the room of the same Father where the admission of novices was in progress. There I saw four Fathers Definitors[1] with the Father Provincial. They gave me an oral examination according to the Constitutions of their Order. Then they wanted to see my papers, meaning the certificate of my baptism and of the municipality where I lived. One particular was missing in these papers, an attestation to the effect that I did not belong to the Jewish race.[2]

A disagreement started among the Definitors over this deficiency. On this point one of them strongly opposed the others, and his word was so respected that all agreed to accept another document if signed by a notary. The very Father who had taken my part so much drew up a paper containing what I needed. Then he told me where the notary's office was, near the Ponte Sisto, in the district as you go to St. Peter in Montorio. I went there with my companion who stayed with me all the while, to see how this would turn out.

This is when the devil got the upper hand. I found the office and told the notary what I wanted. Then I showed him the paper the Father had drawn up, so that he would understand my situation the better, and we agreed on five lire as the fee since this is what he asked. Two witnesses would be needed to make the document authentic. My friend, who was

---

[1] Counsellors to the Minister Provincial.

[2] The Constitutions of the Order at that time forbade admitting descendants of Jews to the fourth generation.

inexperienced in these legal matters, said he would be one of the witnesses himself and the second would be another man from Sezze who was at the hotel, but would not be actually present. I had told him as we came along the street that this could not be done. The witnesses have to be present when documents of this nature are drawn up.

The notary did not appreciate the simplicity of the young fellow but got so angry and suspicious that he began to swear at us, calling us rogues and treating us like spies who were trying to ruin him by getting him to draw up false documents. When poor Peter saw the man so upset and cursing he knelt down and asked pardon for what he had said. He had no idea that his suggestion would hurt the notary's good name, but thought it quite proper.

At this act of humility the notary became more enraged. With words worse than his anger he started to chase us out. He said he would have us whipped and put in prison like sly criminals. Then in a rage he went outside to call the police. The good Lord permitted that there should be none about just then, as only a corporal and a few others were assigned to that district.

Once I saw how badly our business had turned out I said: "Peter, my friend, this is no time to show humility but just to run and save our lives!" That is what we did. Once out of the office we more than just walked, fearing that any moment we would be taken prisoner.

After this mishap and realizing the many difficulties involved, I began to lose courage and to waver like any youngster of little courage and less experience; perhaps it would be better for me to go back home, I thought. But my friend had a lot of spirit and he bolstered up mine; he urged me to keep trying and to use every help in the difficulty so as not to fail altogether. He was determined to go to my priest uncle without delay; he would straighten out everything. And off he started.

Just as he was leaving, my uncle came looking for me. He asked me how things had gone with the admission. I told him briefly of the difficulty of my not having a good certificate and that I needed another one. He took me to a notary from Sezze by the name of Santi Cola, with whom I had gone to school. He drew up the required certificate and I went back to St. Francis with my companion.

As I was going into the monastery I met the Father Guardian of St. Francis of Nazzano. He made me walk along with him. He asked for the certificate and after reading it said that it was useless because it did not have the seal. I was amazed at this. I wanted to get the opinion of the Father who had helped me before and he was just going across the garden. He told me not to worry any longer; he would settle things. I was not to return to the hotel but was to stay in the monastery and should quickly arrange for getting the clothes and whatever else was required, for he wanted to send me as soon as possible to the novitiate with the aforesaid Guardian.

Now that all these difficulties had been overcome with the help of divine grace, I gave thought to buying cloth for my habit and other necessary articles. A young artisan had been admitted with me and I gave him some things he needed, because he was poor.

The next day I had not yet left Rome, so my friend and I went to visit the church of St. Mary Major. We said our prayers, and as we were going out the door some poor people were there asking for alms. Out of love of God I gave them all the money I had left. Then we went to visit our Lady of Victory and I recommended myself to her with great devotion. I begged her as a special favour to give me the grace of being able to report a victory over my enemies during the year of novitiate and I promised that I would come to visit her in thanksgiving after I made my profession. That night the friars asked me to attend Matins. A special consolation came over me in listening to them sing the divine praises, and a wonderful devotion rose within me as I heard them taking the discipline[3] made of metal links.

On the morning that I had to leave Rome for Nazzano, the place of the novitiate, my uncle, Don Francis Maccioni, came to St. Francis a Ripa very early. He had them call the Father Provincial. The two went aside and my uncle told him that it would not be good for me to receive the habit just then, but suggested that I should go back to Sezze for another year's study, or more if necessary, and then to be received as a cleric. The Father said to him: "Let us see what the young man says; if he is satisfied with this I will gladly do it". My answer was: "Very Reverend Father, if you please, I want to receive the habit now and to be a lay-brother". Then he embraced me warmly and said: "Go, my son! A blessing on you, and may our Lord be with you and accompany you!"

We thanked him then for his great charity, and left. All this happened with my companion, Peter de Vecchi, who did not want to leave till that time. This certainly proved him a true friend.

---

[3] "Taking the discipline" is an ascetical practice many centuries old in Religious Orders. The instrument used, called a discipline, is a kind of whip or scourge ordinarily made of several strands of stout cord whose ends are tied in knots. With this discipline one scourges oneself while saying psalms of a penitential nature with other prayers.

Chapter 14
Departure from Rome for Nazzano

LESSED be our Lord, for under his care I left Rome on the twelfth of May,[1] in the company of the Father Guardian of St. Francis of Nazzano and his companion, and also with the other young man who had been admitted, as I mentioned. We started off and went along the road very devoutly as we recited the seven Psalms of David, the Litanies, the crown of six decades of our Lady,[2] and the most holy Rosary.

The Father Guardian wanted us to travel with eyes downcast, with only little talking, and then it should be on the things of God. Because of the lessons he kept giving us by way of instruction in holiness I did not dare raise my eyes, so as not in any way to go against what he had told us; nor did I speak at all. The young artisan, who had been about in the world and had a fine command of speech, enjoyed talking with me about innocent things; but since I was not much of a conversationalist and at the same time was afraid of the Father Guardian, I for the most part refused to talk to him. Once, however, noticing how quiet I was and hardly paying attention to him, he remarked: "You, with your silence, will stay in religion and I, with my talking, do not know if I will stay". He was foretelling what was actually to happen, for he left in the middle of the novitiate.

We continued our journey with some discomfiture—the sun was hot for going along on foot, and besides each of us carried a pack on his back. The first day we reached the

---

[1] 1635.

[2] The so-called crown of St. Bridget consisting of six decades, to which are added three *Hail Marys* in memory of the sixty-three years that, according to a tradition, the Blessed Virgin lived on earth.

monastery at Fiano, called St. Stephen.[3] There we were welcomed with marked joy by the Guardian, Father Paul of Fiano, a very religious man. He treated us all with great charity and we spent the night there. On the following day, our Father Guardian said Mass early and we left all the priests, thanking them for their kindness, and set out for the monastery of Nazzano.

The cloister at Nazzano had an atmosphere of special devotion that touched the soul and lifted it up to God. The Friars were very happy at the return of their Superior and spiritual father. When they led him inside the bell was rung and all came together, including the novices. They knelt down to kiss his hands; then with towels they wiped away the perspiration, for really he and his companion were soaked through and through because of the hot sun and the heavy habits. After that they washed their feet with hot water mixed with sweet-smelling herbs, while they sang hymns and psalms.

In this little ceremony of charity and humility they acted with such loving attention as to enrapture one. To witness it was refreshing to body and soul. A meal of vegetables was prepared, so that with joy and gratitude in the Lord they might enjoy their holy poverty. We seculars also were treated with great charity.

Then a poor but clean room was assigned us, and our thanks went up to His Divine Majesty for having conducted us to this holy place in the woods, far from the world. Our older Fathers claim that this monastery was established by St. Anthony of Padua.[4]

---

[3] The monastery of Fiano, dedicated to the protomartyr St. Stephen, was given to the Friars Minor in 1602; it was abandoned, with so many others, following the suppression of religion by the Italian Government.

[4] According to a tradition recorded by Gonzaga and Wadding, this was in 1229. The mortal remains of the servant of God, Sister Elisabeth of Vissio (died 1615) and of Blessed Stephen Molina (died 1579), promoter of the

For about three days the Fathers treated us as seculars, keeping us busy at manual work in the monastery.

At last the time came for our clothing in the holy habit. Since the Father Guardian wished to hold the ceremony the following morning, he informed us through one of the Friars that if we wished to receive the habit, we should go to the refectory to ask for it for the love of God, that evening just before six o'clock. There were three of us, for one had arrived before we had. We all went gladly, to be there when the Friars assembled for the blessing of the table. When it had been given they sat down. They had us young worldlings kneel up straight in the middle of the refectory, and in a line. The first one, from Valtellina, the tallest of the three, was at the right; the second was the one who had come with me from Rome; the last was myself, the smallest of them all.

In a voice like that of a stranger, as if he had never known or seen us, the Father Guardian asked us as a group why we had come there and what was our wish. Then he asked the first one what he wanted. He answered that he desired the holy habit for the love of God; the last two of us gave the same answer. Once he had listened to our wishes he began to gesture threateningly and to scold us in a loud voice: "I have taken care of you the last few days and I can see very well that you are a lot of lazy do-nothings who are anxious to get out of work. You were dying of hunger in your own homes and now you have come here to starve us. So, go away! We are not going to keep this kind of people in our monasteries! All right, Father Master, open the door and send them away!"

It had astounded me to hear this kind of talk, but when he told the Father to dismiss us I was like one in a dream. The Master got up from his place and without saying a word put us outside and then locked the door.

We were dismayed and stupefied. Each of us bemoaned the

Reform in the Roman Province, lie here. But at present this monastery does not belong to the religious.

misfortune and bad luck that had come without any warning. Everyone had his opinion as to what was to be done. The one from Tuscany, my companion on the journey from Rome, said very decidedly that he wanted to leave and not to do anything about it. I told him that for many reasons it would not be well to leave right away and that it seemed very strange to me that these Fathers would want to insult us the way they had without telling us why; after all, we had not committed any crime that would merit being turned away shamefully, especially since they had lodged us for several days and made us spend so much money. It would be a waste! "So it seems best", I said, "to go back in through the garden gate and see what they do." This was satisfactory to them and we determined to do it. First we said the Litany of the most Blessed Virgin. We recommended ourselves to our Lady and asked her to be our help in this extreme need. We prayed until we reached the gate leading into the garden, a lattice-gate which was the exit for anyone going down into Nazzano. It was shut and none of us knew how to open it. But our Lord never abandons his servants and he took care that it came open for us quite accidentally. We went in and saw two Friars who seemed to be on a tour of inspection, perhaps because they suspected that we had left, as we would have done had we agreed with my companion. As soon as they saw us they went off without saying a word.

Now, to get into the monastery there was a little door that did not lead directly into the garden, but into a walled enclosure with its own door made of planks. This the Friars locked from the inside with a chain when they went in to pray. With the help of the other two I scaled the wall and opened the door. The others came in.

We knocked at the little door which was near the refectory. The Father Guardian sent the Master to see who was knocking there. The Master came and opened the door so little that he could scarcely see us. Then he went back to give a message to the Guardian. I smiled at that and remarked to the others: "Would he do that if we were bandits, standing here with guns?!"

When the meal was over and grace had been said, the Father Guardian with the Vicar, Father Romanus of Rome, a man of exalted prayer, came to the door followed by some other Friars. They opened the door without letting us come inside and made us lie on the ground; and as though surprised and amazed at seeing us the Guardian began to upbraid us even more than before. "Boys, I do not know how you could be so impudent as to return to this holy place, to disturb these servants of God at their prayers. Now I told you that you are not meant for the religious life, that you have come to avoid hunger and not to serve God. But since it is late I am willing to keep you in the monastery tonight so that wild animals will not devour you. Tomorrow morning early you will leave here. The Master will see about giving you some bread as an alms and a little wine to fill your flasks, and if there is any food prepared in the kitchen at that time he will give you some of it, outside this door. Now go to bed, so that you can all walk the better tomorrow." Then he left us.

Some food was brought us, small pieces of bread and a salad. As we were hungry, this was a real help. During the night, when we wanted to get our rest, the devils began disturbing the Tuscan with frightful images. Every once in a while he screamed for help. Because of such a strange happening we were disturbed a good deal of the night and try as I would to keep him from being afraid, it was not enough to keep him quiet. As I see it, it was due to the cowardliness he had shown from the start, that the devil eventually got control of him and in time managed to degrade him completely. That is the way it turned out. He did not make use of his vocation and of the miracle that he was to see worked on himself. He was suddenly cured of a skin infection when he was clothed in the habit. He left the novitiate after it was better than half over.

Chapter 15
Clothed in the Habit of St. Francis

THE day came, so longed for. The Fathers had decided to clothe us in the holy habit of St. Francis. That morning, as we hung between the fear of again being sent away and the hope of staying, one of the Friars was sent by the Father Guardian to take us to the refectory. He did so without saying what awaited us. There the three of us had our hair trimmed in the style of lay-brothers. When I saw my hair on the floor I fervently thanked our Lord; now I knew that my longings were being fulfilled after so many disturbing obstacles.[1]

Then they took us to the church to invest us solemnly in the habit; and that this sacred function by which we were to be consecrated to God might be held with all possible devotion and lift our hearts up to the Divine Majesty, they had us attend Holy Mass and receive our Lord's most Sacred Body. We had first made a general confession.

All the Friars met in the sacristy and from there they went out in order to the high altar with the Father Guardian who was vested in cope. We three knelt on the lowest step holding lighted candles. A short sermon was given in which we were exhorted to think of the special grace our Lord was giving us in withdrawing us from the disturbances of the world and putting us in holy religion, the place of peace and quiet, where there is a better chance of serving God. We were urged to perseverance in resisting the temptations of the devils.

After the sermon the Father Guardian blessed the habits; then with the accompanying prayers he put on us the garment

---

[1] The trial given these three aspirants by the Father Guardian may seem strange and exaggerated. But we should remember that it was really necessary at that period to put new candidates for the Order under serious probation, because of the tendency of some families to dedicate their children for the religious life, and sometimes actually force them into it, even if they were not at all so inclined.

of penance of the glorious Patriarch St. Francis. It was the 18th of May, a Saturday, in the year 1635, and I was twenty-two years old. He gave us each a name: Brother Joseph to the one from Valtellina; Brother Alexius to the one from Tuscany; and to me, Brother Cosmas, a name that was changed at my profession to Brother Charles, as I will explain later. All three of us were clothed as lay-brothers.

After the ceremony of investiture the chanter immediately intoned the *Te Deum*, and while the choir sang it the other Friars came to give us the kiss of peace.

Once I had been clothed in the habit the Father Guardian put me under the charge of the Master of lay-brothers, Brother Diego of Catino,[2] to train me in everything required. He was a man of mature age, very wise, and possessed of marked virtue, prayer, charity and austerity. It was said of him by the Friars that he kept all the Lents of our Father St. Francis, living on bread and dried grapes. After dismissing the novices at night after Matins he would stay in the church to pray and to weep over the sufferings of Jesus Christ.

And just as he walked the path of perfection and goodness, so he drew the eight of us novices along the same path. He showed us how to behave well, to speak rightly, and to direct our every action toward virtue.

He also taught us how to fight against temptations and he told us that the best way was to talk them over with a director. He gave me orders to tell him whatever happened to me. To all of us he gave the example of a gardener who stays in the orchard because someone is going to rob it. As long as the thief does not know that he is being watched by the owner, he goes ahead stealing the fruit; but when he realizes

---

[2] Catino (Rieti). Brother Diego was professed on 17 November 1608. Everyone admired him for his gentle simplicity united to rare prudence, patience, and such great meekness that no one ever saw him upset. He was elected as Master of lay-brothers many times. He died on 15 January 1657, with a reputation for sanctity.

that the owner has seen him, he makes off. That is the way the devil acts when through various temptations he comes to rob us of the grace of God. As long as we act like sleeping people and do not make these temptations known to our spiritual fathers, then he carries out his evil work. But when he knows that he is found out by the priest we have consulted he loses his power and goes away, leaving us alone for a while.

CHAPTER 16
MANUAL WORK

THE life of the lay-brothers in the Franciscan Order is made up mainly of prayer, humility, obedience and love in serving the other Friars by manual labour in the monastery. St. Francis actually called them the mothers of the other Friars.

Our Master instructed us in acts of humility, showing us how to help in the kitchen and carry out our assignments there with the greatest possible love. In such a necessary and meritorious work the first of the seven works of mercy is exercised, which is to feed the hungry. In the Gospel this is greatly praised by Christ. That we might do this work with all possible love, he taught us to reflect how with the food we had prepared we were to feed many poor persons who were continually giving themselves over to the praise of God in prayer.

When dinner was over and we were washing the dishes in the kitchen, he wanted us to recite some prayers such as the Litany of our Blessed Lady, the Psalm Miserere, the De Profundis for the souls in purgatory, and other prayers for our benefactors; and during whatever else we did we should give ourselves to God by acts of love and of resignation to his divine will. Our service of the sick Friars should be carried out with all the perfection possible, since our holy Father St. Francis commands this[1] in order to keep charity among his religious at its highest.

Our Master also had us apply ourselves with exactness to other manual work, such as sweeping the house, working in the garden and going on the quest. We should not be ashamed to carry a sack on our shoulder, but go confidently to ask an

---

[1] *Rule of the Order of Friars Minor*, Chapter 6.

alms for the love of our Love who became poor for our sake though he was the king of heaven and earth.

This is a very profitable method of teaching beginners. In all their actions, however tiresome, they learn to find God and to enkindle their love; which is especially true of those who have been called by His Majesty to the active life. They form good habits and are disposed at all times to love God and to taste his unspeakable sweetness.

Out of holy obedience, I gladly trained myself in the exercises of humility and charity, and of prayer also. Besides the lessons my father had given me in it, obedience was very deeply impressed on my heart by the wonderful things the Father Guardian said about it: how grateful, for example, he was to God for his only-begotten Son who had been obedient even to death; to what a high degree of love and perfection it takes a person, and finally the wonderful examples we have seen of it in the lives of the saints. He spoke so glowingly of obedience that I determined to do anything he told me, no matter how difficult. I will recount some of the things that happened.

One day the Father Guardian took me with him into the town of Nazzano. When his business there was finished, we started back to the monastery. As we came into the woods by which it was surrounded, there across our path was a tree-trunk so big that two men could hardly encircle it. He told me to lift it out of the way. Without hesitating or thinking of anything else, I took my mantle off and went to take hold of it. But I hardly touched it when he took my hand and said that I would not have to do anything further about it; what I had done was enough, without looking for a miracle. The truly obedient person, he said, completely satisfies this virtue when he tries to do what he is told, in so far as he is able, even though it is above his human strength.

He also said that if we believed in obedience with simplicity, even bears and lions and other wild animals would be as gentle as lambs if we were commanded to go out and catch them.

Another time, I and a fellow-novice were planting cabbages in the garden at the bidding of the Master, and we were doing this as it is always done, with the roots down. The Father Guardian came along, greeted us, and then asked us what we were doing. We told him that we were planting cabbages. When he saw how we were doing it, he said it was not right, but that we should have planted them with the leaves down and the roots up. He took the dibble from my hand, and put two or three plants in the ground the way he had described. My companion said that they would not take root, but would dry up, since the roots which should have been covered by the soil were exposed to the sun. The Guardian scolded him for this answer and sent him into the monastery; then he gave the dibble back and told me to continue putting in the plants as he had done. I did this with all that were left. I think anyone would have learned the virtue of obedience through the holiness of that Father who had such great faith, because those plants took hold and did very well!

May God be praised in his works, for this as for other things that are not mentioned here.

Chapter 17
Penitential Exercises

HE exercises of penance that are part of the year of novitiate are strange, because in that year the Order is testing the novice and the novice tries the Order to see if it is what he wants. That is why it is the duty of the Masters along with the Guardians to use every means and device in finding out whether the young men who have taken the habit are really moved by the spirit of God. Especially do they use the means of obedience and mortification.

To be sure of a novice's motives, they do not overlook any defect, however small; they strictly correct and punish it by penances, for example, by having the novice use the discipline for the space of one or two *Miserere*; again by making him eat with the hood up while kneeling in the middle of the refectory, or sometimes while standing with a stone around his neck, or while walking.

As I recall, I had passed half of the novitiate year in this way, when greater strictness was used and the hand of penance pressed down very hard, almost to the point of overwhelming my weak powers. I can only guess that this was the case for two reasons: first, my physical constitution had changed very much and lacked strength due to the illnesses I had gone through; and then my head also suffered from weakness because of the little sleep I was getting,[1] and so to all external appearances I looked like a worthless person who gave every sign of not being any good for the duties of the religious life; secondly, they not only wanted to see if my vocation was genuine, but even more to find out whether the

---

[1] What mainly kept him from getting sufficient sleep, as will be related later, were the annoyances he suffered from the devils.

spirit of prayer and mental abstraction that I had, were from God. I say that because one day on leaving the church and having to walk through the monastery cloister, where the Master and the Father Guardian were talking about this very thing—thinking no doubt that I did not hear them—I concluded that they intended to use penance and obedience to see if what appeared externally was gold or silver.

First the Master took me aside privately; he was not able to impose penances on the novices publicly in front of the Superior or the community, but he could do so in a place apart, such as in the big kitchen. In the middle of the night during the winter, after Matins and meditation were over, he called us all together in the kitchen, not only to instruct us in spiritual matters, but to show us more about our work there and how to cook the vegetables.

Because I was often at fault in different things he gave me penances to correct these. Two or three times he had me take the discipline after midnight till almost daybreak. On other occasions he made me put a rock on my neck and hold it there all the time he remained with me, which would be for an hour and a half, and more often two hours.

To punish me if I was at fault in speech I had to drag my tongue many times along the entire length of the kitchen. Once in the summer, when I broke silence before noon during a period of prayer after None, I was given this penance which I kept at from half past two o'clock till eight. Our Lord had permitted the Master to forget all about the command he had given me. There must have been good reason why that member of my body, which the Lord had given me for honouring and blessing him, was getting such punishment.[2]

---

[2] Notice the Saint's great virtue. He always considers the strictness shown him as just, and he thanks the Superiors. St. Teresa of the Child Jesus expressed the same sentiments towards her Mother Prioress, as we read in the *Story of a Soul*, Chapter 7.

These punishments and penances, as described here, appear less than human, exaggerated, and even anti-hygienic to us moderns. Still it must

The Father Guardian was not slow in doing his part also, in the refectory in front of the community. He spoke to me roughly as one who had committed great faults, and he followed up what he said with penances and mortifications. Once in a while he made me take the discipline for the space of a *Miserere* with the *De Profundis*, though this was usual for all the novices. What he had me do especially was to eat bread and water, kneeling on the floor, sometimes without my hood and other times with a stone around my neck.

If the Guardian allowed me to have some soup as I knelt there, two very impolite kittens quickly ran and began eating from my plate. This mortification lasted for a long time until they were trained to behave themselves.

The novice from Valtellina, my friend, was very put out at what these cats were doing. One day he found them in the refectory while the Friars were in their rooms during silence. He shut the doors and gave them a good whipping, and while doing it he made a kind of scratching sound. After that, whenever they heard that sound they ran off at top speed and did not dare enter the refectory.

I think it was in the eleventh or twelfth month of my novitiate year that matters got worse than ever about admitting me to profession. Though the penances and mortifications were very troublesome, still I carried them out with a lot of satisfaction since I knew they were small compared to what I deserved for my sins. I often said to myself: "Brother Charles, if you died, you would go to hell and suffer with the devils for the great offences you gave His Divine Majesty. Bear with these things gladly for a while, because it is really a great grace our Lord has given you, to suffer for a year out of love for him."

---

be remembered that this was in the seventeenth century when such penances were commonly used in all religious institutes, as also in secular ones.

Chapter 18
Interior Desolation During The Entire Year of Novitiate

OUR Lord permitted me to be bothered by not only one kind of trouble in the novitiate year, but by many and diverse ones; not only by exterior trials coming from other persons, but by interior afflictions, especially a spirit of sadness that seemed to penetrate my very bones.

Hardly had I put on the habit of St. Francis when such a deep melancholy came over me that my soul was suffocated by anxiety very difficult for me to describe; difficult, because every part of me was as though abandoned and derelict, without there being a moment of freedom or the least bit of comfort.

I no longer remembered the burning desire and great longing, that for such a long time had been mine, to wear the habit of St. Francis; no longer remembered were the many graces our Lord had bestowed on me through the intercession of his most Blessed Mother. How suddenly things had changed! Happiness into bitterness, joy into tears! I was as though beside myself with sadness, buried in a dark night of anxieties, with everything contributing to making my illness even worse. When I looked at the sun its very rays filled me with gloom; the birds with their songs only served to remind me of my affliction; everything I saw or heard made me sad.

That is why I was very much tempted to put off the habit and return to the world! And I believe I would have done so, had the chance been given me and if a special help of our Lord had been lacking.

For two or three weeks I remained in this trouble without informing my confessor, who was the Father Guardian. But as God planned it and helped me by his grace, I determined to tell him everything. I did so in confession. He listened very charitably and my courage mounted. He gave me very good advice. I was never to keep any sort of temptation hidden, for in that way it only acquires greater strength and easily makes too great an impression. I was often to reconsider the goal that had influenced me in coming into the religious life and the wonderful promises our Lord had made, who rewards good and punishes evil; that is why I should never think of going back but of moving forward courageously, since the vocation to which our Lord had called me is an excellent means of acquiring his love. For these reasons I should be joyful and make no account of these temptations.

By talking this over with my confessor I was not thereby freed from the temptation to melancholy, since it lasted all during the novitiate year. Still, I was really greatly strengthened. The awful thought of leaving left me immediately and I received a great help to keep going. In all this I noticed the power of the sacrament of penance for helping the Christian; it certainly strengthened me in overcoming these trials. They were especially severe when I thought of my brother, the one who had been so sick. Because of the love I had for him and the respect we had for each other, many times he seemed to be right there in front of me and this picture stirred me to the depths. At other times I would imagine my family sitting down at table, and all I could think of was: "Look at what they are having for dinner! And here you cannot get over your hunger!"

To this was added all the good things my father had planned for me. Now I recalled his fatherly affection and the little I had responded to it. Then there was the tenderness of my mother who had loved me without stint, and it seemed I had never really been aware of it till then!

All these recollections came upon me at one time like a torrent and filled me with sadness. I felt it as deeply as anyone can believe, yet with God's help I overcame it. After all, I had not gone to the monastery to eat and drink and to look for consolation, but to suffer for the love of Jesus and to do penance.

But what touched me to the quick was that I began to sense that the Friars did not want to admit me to profession. I knew of no remedy except to have recourse to prayer and to resign myself to the divine will.

Chapter 19
Some Temptations and Illusions from the Devil

THERE were many wars waged openly against me by the demons and they plotted every kind of deceit under the guise of devotion. They would come at night during the time of sleep. I longed to give my body some rest, tired as it was and badly worn out by continuous pain, but they kept me terrified with the different forms they took. If it happened that I had fallen off to sleep I would suddenly awaken again badly frightened. At such times I made the sign of the cross, called upon the name of Jesus, said some prayers, especially the *Sub tuum praesidium*, and that drove them off.

At other times they assumed the human form of a religious, more specifically of another novice whom I had known in the world and for whom I had a high regard in religion. They came up to me in a friendly way, sometimes in silence, and on other occasions saying things meant to win me over.

One of them came along one time in the form of the Father Guardian, to tell me to come to his room for he wanted to speak to me. Immediately I arose and went there. The Guardian was astonished to hear me tell this. He said it was not he who had called me and that I should go back to bed with God's blessing.

More often these evil spirits brought a fainting spell on me. They then severely vexed me interiorly without my being able to do a thing about it, not even by saying a word, or by calling upon the most sweet name of Jesus. As a boy I had used this means and it often awakened the memory of my good grandmother who, with this effect in mind, made me carry some holy object on my person.

The good Fathers taught me to say the crown of seven

decades of our Lady in memory of the seven joys that were hers in this life and in which she exults in paradise.

One evening after I had finished my duties and had gone to my room, I prepared to say the above-mentioned crown. When I came to the seventh decade I became so drowsy that I could not continue this devotion. The Master had shown me how to stand on one foot and to hold the other up in the air with my cord, as a help against sleepiness in prayer. I made use of what he had taught me and I took precautions not to hurt myself if I were to fall. I stood at the foot of my straw mattress and in spite of the drowsiness finished the last decade, the one in memory of our Lady assumed into heaven and crowned with glory by the most Blessed Trinity.

I had scarcely finished it when sleepiness and tiredness enveloped me immediately and I let myself fall on the mattress. Then I realized that the entire room was lit up very brightly. This was something new. I lifted my head and opened my eyes to see from what direction this bright light was coming. At the other end of the room, near the ceiling, I saw with my very eyes the mystery I had just been meditating on; and I saw it so distinctly that I would have believed that the lady who stood in the centre with such majesty and glory was the Virgin Mary, and that those who were standing around her, and placing a crown on her head, were the three Divine Persons.

I was overcome with amazement at this vision. It seemed so unfitting that the Mother of God should confer so great a favour on a sinner. I exclaimed: "O Mother most holy, I am not worthy to behold you on account of my sins!" No sooner were these words said than the false vision left the place where it had been. Everything about it changed. The devils were there in various forms; with a lot of noise they attacked and struck me in every way imaginable. I was like a dead person.

At the noise, a fellow novice who lived in that part of the

building came to help me. Because of the blows I had received I could not do my usual work the next day, and so I talked the whole incident over with my Master and also with the Father Guardian who called me to his room. After listening to my story, he told me that if I had not spoken the words about my being a sinner and unworthy of such a vision, the devils would not have maltreated me. But since they cannot stand humility they would have torn me to pieces, if they could. On the other hand, had I been pleased at having this vision they easily would have led me to believe that it was true; in short, under the appearance of good they would have tried to ruin my soul.

Seeing that he could not have his way this time, the deceiver just bided his time; and when I had forgotten the vision he came again under the appearance of the Mother of God with her little Child in her arms. But when he realized that I saw through his trickery, in his rage he stood over me and struck me fiercely.

He did not give up, however. He tried to set another trap at night in the church when I was favoured with mental rapture during prayer. He took human form and came so close as to touch me. Then with a little spoon he put a liquid in my mouth. This happened on two nights. I thought it over, trying to find out what it could mean. Then I spoke of it to the Master, who said it was a trick of the devil and that I would soon be sure of this. The next time I was to say to him: "Evil beast, open your mouth; I want to fill it with dung", and he would quickly flee. But if this thing were from God, it would not leave. That is what he ordered me to do.

As I was praying the following night, this false friend came with his poisonous liquid and as he approached me I said what the Master had commanded me, and I spat in his face. He fled shamefully and never again appeared in that form.

Chapter 20
Temptation to Vainglory

MONG all the trials of the novitiate I had one relief: peace of conscience. This helped me very much to carry joyfully all the heavy burdens and crosses my vocation placed on me, and to preserve union with God. It made me enjoy a paradise on earth in spite of the troubles of this world. The main thing to attend to in the spiritual life is to have a pure and tranquil conscience at all times, because when a person is without sin he reaches union with God through grace, he gains merit continuously and he is disposed for the exalted enjoyment of divine contemplation, the state of peace and consolation given by the Holy Spirit.

For some months in the novitiate year I enjoyed a peace and serenity of conscience so delicate that it was more divine than human. In this state I seemed to be living a more devout and truly Christian life, for I was not offending my Lord so much—the evil occasions for that were lacking—and still more I had a motive for serving, loving and blessing him in all things. It was like being in paradise, which we really possess in our souls here on earth when we are united to God; and it is so wonderful that even our bodies share in the happiness, as we sing with the saintly King David: "This is the day which the Lord hath made: let us be glad and rejoice therein; for he is good."[1]

While I was taking satisfaction from this peace of soul, it turned out that two of the Friars came to where I was busy with some work and they started to talk about the perfection and holiness they noticed in some of the novices. No doubt they thought I could not hear what they were saying. What I heard particularly was: "That Brother Charles of Sezze is an

---
[1] Psalm 117. 24 and 29.

angel in the flesh!" I felt some natural complacency and pride at hearing this, without thinking that I should completely dismiss this sort of temptation.

When the reaction to complacency had passed and the darkness of mind that it brought on had lifted, I felt that I had become a devil from hell rather than an angel in the flesh! My peace and serenity of conscience left me and I was so disquieted that I did not know what to do, for all the sins I had ever committed came before me. They bit me savagely as though with sharp teeth; with frightful shrieks they cried out as a group that I had not confessed them rightly. The pain I experienced was intense because I could not receive Holy Communion even once in peace, as one thing after another came back to me.

How careful we should be in speaking, so as not to be the cause of ruining a soul and making it lose what it took a long time and much suffering to acquire! Sometimes when we are with a good person we think it is proper to speak of his virtues. If we only knew, we should be startled at the damage that can follow on such praise. It is a poison that attacks quickly and brings spiritual death.

It was about the sixth month of my novitiate that our Lord struck me so as to check the empty self-esteem that we create when we try to credit ourselves with what does not belong to us. Not only did I carry the cross of an uneasy conscience for the rest of the novitiate, but it lasted for six years without in any way diminishing.

Though I had learned and practical confessors all during this time, I could not find any rest until, as God willed, I fell seriously sick. I confessed my sins to one of the Fathers and told him of my trouble. Some of my peace was restored, but I have suffered right up to the present, even though I have made a general confession many times.

Chapter 21
Profession of Vows

IN the ninth month of the novitiate, while the good Lord was taking me into the home of his love along the safe way of suffering, my Master and the other Friars, all conscientious men, were reluctant to give me the votes needed for my profession. The principal reason was that I could not carry out the tasks that are assigned to lay-brothers. Only God knows how much this increased the affliction of my heart.

In the novitiate house there was a professed brother, by name Thaddeus, who thought very much of me. He worked in the garden and when he went to places nearby begging for alms he would ask the Father Guardian if he might have me as his companion. He was very displeased that the Friars had formed an adverse opinion of me and he greatly encouraged me to persevere as I had begun, and to hope in God. I looked on him as my father for the great love he showed me and for his other fine qualities.

I greatly enjoyed his method of prayer which was simply this: he knelt down, made the sign of the cross, and began the Our Father. After saying the first petition of that prayer, he was lifted out of himself, as it were, and withdrawn for quite a time. On coming back to himself he said the second petition and again was lifted up and withdrawn; and so it went on for the rest of the prayer. When he went into the church during the night—and he used to go rather early before the bell for Matins—I sometimes went ahead of him and secretly kept him company.

As time went on and I saw that my case was desperate, humanly speaking, and that all the Friars, including the novices, said I should be deprived of the holy habit, I had recourse for help at this difficult time to the most glorious

Virgin Mother of God, my principal advocate; and then I also took some steps of my own not to be turned aside from what had begun well.

My first determination was that, should the Fathers put me out of the novitiate, I would take the habit with me and keep it out of devotion to St. Francis; the under-tunic I would leave for some poor novice who had been clothed gratis in an old habit.

The second determination was that, since it seemed very shameful to go back to the world after being dismissed, I thought of staying in some hermit's cave in the woods and doing penance for my sins. But on thinking ahead of the danger I could run into and the many difficulties of persevering in that life, I gave up the idea.

The third and last determination was to go back home and live in chastity, and as calmly as possible take everything from the hand of God and bear that mortification for love of him, with the consolation that for all the years up to then that I had lived an evil life in the world, I spent one for Jesus Christ.

While I was at the peak of my trial and swam in a sea of afflictions, His Divine Majesty did not fail to give me some relief through a lay-brother, Brother Stephen of Sezze, whom I had known at school and who happened to be at Nazzano for a while. When he learned that I was making my novitiate he came looking for me in the kitchen, to talk to me. But since the novices may not speak to anyone without the special permission of the Father Guardian or of the Master, I knelt down and kept my head bowed when he came in, until he said all that God had inspired him to say.

After a holy exhortation to keep going, he said specifically that because I was pleasing to our Lord I would be admitted to profession. So I should not doubt, but be of good cheer. He blessed me in the name of God and left for wherever obedience called him, leaving me very consoled.

At this time I recalled what a holy hermit had once told

me. This man never left Sezze but stayed in a hermitage called St. Lucy, a place my family knew very well.[1] He clearly said that the first eight months would be passed very happily and that I would have all the votes of the Friars, but that from the eighth to the eleventh month I would be in great danger of being sent away; and if the eleventh month passed, then everything would be all right and I need not have any more fear.

All these things started coming back to me and when I realized that all that he had said had been fulfilled up to then, I had great hopes for the rest if only that eleventh month would pass. I often begged our Lord that it would.

It finally did pass and then the time for the Provincial Chapter came when a good many of the Friars are changed from one monastery to another. Before any of them left, if that were to happen, the Fathers wanted to vote on the novices. So on a set day they all met in the refectory; the novices were sent off in procession to the church, with them myself more than ever full of fear.

In church I knelt down before a lovely painting of the Madonna which stood in one of the chapels. I had a special devotion to it. With a great deal of familiarity I began speaking aloud from my heart. "You know very well, O most Blessed Mother, that I came here to do what I promised you, and that is to serve you in chastity in the holy Order of St. Francis. Now the Fathers want to send me back to the world. I really think that I have corresponded with my vocation and carried it out as much as I had to, and I do not know of any fault committed maliciously. Nothing is left now but your help; I humbly beg you, give it to me."

At this prayer I experienced an unusual relief and it brought a sweet tranquillity to my soul. I was completely

---

[1] It still exists on the spot where in ancient times a Benedictine monastery stood. Priceless frescoes of the sixteenth century will delight the visitor.

changed by this indescribable conversation with Mary and I sensed such a marvellous peace in the depths of her motherly love that I felt I wanted nothing else but to be united to the divine will and to conform myself completely to it.

While I was being consoled by our Lord through this gracious gift of his, the Fathers sent word to have us come to the refectory. We went there at once. As we passed the high altar, one of the novices in the pair just ahead of me genuflected and then said as he turned around: "Your turn this time, Brother Charles; just wait!" And though during my prayer in church I understood what conformity to the will of God was, still my weak flesh wanted to show its fickleness. Those words were like a sword passing through my heart and it was all I could do to catch myself and say: "The will of God be done!"

On entering the refectory we kissed the floor and received the blessing. The Father Guardian then told us to stand up, but only after he had first exhorted us strongly to be ready for whatever God had provided for each of us. Then he called one of the cleric novices, told him to prostrate on the floor, and upbraided him severely for some of his defects. And immediately, publicly, he had two Friars take the habit from him and give him his own clothes. If I remember rightly, he did the same to another novice.

Then my turn came and while I lay on the floor with more dread than you can imagine he told me of my worthlessness and inability to learn what a lay-brother should know; and that consequently he had made up his mind to do with me what he had just done to these two, but since I still had twenty days left, I should get busy in the kitchen and if I did not do well there he would carry out his intention. With this small hope left, I got up from the floor; and the Master of lay-brothers assigned me to the kitchen. With the help of God I gave entire satisfaction there.

The provincial meeting took place and among the Friars

changed were the Father Guardian and the Father Vicar. Father Francis of Rimini remained in charge of the monastery for the time. In a few days the new Guardian came, Father Angelus Maria of Rome, a kindly man gifted with the love of God. He had a special way of leading souls along the path of love after the example of Christ our Lord. His rigorous penances were accompanied with such a warm cordiality that they seemed little and light, showing that they contained a special love. He was a great comfort to me.

The last day of my novitiate came and Father Angelus Maria was willing to profess me. He told me to go to my room in the morning after I had received the most Holy Body of our Lord. I could better recollect myself there and would offer myself as a holocaust with that much more fervour when I took my vows. I did this as best I knew how. I recommended myself to His Divine Majesty and to the most Blessed Virgin, as I thanked them for the help they had given me in bearing so many trials and in conquering the infernal enemy.

It is impossible for me to say how I felt then, once I realized that my espousal to my vocation was accomplished. I experienced a marvellous composure, a withdrawal from everything created and a union with the Highest Good. In a sense I saw and felt nothing, for my soul was separated from bodily senses and transformed by the unspeakable sweetness of its Creator. I understood really that it was not I who was acting and working but rather the omnipotent Lord who was doing everything in me, while I revelled mysteriously in his uncreated love.

Oh what a good paymaster our God is, liberally rewarding us for every suffering borne for him! O holy sufferings that so happily unite our soul with God in the room of his heavenly treasures!

The time for Vespers came. All the Friars went to the church when the bell sounded. The Father Guardian was vested in a cope. He went to the high altar and there he had us two novices approach and kneel on the bottom step. After a very fervent sermon he received our profession. My name was changed from Brother Cosmas to Brother Charles at the request of my mother. All this took place on 19 May 1636, a Sunday, the Feast of St. Pudentiana, Virgin. I was twenty-three years old.

Chapter 22
Assignment to the Morlupo Monastery

FTER my profession I was immediately given an obedience by the Provincial Superior to go to the monastery of St. Mary Seconda in Morlupo.[1] This was the first place I was assigned to after the year of novitiate. Through the intercession of the Mother of God, to whom this monastery was dedicated, our Lord was pleased to give me many favours.

Before leaving Nazzano the Father Guardian first made me ask pardon of all the Friars for not having given them a better example while I was among them, and then he went to the door with me and my dear friend Brother Thaddeus who would be with me on the journey.

His companionship was especially consoling and profitable because of his kind lessons and saintly advice, all the more welcome since he was very experienced in the religious life, besides being rather old. One of the counsels this fine Franciscan gave me was that I should try very hard to be a genuine Friar Minor, obedient, chaste and poor, so as to obtain what our Lord has promised me.

It was late when we arrived at the monastery of Morlupo, for we had walked twelve miles from St. Francis in Nazzano. The porter let us in and we presented ourselves to the Guardian, Father Innocent of Rome. He brought us to the common room where all the Friars had assembled when the bell rang, to bestow on us the marks of charity shown to travellers. They were quite surprised on seeing me, for word had got around that I had been dismissed from the novitiate. Several times the Father Guardian said with a surprised air:

---

[1] This monastery is called St. Mary Seconda because of a tradition that the picture of our Lady there is the second painting of her by St. Luke—the first being in St. Mary Major. It no longer belongs to the Franciscans.

"Are you Brother Charles of Sezze?" "Yes", I answered. "By the grace of our Lord!"

They very happily thanked His Divine Majesty. The Father Guardian showed that he sympathized with me very much; no doubt he had heard how much I had gone through. Then he saw that I was given a room.

Our Lord willed that this Guardian have a special affection for me, as a true father in Christ. More often than not, he called me son. Because of the great charity with which God had richly endowed him I returned his love very sincerely. When the occasion arose for his giving me some task to perform, he would say: "Son, do this or that". It sometimes happened that I committed a fault or broke something. "Son", he would say, "next time be careful; pay attention to what you are doing."

I think that in a person placed over others these traits are exceedingly pleasing to His Divine Majesty: gentleness in word, kindness in treating others, and a modest gravity in giving commands. His genuine humaneness was like a holy unction that drew me to fulfilling his requests. The idea of what he wanted done no sooner entered my mind than I felt within me a special inclination to obey him; and then I did it with such love that there was no weariness about it; in fact, I experienced a refreshing comfort. It was love making the burden light and sweet.

Among the first instructions he gave me, one was that I should do my work in the monastery with charity and love, to make it meritorious; that at prayer I should be very fervent and never for any reason miss the prayers in common, regardless of how urgent it might seem.

My confessor was of the same opinion. I was put under his care to learn the spiritual life and also the different ceremonies. He was the Vicar, Father Raphael of Poggio San Lorenzo. The custom was that the Vicars of monasteries had charge of the young Friars and were their Masters and spiritual guides.

The monastery had no gardener, and until provision was made for one the Father Guardian gave me charge of the garden. I worked at it very devotedly and carefully, trying to keep myself recollected in God by meditation during my work there. By some force that could only have been supernatural I was drawn to lift up my hands and eyes to heaven, and to fasten the eye of my soul on that incomprehensible object, God, where I remained fascinated, as before a mirror, wondering at the eternal light.

When this happened to me over a period of time, my soul acquired such a light for knowing God, affection for loving him and strength in serving him, that I could well say with St. Paul that nothing could separate me from the love of Christ.[2]

Because Jesus Christ at his resurrection permitted Magdalen to see and think of him as a gardener, I took a great liking for this kind of work; the year of novitiate had not quite changed me into a new person, for I liked this assignment very much, as I thought how, here in the garden, was grown the food for the needs of the Friars. No doubt the clever, infernal enemy wanted to use the diligence and love I showed in this assignment to turn me aside from the sure way of holy obedience and to make me dishonest with myself by an excessive zeal. When my superiors gave me some work other than that of gardener, such as going on the quest or performing some other duties, I began to sense an unrest coming from rebellious thoughts. This bothered me very much; still I did not notice the damage I was doing and that this was the work of the devil.

One day when the Superior gave me a different assignment, this temptation to rebellion arose stronger than ever, although I had immediately set aside what I was doing to carry out his will. This rebellion filled me with such a deep chagrin and fierce unrest that I cannot describe it.

---

[2] Romans 8: 35; 38-9.

Our Lord wanted to help me enter into myself and he began speaking to me with his usual gentleness: "Brother Charles, tell me now, what did you promise God when you made your profession?" I answered that I promised to obey my Superior in everything he commanded me, so long as it was not sinful, and not to do my own will. He replied: "Well, then, if that is so, why are you so disappointed and disquieted when the Superior commands you? Do you not see that it is a good thing for one in the religious life to have no other will but that of the Superior, and to be like a dead person in his hands?" The temptation that had tried to take away my peace and prevent my spiritual advancement vanished at these words. I became very calm and resigned to obedience. Greater elevations of soul were granted me, for our Lord listens more readily when we simply do his will in our superiors.

The monastery enclosure was in bad repair for the most part and oxen came in to cause great damage in the garden, destroying some vegetables and eating others. One night two young bulls and an ox came in. Very early the next morning the Father Vicar saw them. The Father Guardian was not in the house at the time, so the Vicar had all the Friars assemble with the exception of myself, for I had been up almost the whole night helping to care for a dying woman. The Superior had ordered me to rest and I was not to leave my room without his permission. He now sent someone to call me immediately. When I saw the Friars with sticks and long poles in their hands, busy chasing the animals as they kept running around in their fright, a great desire to laugh came over me.

But I went over to the Superior, who commanded me in virtue of holy obedience to catch the animals. He gave me the rope himself. I went up to the beasts and in the name of God told them to stand still; they stopped, and did not move a foot, just turning their great heads towards me and staring at me. Going up to the one that was closest, I put the rope round his horns while I prayed to God, and I tied him up as easily as if he were a meek little donkey. Then again in the name of God I told him to come near me; he took a few steps and came closer and so did the other two. Then in accordance with what the Superior wanted I led them inside the monastery and put them in a stall where we had a donkey.

The owner was amazed. He marvelled, for he said he had never been able to catch the two young ones. The Superior told him that all this had come about through the virtue of holy obedience!

Chapter 23
The Cook

WHEN some months had passed, the Superior saw fit to put another Friar in charge of the garden, and he assigned me to the kitchen under the direction of a devout and charitable confrere. It was customary that the young Friars be given an older one as instructor.

This good religious had a very nice way of teaching me, and he made use of every possible means. He wanted me to profit from the kitchen work because of its being so pleasing to God. When he saw things nicely arranged and the food prepared in the way he had taught me, he would very politely bring the Father Guardian in and say: "Look at the nice kitchen Brother Charles keeps! Everything is in its place and the food is nicely prepared and seasoned!" Father Guardian was happy and thanked God.

I greatly admired the goodness of this Friar. The love he had for Christ Jesus was extraordinary. He spurred the young Friars on to virtue by his pleasantness and at the same time he kept me in the good graces of the Superior. When he noticed that I had done something which could offend the others, he very tactfully had me change it.

This Friar showed great charity not only towards us religious but also to the poor. One point of the lessons he gave me was that I should never refuse an alms to any poor person, especially the one I met first; and if I had nothing to give, then I should say something to console him and recommend him to God by saying the *Our Father* or the *Hail Mary* or the *Hail, Holy Queen*.

Whenever he went out on the quest he left me to take care of the kitchen. On his return he would empty out the sacks of bread into a bin. He always noticed that there was only a little bread left of what he had put there. I had given it to the poor who came in great numbers because of the bad times. "What have you done, Brother Charles?", he used to say. "I did what you taught me to do!", I would answer, smiling, without a further word, for I wanted to praise the name of our Lord who generously took care of our needs as he had promised in the Gospel.

There is something similar to this I would like to tell, that happened to both of us when we were sent on a journey, and I recount it that you may see the providence of God. We travelled along very happily the first day, and in the evening reached a monastery where we were warmly welcomed. Very early the next morning after our prayers, we left without asking for some food to take with us. We had scarcely walked three or four miles when a pauper came up, barefoot and ragged, asking an alms for the love of God. It made me sad to see him in that condition and I gave him a piece of the bread I still had. Since we two friars had been walking about three stone-throws apart, my companion had not seen the beggar. Further on we stopped for lunch and he asked for some of the bread. I told him a poor man had come up to me, and I had given it to him. Instead of being upset he thanked our Lord and we continued our journey in peace of soul.

We became very hungry and tired. After we had walked about a third of a mile further I thought I heard someone calling out. My companion also heard it, even though he had gone ahead again. When we turned round we saw a rather old and serious-looking man coming our way. He stopped as he reached us and greeted us in the name of our Lord. Then from under his mantle he took out a beautiful bottle of wine and a loaf of bread. He asked us to be so kind as to take them and strengthen ourselves for the rest of the trip. We heartily thanked him and our Lord. Shortly after, we reached our monastery of St. John Baptist of Piglio, on the vigil of the feast of St. Anthony of Padua. When we had arranged the business that had brought us there under obedience, we returned to

Morlupo. I continued in my kitchen work there with greater diligence.

As much as I could I tried to understand and grasp what my confrere taught me. Our good Lord helped me to learn how to do things, though they were not done with the exactness and neatness with which my teacher did them. Anyway, since this was the kitchen of poor Friars, they were easily satisfied, for they were given more to mortification than to tasty food. They lived together very peacefully, feeding more on the spiritual food of devotion than on bodily food.

The work delighted me in that I was close to God, far from worldly concerns. Really, for beginners such as I was, not very solidly grounded in virtue, this kind of work is an excellent means of keeping oneself recollected and at the same time enabling one to carry out the works of charity; for especially in the kitchen is fulfilled one of the seven works of mercy, to feed the hungry. I was feeding many servants of God. Really, whoever has the spirit of humility will not look upon such work as beneath him, but will value it as a great favour of our Lord.

To keep myself recollected I would devoutly represent to myself certain events of the life of Jesus Christ. Sometimes I found myself in the poor cave of Bethlehem where the awesome mystery of the birth of our Lord took place, and I said to myself: "Come on, Brother Charles, this morning we will work in the kitchen for the most glorious Virgin, our Mother, from whom we have received such great favours, even that of her bringing forth the Divine Word and Saviour of the world; and we will work also for our special advocate, St. Joseph and all who were there, such as the shepherds".

On other days I imagined the coming of the Magi. On seeing the appearance of a new star in the East, they were inspired by God and came with many people to adore the promised Messias, the eternal King, now newly born. I considered it a great honour to serve them spiritually in my work, and I would have gladly shown them every mark of love possible, since they suffered many discomforts on that long journey.

At other times I pictured myself making meals for our Lord, for his holy Apostles, and for those whom he had chosen as the foundation of the Church. I considered that all this was being done for the Son of God from whom I had received my existence and its continuation, and who had redeemed us with his most Precious Blood.

Mentally I would put myself in the company of my Angel Guardian and of St. Martha, and going ahead with some work I alternately recited with them the Litany of our Lady and other prayers, along with a few ejaculations. While doing the dishes I said with my lips and my heart: "Jesus, Mary, wash my heart and my soul that I may praise and bless you!" And while sweeping: "Jesus and Mary, cleanse my heart and my soul that I may always praise and bless you!"

As I became used to my work, my soul too grew accustomed to it and I experienced delightful consolation and wonderful sweetness in God. I now realize well what I did not then realize: these lowly tasks were the means of leading my soul to its true goal, God; there I stayed and rested in the ecstasy of a mental union, and resting, tasted the peace and joy of the Holy Spirit.

O my confreres,[1] we should employ every talent we have to gain such a large profit. If we look at it rightly our Lord has already put us on the road to it in choosing us for so humble and lowly a state, out of pure generosity; lowly, in the judgment of the world, but very high in the sight of God for those who know how to profit from it. Our Lord is wonderfully pleased by the humble of heart. Just look at our great saint, Brother Didacus of Alcala, and other saintly lay-brothers, and think of the path they held to. They were humbled and scorned in this life, to become really great in the

---

[1] He is addressing the lay-brothers of his Order.

court of the heavenly King. We should not listen to the devil or to our own vanity which would have us believe that the work we do is unimportant; rather we should think of the great reward it brings.

Chapter 24
Further Points About the Time He Was Cook

ROM the mental prayer in which I kept myself occupied and united to His Divine Majesty there grew a certain inner and supernatural pleasure. I experienced this in my soul and therefore gloried in God at being a cook of St. Francis. Many times I said to myself with real feeling: "O Lord, I am the cook of so great a Saint! How did I merit this? I merited hell for my sins and you have treated me so well! Be blessed forever and may all creatures praise and thank you for me!"

What very much increased the ardour of divine love in me was not only the charity towards the poor who came to the door, but also to the religious of other Orders who passed our monastery in large numbers. So as to help them, I abstained from meat and kept it for these occasions. And in some of the serious needs, our Lord did not fail to provide.

One day eleven of these religious came from different places and that evening there were not enough provisions on hand. I began to pray to the Father of the poor, begging him to provide for his servants who had to go weary and foot-sore through the world to make a living. Only a few hours passed before a man by the name of Francis, who was very devoted to me, sent someone to get a little salad, and in return he left a good-sized leg of mutton. I cooked it and fed all the religious. It came to me with a lot of pleasure that I could not remember ever having made anything so well seasoned and tasty as that mutton.

Another day when dinner was over, six of these religious came in without any notice. There was enough left in the pot only for two. They were really famished and could hardly wait any longer; and I did not know where I was going to get the food. I relied on our Lord and with great faith made the sign of the cross over the cooking-pot. The contents were increased so much that what was going to have to do for two was more than enough for six!

As I went on thus, very happy in serving God in the kitchen, the same holy God, who knows our weakness well, put a little counterbalance to this work of mine so that the spirit of self-esteem should not get into my heart and conquer me. The kitchen utensils, pots and pans, plates and soup-dishes, began breaking. This was more than a little mortifying to me, because sometimes when others took these utensils to hand them to me, they broke into pieces even though they were very careful about it. Besides, when I was taking a small tray of dishes from the refectory to the kitchen, I slipped—how, I do not know—and not one plate remained whole. When I was serving Mass, the cruets quite often broke or else I upset them. This put a great fear in me and made me blush terribly.

What upset me interiorly in all this more than anything else, was that the Father Guardian was displeased at it. He did not want the other Friars to take me for an awkward dolt. And so he often corrected me charitably in private, finally telling me that I should no longer put some such broken utensil around my neck in the refectory as a penance, as was the rule and the custom for the young Friars.

Something worse and more disturbing happened, and it had to do with the kitchen fire. In the summer some of the Friars asked me kindly to make some fried onions for them. They were making a Lent of devotion, and besides they were very used to eating poor food.

As yet I had no practice in preparing onions in the way they asked. There was a different Master now, as I shall tell later, and I talked it over with him. He taught me what to do. First I was to boil some onions and then drain the water off well; after that I should roll them in flour and put them to fry in a pan with hot olive oil. I did this. I suppose they were not drained well enough, for when I put them into the frying-pan, all of a sudden the boiling oil began to jump out of the pan and the fire took hold of it with such suddenness that flames were scattered all over that part of the kitchen.

It was easy to see that I was in great danger in that narrow place. I went to the window to jump out, but it was too high from the level outside; so the next thing to do was to go through the flames and out the door to where all the Friars were standing helpless to assist me. There was a statue of glorious St. Joseph in the kitchen and with much faith I put myself in his care. Then I threw a fold of my habit up over my face and ran through the fire. Our Lord watched over me because I got out without any burns. When the Friars saw I was safe they all came up and began to joke: "Wasn't it enough to break dishes and other utensils? Did you want to fry us alive?" Once I was out of the kitchen the fire died out by itself and no damage was done, except that all the oil in the frying-pan was gone.

My good father, of whom I had such wonderful memories, passed to a better life at this time. This is how our Lord let me know about his death, so that I could help him, since I was greatly indebted to him. When I had retired for the night, my father came to me in a dream very distressed, as one who is suffering terrible pains in his last hours. He kept begging me very urgently to go to church to pray for him, and this awakened me. I went down to the church before the Blessed Sacrament, knelt on the floor and said the seven Penitential Psalms[1] with other prayers.

When I received Holy Communion that morning I applied the holy indulgences to him.

This lasted many days and his requests grew more urgent, until all at once I understood, without knowing how, that his soul had gone to heaven. I was greatly comforted, though the

---

[1] Called the Penitential Psalms because they are very well adapted to expressing sentiments of compunction and penance.

devil who hates everything good tried to afflict me with some false apparitions. He wanted me to believe that my father had not really been saved but that he was in hell. Many times my father appeared in his own bodily form suffering the very pains which the devil endures. But I paid little attention to all of this and simply continued to pray for his soul.

Not many days had gone by when a letter came from Sezze advising me of my father's death. He had been marvellously resigned to it, after having received the sacraments of the Church with marked devotion. Like another Jacob he had blessed all his children and though I was not there, as he wished, he also gave me his blessing wherever I might be, mentioning my name many times.

Chapter 25
Determination to Practise Rigorous Penances

THOUGH I had often transgressed the divine law, still the Father of mercies brought me to the sheepfold and the safe harbour of the religious life. The attractions of his grace led me there. He formed in me a great desire to love him and to perform very severe penances for his sake, in satisfaction of my serious sins. This desire grew greater when I saw that my Father Guardian and spiritual director were of a mind to allow this. So I determined to bring about a betterment in myself by moderating my use of clothing. With the permission of the Father Provincial I stopped using the inner tunic and got ready to suffer the cold of winter. For thirteen years I wore one old habit until the Provincial Superior commanded differently.

In eating and sleeping I held to the same rigour, abstaining from meat and fish. Still I did not refuse the body its needs, giving it sufficient bread and watered wine, vegetables and fruit. For a bed I used a table on which I put a straw-mat. I rested poorly and I slept worse, so that in my waking hours I was like a person who had been knocked about. The hours I spent in sleep were few since for a good part of the night I kept vigil in church in mental prayer and in calling on God aloud in affectionate terms, taking the discipline for half an hour. On Fridays especially, in memory of the most holy Passion, I took the discipline to blood, for I had one with well sharpened iron points.

When he saw that I continued determinedly in prayer and penance and that in these I put myself under holy obedience, the enemy tried another kind of warfare. Once again he enkindled the fire of sensuality in my flesh with the fuel of shameful thoughts and evil images. During the novitiate it had lain dormant, as it were. Now I was forced to think of what I was ignorant of and to imagine what I had never experienced.

Right in the middle of my sleep at night when I wanted to get my rest, he presented disgraceful things that caused the most awful dreams against the vow of chastity. I awakened very much upset and miserable for fear of offending my Lord. I felt as though I was talking to people who kept saying: "How much better you would have done to stay in the world, for you have committed very serious sins even though you are a religious". They chid me terribly as though I had deliberately offended God, to make me fall into the sin of despair. That is how far the enemy went.

But no matter how much he tried, all this was against my will; I was not my own master. I would have preferred to be killed many times rather than offend God. In my conscience I knew that I had no part in this, so I recovered somewhat and thanked our Lord and the most glorious Virgin with St. Joseph, her spouse, for the help they had given me.

These infernal monsters raged so fiercely against me that I think they would have destroyed me and reduced me to ashes, had they been able. Often enough when I was trying to sleep, two or three devils would come and invade my heart with their diabolical suggestions. It was as if they took a long iron nail, red-hot, and pierced my head as they made it go through one ear and out the other in a great blaze. The pain I felt was immense. My hearing was impaired, even ruined for life, but I myself was uninjured by the piercing fire.

One night they formed a line in my room and attacked me like mad wolves. Acting as if they were going to eat me alive, they strangled me and kept saying: "Renounce God or we will kill you!" I answered that I would die before doing that! Then they went off in a rage and I thanked His Divine Majesty for having freed me from their dreadful mouths. I considered all these divine permissions a great grace because it is far worse to be tormented for ever in hell in the company of the devils. Perhaps this was the reason why our Lord let me in spirit see that place of misery.

One day when I was in my room during the time of silence and prayer I found myself in a very deep place without realizing how. Since I was right on the surface I saw great fiery flames rising toward the heavens; these flames were full of damned souls all afire, and of devils tormenting them with every sort of torture. I heard the pitiable screams of these miserable wretches; the whole world was filled with frightful terror at the horrible blasphemies they uttered against God. I trembled from head to foot at seeing the pain of these condemned creatures and more at hearing what they said against God. I do not know if I was there bodily or if this was a vision, but I began to beg our Lord to give me the grace not to blaspheme him as they were doing in that fire, since it pleased him that I be there without suffering any bodily harm. As I prayed I came back to my senses and cried out: "Oh, if one moment in that place seemed like a thousand years, what would it be like to be there for all eternity?"[2]

---

[2] The canonization of St. Charles after his having remained unknown for several centuries should serve to indicate that his life and writings carry a message for modem man. His complete obedience rebukes the present-day lust for self-determination; his humility, its pride and boastfulness; his poverty, its precipitate rush after material pleasures. What he suffered at the hands of the demons also carries a lesson for modem times. It is that the devil is very much in existence, and deliberately to close our mind against the thought of him will only serve to give him greater power. St. Charles teaches us the way to oppose the devil and all the fallen angels in their incessant warfare against our souls. Very few will ever be asked to suffer bodily harm from the devil, but all must suffer, and overcome, his temptations to pride, lust and ambition (*Translator*).

Chapter 26
New Guardian and Master

THE Provincial Chapter was held during Easter week and Father Berard of Bologna was elected the Provincial Superior. I had been at the Morlupo monastery one year. The Father Guardian and quite a few of the Friars were changed. Father Romanus of Rome came as the new Guardian. A man of prayer, he was held in high esteem. The new Vicar was Father John of Filacciano who became my new spiritual director.

The new Guardian took good care of me. He wanted to keep me in the strictness that is expected of novices. Above all he watched to make sure that I was with the others at common prayer and the ceremonies of our Order. Each little negligence was punished rigorously. Wonderful observance and silence were kept in the monastery. Our Lord was favouring my desires.

Since the Friars who had to come from a distance had not yet arrived and the others had gone, I had to be the porter and also continue my work in the kitchen, and this meant a lot of inconvenience. Because the monastery was near a road to Rome, many different religious stopped there on their travels, and I needed the Superior's permission to bring them inside and give them some food. When the good Superior saw the numbers who called to ask for alms, he became somewhat scrupulous because it meant taking the food the benefactors had donated to the Friars and giving it to strangers. So he commanded me not to give anything to anyone in the future, except to our own religious.

I felt some displeasure at this order but still I carried out the obedience without a word about it. However, our Lord remedied the situation, for as we had withdrawn the hand of charity from the poor, so he withdrew his hand from us, his religious. We have to be full of love in helping our fellow men to save their souls and in giving them whatever pertains to their bodily needs.

When I saw the alms to us decreasing I spoke respectfully to the Father Guardian about it, since I felt this was the right time: "Father, I think the reason people are no longer sending us alms is that we withdrew the hand of charity from the poor, and so our Lord has done the same to us. We should therefore give a lot of thought to what we are doing!" The Father Guardian listened to what I had to say, thought it over carefully, and then quickly changed his outlook. He told me to do just what I had done previously. That is what I did, and our Lord quickly provided for us as before.

My Master in the kitchen was a very fine cook. He also guided me in the matter of perfection, keeping more to the strict side than to kindness and gentleness. Whenever he noticed something poorly done or some food not well prepared he not only corrected me on the spot but brought the Father Guardian into the kitchen to see where I had failed and had him give me a penance in the refectory. I tried to benefit from this, especially since the Master had only the best motives. I am sure he did this only to keep me humble. But though I took all these penances gladly, still I had all I could do to bring this weak and very sensitive nature of mine into line, since it longed for nothing but to be coddled and held in great esteem.

That we may see how much a person can do when God assists him with his grace, and how quickly he fails if God abandons him only for a moment, I should like to tell how I was somewhat humbled on one occasion. At the request of the Master I was given a penance by the Father Guardian and I felt the mortification so much that it not only made my blood boil but I could not even think correctly.

I went back to the kitchen after dinner and I was still just as much disturbed. The Master came in after a while to see what I was doing; he was smiling and began to talk. Just as soon as he started to speak the devil put I do not know what into my head; there was nothing more I wanted to do than to ridicule him for what he had done to me. Oh, the blindness of that moment! Instead of thanking him for his charity I took everything wrong and answered him angrily, though thanks to God's grace I did not use any harmful or disrespectful words. He had to smile at my foolishness and because he was very wise, he graciously left without saying a word.

Once he had gone a terrible remorse of conscience for what I had done settled over me and an inner restlessness lashed me, for it seemed that I had committed one of the greatest sins in the world. As I thought about it I asked pardon of God with great sorrow, blaming myself for a lack of reverence toward the Master. For this act of pride I judged that I was not worthy to wear the holy habit. For the rest of the day I could find no peace of heart, not for fear of my reputation in the community, but at what I had done and at my helplessness in finding the means to crush that pride of mine.

After much thought I made up my mind to take off the habit, put it around my neck and go into the refectory that way when all the Friars were there. If the Superior under God's direction thought that I should be given a chance to be clothed in the habit again, he would make a concession such as was made when I was first received. I did not budge from this resolution, but begged our Lord all along to be there to help me in carrying out his will.

When the evening meal came I sent out the little food we had that the Friars might refresh themselves in the Lord. Then I knelt before the statue of St. Joseph, beseeching him together with the Virgin to help me in what I was determined to carry out, and that our Lord should inspire my Superior in what was to be done with me. I made the sign of the cross, took my habit off and made a bundle of it; then I put it around my neck and went into the refectory. In the presence of all the Friars I prostrated on the floor, admitted my fault of pride in answering my brother angrily and said I was not worthy therefore to wear the habit. After he had listened to me, the Father Guardian gave me a fitting penance. He commanded me to go back to the kitchen, put the habit on again and do my work with charity and patience. My consolation was complete, for in my Superior I saw the charity of God and I did what he told me.

When the meal was over, the Master came in and embraced me affectionately. He said that once this happened he had given it no further thought, for such resentment will often arise as long as we are in the flesh. At times it is so strong that we cannot bear it any longer and are not masters of ourselves. And so I should be at peace and trouble myself no more, for uneasiness is at times worse than faults themselves.

Chapter 27
New Spiritual Director

Y new spiritual director also saw to it that I advanced in perfection and in striving for total self-renunciation. He did not permit me to do anything on my own judgment.

Concerning prayer he told me that I was not to spend any time in it beyond what is customarily required in the Order. Once the Ave Maria bell of the dead rang[1] I was not to stay in church but go straight to my room and go to bed, folding my arms in the form of a cross, and I was not to get up till the Matins bell had rung. When Matins was over I was to go back to bed again till the morning. To know whether I was obedient in this he would come into my room unexpectedly, to see whether or not I was praying. He further questioned my not having any order in my prayers.

As for penance, he completely forbade the discipline to blood and ordered me to take it with the others the usual three times a week; and at no time was I to wear a hair-shirt. All this I observed to the letter.

To have me avoid singularity in all things he wanted me to eat what all the others ate; and to break my own will all the more he told me that when meat was served I was first to eat the meat, and then the other food. I did the same on a fast day when fish was served.

Sometimes when I had cooked one kind of food he would come in and make me cook another, and leave the first one there. At times it would be quite late, near mealtime, and it

---

[1] The *Ave Maria* of the dead is the ringing of the bell that is customary in many places one hour after the evening *Angelus*, to call the faithful to pray for die faithful departed.

made me very nervous; still I did everything he told me, obediently, with the help of His Divine Majesty.

On other occasions, right in the middle of my work he made me leave the kitchen and do something in the garden. Hardly a quarter of an hour would pass when he would come to call me back to the kitchen again. Sometimes he ordered me to do very difficult things, and, after a little while, would dispense me from the command. In short, he did everything his office of spiritual director called for to remedy my imprudence and have me act always under obedience, with complete renunciation of my own will—something that is of great help to beginners.

During this time I did not cease helping the poor, of whom one morning there were many, besides the religious of other Orders. As the time approached for me to get the meal ready for the community there was not enough bread in the basket; and because it was late no one had time to go for some. I became a little restless at this, the more so since the brethren were aware of it and raised a big fuss; they went complaining about it to the Superior.

When I noticed the disturbance I took steps to remedy it by hurriedly sending for bread a young lad who used to go on errands for the monastery. But God is really wonderful in all his works and while I was talking with the lad I was summoned by the Father Vicar. A young man, he told me, had brought a large amount of bread from a great distance and I should be hospitable to him before he left. I was surprised. I could not understand how he had come in, since I had the key to the door. But I immediately carried out the obedience to find him and give him a lunch. But though I looked through the whole monastery and asked everyone in the house if he had seen this person, a young man with a little dog, I never found him.

When the Father Vicar realized that a miracle had taken place he gave a fervent instruction in the refectory and ordered me never again to deny an alms to the poor; and if there was no bread left, then even what was to be put at his own small table should be given to them, for nothing more pleasing to God could ever be done for them than this!

One day His Divine Majesty arranged that I go on a preaching trip with one of the Fathers into and about Morlupo. He first had to go to the city of Nepi to ask the bishop for his blessing. We left the monastery in the morning without taking any provisions with us. When we reached Nepi we were told that the bishop had left for Sutri, so we started walking there. Night came on and we still had about half a mile to go. The Father became afraid. He stopped to ask me how we could spend the night, since it was cold and late and we were strangers in that region. I said that we had to have recourse to God and have confidence that he would help us find some young fellow at the city gate who would take us to whatever hotel there was.

We recited the Litany of our Lady devoutly, with some prayers for the dead. It had already been dark about an hour when we came to the gate of the city. A young man was standing there with his hand on his belt. He gladly offered to take us inside the city; in fact, he took us to a mansion whose owner warmly welcomed us when he saw that we were Franciscans. Because we were suffering and shivering from the cold he brought us into the great hall where there was a big fire. As we warmed ourselves a servant prepared a meal. Though he kept bringing in every kind of dish we could not see any women in the house, nor from where the food was coming.

I was astounded at seeing such a variety of food come out so quickly, as though His Divine Majesty had kept these things ready just for us. After our meal the master of the house insisted on having our feet washed in warm wine. Our legs were all inflamed and bloody from the wet, muddy habit rubbing against them. Then he took us to our rooms for a night's rest; each had his own nicely furnished room.

We had to leave there in the morning but first our host personally gave us two loaves of white bread with other delicacies. Then he filled our flask with wine and stayed with us right to the mansion gate. We thanked him and went to look for the bishop who was living in a monastery outside the city. Once we had received his blessing we took the road back to our monastery in Morlupo.

Another time our Lord helped me when I went back to Nepi with the Father confessor of the bishop. A guide had been furnished us. He took a different road from the one we had used before. He stayed with us for two miles or so and left when he thought that we could find our own way safely. But we had not gone far when we ended up in a thick wood at the foot of a hill. There was no longer any road but only some small paths used by animals.

Not knowing where to go we were frightened, so we stopped to decide what should be done. As each gave his opinion, two birds came up very close. They were magpies, very beautiful birds. They are mostly found in pairs and even sing alternately. I said: "Father, we should follow these birds; they may come out on some road". We did that.

The birds went along ahead of us following a valley. When we caught up with them again they flew off singing loudly, and they kept ahead of us at just the right distance for us to see and hear them, as they rested on the branches of a tree. In that way they led us to a wood where a man came by, who took us through it and put us on a safe road. The birds turned and flew back. We thanked God for this and went on to the monastery.

Chapter 28
A Command from the Spiritual Director

HE Father Vicar who was my spiritual director had a sick brother at Filacciano and the poor Father was very much troubled and afflicted over this. He kept recommending his brother to me. But when he realized that the sickness was constantly getting worse he put me under obedience to pray for his brother. In particular I was to pray during the night before the painting of the Madonna at the high altar, nor was I to leave there until I learned from the Virgin what our Lord was going to do.

The first night I prayed without stopping. The second night I petitioned the most holy Virgin in the best way I knew, repeating over and over these words: "You know, O most holy Mother, that I cannot leave here; help me then in what I have to do!" As I kept at this prayer in the deep stillness of the night, the Mother of God appeared to me with the Child in her arms. The Child seemed to be about two years old. He held a little silver cross in one hand and on his face was a smile as he looked at me. The Virgin revealed to me that the sick man was going to die in a few days. I told this to my Father director; he was resigned to the divine will and thanked our Lord. It was not many days afterward that his brother's death became known.

One morning after my devotions as I was going to the kitchen, the monastery of St. Mary of Grace at Ponticelli came to my mind. When I had been there eight months previously, it seemed to be a very gloomy place as I walked through the dormitory. I said to myself then: "O Lord, who would want to come here?" And now, this very morning as the thought of that holy place passed through my mind, a terrible melancholy took hold of me as I recalled in particular that narrow little dormitory.

A quarter of an hour had not gone by when two Friars came to the monastery; they were from Rome, from the monastery of St. Francis a Ripa. One of them was my former Master, Brother Valentine of Spoleto. He came to the kitchen to pay me a visit. We greeted each other affectionately and then he said he was bringing me good news from Rome. I begged him to tell me what it was and to let me see what he had in his hand. He smilingly indicated that it was an obedience[1] to St. Mary of Ponticelli;[2] and so he would give it to the Father Guardian. I prostrated myself on the floor and thanked God as I prepared myself to do his holy will.

---

[1] An order or a permission of the Superior usually put in writing.

[2] The monastery of Ponticelli (Rieti), dedicated to our Lady of Grace, was founded in 1478 by Blessed Amadeus the Portuguese. It was also hallowed by the stay of Blessed Bonaventure of Barcelona who made it a *ritiro* in 1662. St. Leonard of Port Maurice, the Venerable John Baptist of Borgogna, and others, also lived there.

Chapter 29
Monastery at Ponticelli: Gardener

I ARRIVED at this place, sacred to the Virgin, accompanied by its Father Guardian, Innocent of Rome, who was very cordial to me in Christ. The charity with which we were welcomed by all the Fathers and Brothers was great. They did not hide their happiness at the return of their Superior and spiritual father. After the washing of our feet, the Father Guardian himself showed me to my living quarters as he gave me his blessing. My room was in that small and dark dormitory-wing which, as I said, seemed to me very gloomy. But without a word I embraced holy obedience though it was very repugnant to my natural disposition. I thanked God that this was his holy will because it sweetens everything when it is accepted obediently.

The Father Guardian gave me Father Francis of Montalto della Marca as my spiritual director. But this good Father did not take many pains with what concerned the interior life; he gave his attention only to my exterior observance of the rule, customs and religious ceremonies.

The Master who was assigned to instruct me in manual labour was the brother gardener. I was to be his helper in the garden work and go with him begging alms in nearby places. This venerable religious was quite old, but given to a lot of work and great austerity. He went barefoot, and I do not mean without socks, but without sandals, even when it was very cold.

Once he had me under his charge he expected the same austerity of me that he demanded of himself without regard to my constitution which was not vigorous and robust as his was. With the Father Guardian's permission he had me go barefoot. The fact that I was young helped me a lot in imitating him in this as well as in the work, at which he was tireless. He was very sparing in words when he gave me instructions. What he wanted me to do was pretty well indicated by his actions. I had all I could do to keep up with him and to get used to his disposition, but our Lord gave me the necessary grace. When he saw that I was making progress he took such a liking to me that it was a wonder.

In this brother I was able to see a marvellous simplicity. Besides, he had a way with animals and spoke to them as though they were rational creatures. The Friars told me that several times swallows had come into his hands. He was held in high esteem by seculars.

This brother insisted that I was to be obedient in everything he gave me to do and he said that with obedience a religious could not leave the right path because it was the safest of the virtues. At times he commanded things of me that seemed exaggerated, as, for example, when we went into the garden to work or into the woods to cut wood, he always wanted me to keep the axe tied to my cord.

During the period in which my Superior kept me at work with this servant of God I experienced little of the prayer of quiet because I was wrapped up in the garden work so that the Friars should not lack food. In the morning I heard the first Mass and after we had said our devotions we went to the garden and worked there till lunch time. After lunch we continued the work till the evening. It is true that the Father Guardian wanted me also to serve a Mass every morning and be at prayer and go to Holy Communion with the others; but when I went to get permission for this from the Master he told me to see to it that I did not place my arms in the form of a cross; by this he meant to say that after I received Holy Communion I should not remain behind saying long prayers, but hurry and get back to work. I gave in to what he wanted and so I did everything quickly.

Besides, since it was a very poor locality, we used to go to the Castelli[1] round about asking for alms. Between one occupation and another, as I said, there was little time for recollection and meditation, so our whole profit lay in obedience alone. This was not little, since it is one of the greatest things a religious can do to please God. If we did nothing else in religion, great would be the gain it brings. We should be very happy with it, realizing that our Lord will give us great exaltation of soul right in the middle of our busiest days, if he so wishes.[2] Still, we should not look for that, because if we do, it would simply be a looking for a reward from His Divine Majesty. We have to do our work out of love for our Lord Jesus Christ who will grant an eternal reward for our labour. This reward will be himself in an enjoyment that beatifies.

---

[1] The Castelli are picturesque towns and villages situated in most cases on the tops of mountains. They are so called because they were built for the purposes of defence around a castle (*castello*) which was at the same time a fortress.

[2] Interior recollection and the spirit of prayer and devotion are meant. The Saint intends to say that this may happen when we omit our usual practices of piety not out of negligence and whim, but out of obedience when it requires unusual work.

Chapter 30
Cook Again: Trouble in the Kitchen

BOUT four months had gone by while I was under the care of the Friar gardener, when the monastery lost its cook. The Father Guardian asked me to do this work of great charity and he gave me Brother Jerome of Rieti as my master.

Not only was Brother Jerome a good religious; he was very experienced in manual work and he had his own way of instructing and bringing others to understand something. What had to be done the next day, he would show me the day before; and he was strict about it. In order not to make any mistakes I had to pay close attention to what he told me, for he did not hesitate to correct whatever errors I made. I learned some points from him, especially how to work dough. However, the good Lord kept me humble by the many utensils I broke. All this made me praise his infinite goodness since he is pleased that our accomplishments have certain counterbalances, even when they are good and carried out for him. It was well for me that my Superior was indulgent. He knew me, for he had been my Guardian in the monastery at Morlupo.

One day some of the Friars were told to go fishing in a place nearby, called the brook Corese. They caught enough fish to provide a meal for all the Friars. I fried them in the copper pans we had and I kept them in the closed oven, after putting some live coals beneath it. Meanwhile the bell for one of the Masses rang and because I saw that all my work was done for the time, I went to serve it. When I came back into the sacristy another priest was vested for Mass. I thought there was time for it, so I served his Mass also, but when it was over I found the Guardian waiting for me in the sacristy.

Just at that time the Lent that we call the *Benedicta* was

on.[1] The Superior called me aside and asked me if I was preparing a Lenten meal or not. My answer was that it was a Lenten meal and so I had prepared it accordingly. He said that he had very definitely smelled sausages cooking in the kitchen. I went there immediately to see what had happened. The Guardian went too and when I opened the oven where I had put the fish, we found it had been all burnt and the smell filled the whole place. Because the Guardian was a prudent man he did not get upset at this. He restrained himself. He thanked God calmly and told me to mention this fault at *culpa*.[2] Something else could be served for the meal.

The fault could not be hidden, for all the Friars knew that I had cooked the fish. By having me mention it at *culpa* the Guardian wanted the penance to be known also. I went into the refectory during the evening meal, confessed my fault as I knelt on the floor with head down, and in a particular way admitted the damage I had done that morning. The Father Guardian charitably reprimanded me. He showed he was displeased, for through my forgetfulness I had deprived the poor Friars on a day when all that they had was a little fish. For fifteen days I was to eat bread and water on the floor of the refectory, because fifteen or sixteen Friars had to go without the small provisions the Lord had sent during a fasting period. I did this penance gladly for the love of Jesus Christ because I knew I well deserved it. After the tenth day the Father Guardian very compassionately dispensed me from the rest of the penance at the request of the entire community, and I was able to sit down at table.

Because I was a youngster in the religious life the good

---

[1] So called because of the special blessing of St. Francis attached to it. The Benedicta begins on Epiphany, January 6, and lasts for forty days. It is not of obligation.

[2] He is alluding to the custom, found in almost all religious institutes, of manifesting one's external faults in public; this is followed by an admonition and a penance given by the Superior.

Fathers at times discussed with me the paths to be taken that I might go ahead in Christian perfection. To see what virtue I had, they would sometimes say a little thing calculated to try my patience, as did the saintly Fathers of the desert with someone who had recently left the world.

One morning I was cooking a vegetable and one of the Fathers, who more than the others wanted me to be perfect in the virtue of patience, told me that it would not taste good to the Friars if I made it that way, and besides it was not how he would do it. I was very friendly with him and so I said smilingly: "If it does not turn out well this way, the way the Master showed me, the penance will be for me to eat it all myself". He seemed displeased at this and so he told the Superior what had happened that he might use this to keep me humble and mortified.

When I went into the refectory to acknowledge my defects and shortcomings, the Father Superior held a long chapter.[3] He reproved me for the little respect I had for the Friars when they came to the fire to warm themselves. I was to revere them as angels from heaven, especially the priests who administer the most holy Body of the Lord. In their presence I was to stand politely without saying a word. It was not becoming a young professed religious to talk much.

Then there was a change in what he had to say. "My son", he said, "if you try to satisfy the taste of all the Friars, then each of them would need to have his own little cooking-pot, and I do not know if even this would be enough! So avoid making some speciality, even if it is a little thing, but gladly cook what is customary and in accord with our life, and whatever the Master tells you."

---

[3] This is a discourse given by the Superior to the assembled religious in which he exhorts them to correct their defects and to keep improving themselves.

In that way he corrected my lack of respect while talking to the Friars, and the Friars also for wanting things made their own way, each to his own taste.

Chapter 31
Renewed Temptation to Vainglory

HOUGH I was no longer under the brother gardener, I continued to go barefoot for no one had told me differently. And because we become very much attached to these external things they can be a great danger, especially when a solid firmness is lacking in us. Our common enemy, who goes about ceaselessly looking into our inclinations and observing our habits, puts a rope across our path to make us fall and he puts it where he sees we are leaning the most, even to good works.

When he noticed that I persisted in the mortification of going barefoot he began tempting me very much to vainglory. He filled my heart with self-praise, putting conceited thoughts in my mind, making me think I was regarded as a saint and a perfect man by being seen barefoot. Especially when I went into the church to serve Mass he invaded my soul with the thought that everyone there saw me, and this brought on such self-esteem that as I walked along I felt that I was being lifted up in the air by the hairs of my head! If I had not actually experienced this I would never have thought it possible.

We do well to note the risk to our soul in wanting to be even the least bit singular, even though we have permission not to follow the common life. This is a permission that should not be granted readily and then only to those who are fully mature in the spiritual life.

As I watched myself constantly I continued as before, often recommending myself to the help of God. He is everywhere, diffusing the rays of his infinite mercy. After I had suffered this troublesome temptation for some months the good God saw fit to free me from it in a way far removed from human wisdom.

Near the end of July and the beginning of August the

people who lived near one of the Castelli were having a great feast day. They wanted us also to share in the blessings of the Lord, so, in their charity, they sent us different things, including some snow. I was not only able to cool our wine with it, but also some fruit. When the next meal came I sat down to eat some of the fruit. I was very warm, since I had been near the stove, and besides I had eaten some hot food. The fruit was so chilled that I caught a cold in the stomach and the rest of the day I was quite sick. But when night came I thought I was going to die; there was no end to the pain!

No one else had fallen ill, as I had. When the Superior came to see me he decided that all this came from my going barefoot and so he said that as soon as I was well again I was to put on sandals. I did this and considered it a great grace from God, for hardly had I carried out the obedience that the temptation to vainglory disappeared.

CHAPTER 32
INCREASE IN THE DESIRE FOR PENANCE

THE desire I had of doing penance for my sins was very great. It increased daily and to such a degree that I was left without a way to satisfy it. At this time our Father Provincial came to the monastery and I told him how I felt. He ordered me to keep the common life and said that I would be doing a great thing if I carried it out exactly. One can say that those who faithfully observe the common life are safely walking the way of holiness.[1]

Though this did not give me as much as I had longed for, still I was very consoled in knowing the will of my major superior, for I had always firmly held that every other virtue is perfect when linked with obedience and that, without it, no other virtue has any worth. Now the reason for my wanting to do more was that I looked upon penance not as a means but as an end. This showed that I still did not have a practical foundation in the spiritual life.

Beginners should put themselves under the direction of their Master and, though they may think they are not progressing— because they do not receive directions from their Master corresponding to their own wishes—still, if they follow his guidance exactly, this will become the shortest and the easiest way to perfection. And not only is it advantageous to the soul but also to the body in keeping it healthy.

Though I could not extend my practices of penance as I wanted, I did not, however, give up suitable mortifications. It is mortification which keeps natural imperfections in check, and surely we know well how they make us slip. So I kept at

---

[1] St. Charles here touches upon what the Saints and ascetical authors emphasize greatly, namely, that the common life is the very backbone of the religious state, and that without it every type of irregularity and singularity will enter because of self-delusion.

this work against myself, and to conquer myself I took to distributing the days in honour of God and of the saints.

For a time I used this exercise of mortification without seeing any of the gains I had hoped for; in fact, I seemed to be going backwards. I think it was because I lacked humility, for at times I thought I was overcoming myself by my own strength. But to do this one needs a special grace of God without whose help human diligence means nothing. No sooner had I formed the determination of not committing any fault than I began to fail a little. Our Lord allows this to happen to anyone who presumes too much on himself, in order to humble him, so that he may acknowledge his nothingness and the omnipotent power of God on which he depends.

Though this type of mortification is good and helps in checking our evil inclinations, still it came to me one day at prayer that I should give it up and use another exercise that seemed better and likely to yield greater profit from the mortification of my senses. The exercise is confidence in God. This placed me under his fatherly protection as a child lies in its mother's arms and is defended by her against every danger. Still, I did not want to omit doing anything that depended on me.

Once I grasped this truth shared with me by the Father of lights, I made an act of love of God and of true confidence as devoutly and humbly as I could, distrusting myself completely. I put all my reliance on God, asking his pardon if I was late in doing this and promising him that I would never again leave his protection, because he had never abandoned me but had always come to my help.[2]

As time went on the affairs of my soul turned out much better. I grew in spiritual vigour and in resignation to daily

---

[2] The childlike confidence in God demonstrated by St. Charles reminds us forcefully of the same simple reliance on God which was later shown by St. Teresa of the Child Jesus.

occurrences, and instead of becoming sad and discouraged over my faults I peacefully lifted myself up again from them.

To check my natural desire for fruit, especially grapes and figs, for which I had an unusual fondness, I used to say as I went into the garden to pick them for the brethren who allowed me to eat some of them: "This time let us leave them be; the next time I will allow you to eat as much as you want!"

Chapter 33
Rome, Palestrina

AFTER I had lived a whole year at the monastery in Ponticelli an obedience was sent by the Provincial Superior to one of our Fathers, transferring him to Rome, and in the same obedience it was stated that I was to go with him. When Father Guardian saw this he was very upset because of his affection for me. He guessed that I would not come back.

On the first of November after we had asked the Superior for his blessing, the Father and I walked to Rome. It was a very happy trip, as we went along praising and thanking our Lord and saying some prayers such as the Psalms of David and the Litany of our Lady.

We had covered better than half the way to Rome when I began to sense an awful disturbance. It bothered my whole being without my being able to discover the reason for this unusual restlessness. I did not know what was going to happen. I took courage by making acts of faith, hope and love, and prepared myself to meet whatever the divine will had in store for me.

When we reached our monastery of St. Francis in Rome I met at the entrance the Guardian of the monastery at Sezze, Father Augustine of Velletri, a man of great virtue. He asked me if I was Brother Charles of Sezze. "Yes, by the mercy of God", I told him. "Son, your mother has gone to a better life; be resigned now and pray to our Lord for her soul."

When I heard this unexpected news I felt the natural emotion of tenderness that everyone experiences at such a time; but I was not upset and I thanked God for having freed her from the prison of this world and the troubles we suffer in it, for she had gone out of her way to help many people. I assisted her by prayer and by receiving the most holy

Sacrament of the Altar, applying the indulgences to her soul until our Lord in his mercy revealed to me that she was in glory.

We went to show our obedience to the Father Provincial.

He was in his office with some other Fathers, treating affairs of the province. He was happy to see us and told me he wanted to send me some distance away to the monastery of St. Francis of Palestrina.[1] As my companion I would have the Father Vicar of that same monastery, who was in Rome settling some of its business, and that I should stay a while.

I stayed there several days during which I visited the seven churches.[2] Then I left Rome under holy obedience with the Father Vicar. We reached the monastery of St. Bonaventure of Frascati[3] where we spent the night. In the morning we set off for the monastery of Palestrina where we were received by the Father Guardian and the brethren with the accustomed charity shown to travelling religious.

The fourth monastery thus far to which I had been sent by my Provincial Superior in the Franciscan family, had Father Nicholas of Sospello as its Guardian. Because there was no one there who could cook, he gave me that work, so excellent for the exercise of charity. My Master was Brother Didacus of Catino who had also been my Master in the novitiate. He marvelled that I had succeeded and had learned so much since

---

[1] The monastery of St. Francis of Palestrina was founded in 1426. On the main altar of the church is a priceless triptych of that age. Under the altar is the body of St. Constance, Martyr.

[2] Namely, St. Peter's Basilica, St. John Lateran, St. Mary Major, St. Paul outside-the-walls, the Holy Cross in Jerusalem, St. Sebastian, and St. Lawrence outside-the-walls. From ancient times pilgrims visited these seven churches in order to gain the plenary indulgence. More recently this indulgence has been gained by visiting only the first four, which are the Major Basilicas.

[3] The monastery of St. Bonaventure of Frascati was founded in 1610. At present it is the house of philosophy and theology of the Franciscan Roman Province.

leaving his charge. He noticed also that I busied myself as much as possible so that the Friars would not suffer, and that I took such good care of them at table that they had no reason for going elsewhere for their meals.

Father Guardian was a very austere religious. When he saw what I was making he felt it was too much, as he wanted the Friars to be more abstemious. Yet everything was in moderation and it did not go beyond the requirements of poverty.

One day he came into the kitchen and very pleasantly told me that I was giving the Friars too much to eat. With his permission I said that I was not doing any more than what he had ordered me, and since some of the food came as alms and did not exceed the moderation of poor living, it seemed a good thing to be charitable to the Friars, instead of wasting the food, especially since some of the Friars there were weak and needed more to strengthen themselves. He was satisfied and at rest with my opinion on this, happy that I was showing the charity I had started off with to the twenty religious who were far advanced in virtue and perfection.

The Easter season came. Some small lambs were sent to us as an alms. I believe there were six of them. They would be slaughtered as needed. Meanwhile they were put out in the woods to graze. When the time came to slaughter one of them I simply could not catch any of them, try as I might and run as I might. I gave up after getting very tired. Then they all grouped together on one of the paths of the woods and set off for the monastery. They found their own way to the kitchen and when they got there, those meek animals all faced me, bent their knees to the floor and lowered their heads by way of asking pardon.

When I saw all this I was full of wonderment and compassion. I looked up to heaven, thanked God and gave them a blessing in the name of the Father, of the Son and of the Holy Spirit, telling them to leave with the peace of our Lord for they would never be molested or killed by me. When they were blessed they stood up as if they knew what all this meant and went back into the woods along the same path.

CHAPTER 34
BEGINNING OF ECSTASIES: THEIR CAUSES

URING my first year at Palestrina my spiritual director was Father Eugene of Rome. He was Vicar of the monastery, a very prudent man and a good preacher. He took great pains in teaching me how to walk in the way of perfection in the life of the soul. Father Eugene was not very concerned as to whether I performed great penances. His programme consisted essentially in the common life as lived in the Order. This is a holy and safe way and through it many have gone to heaven with a name for great sanctity.

Since the Father Guardian was an expert in spiritual matters he also carefully observed me, and above all he saw to it that I did not converse with secular persons. It is not becoming for young religious to associate with secular people. By avoiding them, they stay in humble mortification and religious retirement, as if dead to the world. This point was very helpful to me in keeping recollected and disposed for mental prayer. The time that is uselessly spent with people not only detracts from devotion but also interferes with one's work, the work obedience gives us to perform with all zeal and purity of heart.

Through our Lord's grace I began to have at this time a type of very sensible ecstasy that affected even my body, making it experience in an extraordinary manner what it lacked naturally. This seemed to stem from three causes:

The first was that when I listened to a discourse on God I was inflamed by an affective love for him. I understood his great goodness, majesty and grandeur. Through this my soul was carried away and lifted above itself, while the violence of the love drew along with it every bodily sensation. The second was that when I raised my thoughts to some mystery in the life of Christ I became wrapped in such wonder over it that I was as though senseless. There was a third cause: it was present when His Divine Majesty was pleased to stir my soul with the pure spirit of his divinity which, like a heavenly and most gentle breath of air, drew together in my innermost being the soul's scattered powers and attracted to itself all my bodily movements and powers, making me like a slave of love, a prisoner who is unable to move because he is delightfully bound by the presence of God.

Concerning the powers of the soul being gathered into one in its own depths—and this is actually experienced—one can better understand how this happens from the analogy of the shepherd. By a simple blast on his horn, as I witnessed many times, the shepherd brings his flocks together. They have been grazing here and there on the slopes and plains and now they lightly and merrily run towards the sound, stopping now and then to listen to their master as he entertains them with the sweet sound of the pipe.

In the union of ecstasy one experiences and enjoys God through faith whereby the soul receives a special light to know God better and a disposition to love him more.

It is very important not to permit ourselves to think that we have ecstasies, visions and revelations, especially such as become known publicly. We have to ask God to dispose us to love him perfectly, keep us humble, and give us patience in bearing calumnies and persecution, since there can be no deception to our souls in these as there can be in ecstasies and visions, though they appear to be good. Sometimes the devil leads us along this false way to destroy us; as happened during my stay in this city to two persons, a man and a woman, both Franciscan Tertiaries.

The man had ecstasies and visions. His confidence in himself was excessive and the devil played a great deception on him. No doubt it was his way of making this person despair, for he made him predict some things which simply did not happen. For instance, he foretold that a woman who had been ill many years would become well if she were taken to a church of our Lady outside the city and Mass celebrated there. My Father Guardian was called to say the Mass and the sick woman was brought to the church. Many devout people were present. When the Sacred Host was raised at the consecration this poor man who had been deceived by the devil began to do the wildest things and would even have laid hands on the priest if he had not been restrained by the people who were there.

This strange happening caused a great disturbance among the congregation, once they saw that everything had turned out contrary to what they expected. Though they had been made to look very foolish, still they treated the man very charitably, for he was really a good person. And as it pleased God—who at times wills to mortify us in this way to repress our curiosity—he came to his senses and paid me a visit at the monastery.

He very confidentially told me everything: how in the ecstasies the devils appeared to him in the form of our Lady, the saints and angels, and made him dance and jump about with them. I asked him if he had an ordinary confessor and whether he had told him these things. He said, No. This disturbed me and I told him that he had done wrong and this should teach him never to keep anything back. In this way, the devil would not deceive him again, if he would go back to serving God with greater fervour. That is what the man did and his life became an example to everyone.

The deceit the devil foisted upon the woman took this form: she did not want to be obedient to her spiritual director who was the servant of God, Father Augustine of Velletri, Guardian at the monastery in Sezze. By a revelation given him while at prayer in his monastery, he understood how the devil had deceived his penitent and that he should quickly go to help her. With the permission of the Provincial Superior he went immediately and found just what our Lord had revealed.

Father Augustine took me into his confidence. He told me everything under secrecy and wanted me with the Father Guardian's permission to accompany him on this great work of charity. The first time we went to the woman she became very disturbed and gave us to understand that she no longer wished to see the Father who had come to care for her soul, nor to listen to him any more. I do not remember what reasons she gave, but it was easy to see that her actions were like those of a possessed person. She was very afraid of the poor Father because she realized how she was resisting his directions, no matter how obedient to them she had once been. He begged me to recommend her soul to our Lord and put me under obedience to make the sign of the cross over her—a sign that has great power due to the death of our Saviour. I did this, though I experienced great fatigue. Because of this and the merit of obedience the devil lost his power; he left the woman alone and to the joy of all of us she went to confession to Father Augustine.

From then on the woman lived in an exemplary manner, with a great reputation for holiness. She was the first sister in Christ[1] that I had after putting on the habit. Her name was Sister Geronima Ciprari.[2] Our Lord granted her a high degree of prayer.

---

[1] What St. Charles wishes to say is that, like the holy familiarity between St. Francis and St. Clare, this was his first such friendship, in which one helped the other to walk the way of holiness.

[2] She was of the Di Flaminio Ciprari family.

Chapter 35
Many Contests with the Demons

HE battles I fought with the devils in this monastery were not ordinary ones; they were frightful and quite indescribable, for these evil spirits turned on me with greater force and disdain than ever before and they did to my person what they had never done previously. The nights were very few when they did not come to trouble me in a way that brought me close to death; all that was needed was for my soul to leave the body.

It seemed the whole monastery was full of demons and that each had sworn an oath against me. If His Divine Majesty had allowed it I think they would have buried me in the deepest part of hell. To get some little relief I had to run to the altar of the most Blessed Sacrament and there hide under the shadow of our Lord as in a safe place, for the greatest powers of the world and of hell tremble in his presence.

One day just a little before Compline I had retired to my room to pray for a while and to recommend to our Lord his servant Sister Geronima, after the event previously mentioned. Those hellish monsters came and, like ferocious lions, fell upon me to devour me alive. In the face of such a fierce attack I could not resist at all, nor take up spiritual arms. While I was right in this struggle the time for Compline came and no other Friar was left in the dormitory. I was alone and very downcast.

One Friar, however, had passed by my room and heard my voice. Later when he did not see me in choir with the others he wondered if something had happened to me. As soon as the Litany after Compline[1] was finished he spoke to Father

---

[1] The Litany of Loreto which the Friars used to say after Compline before starting their meditation.

Guardian about it. The Guardian came with some other Friars and when he entered my room he saw that I was more dead than alive, because I could not say a word. Those evil beasts had entered my heart and I believed I would die!

The Father Guardian immediately sent the Friars into church to pray before the Blessed Sacrament. He stayed in my room with one or two, kneeling on the floor and praying to our Lord. After a little while he put his hand over my heart and made the sign of the cross many times, telling the demons to leave in the name of God. I began to feel a little relief and called upon the most powerful name of Jesus. And since I really thought I had come to the end of my life I asked to go to confession. Father Guardian himself kindly gave me this sacrament.

When the confession was over my mind was enlightened by a great light and I saw our Lord Jesus Christ near me in bodily form. His face was majestic and adorable; the brightness of that most holy humanity joined to the divinity cannot be described. My whole interior being was filled with a divine light, clearer and more resplendent than the sun. So much consolation took hold of me that what I had suffered was as nothing in comparison with what my soul was tasting. Carried away spiritually I hurried to embrace my Lord, but that was not permitted me because of my many sins.

The Father Guardian had them put me on a straw mattress for he thought that I could not last more than a few days. But early the next morning I got up as though nothing had happened and made breakfast for the Friars.

The Provincial Superior was making his visitation at that time. He came to see the Friars of our monastery and his room was opposite mine. From what happened I imagine the infernal demons wanted me to fall into vainglory, because that night, when I had gone to bed, I thought they were speaking to me through a third person who said: "If you call out tonight when we come to molest you, the Provincial will hear you and take you for a saint." I knew who they were for I had been on the look-out for their return; besides, after what had happened, the Father Guardian ordered some of the Friars to hurry and see what was going on if they heard any noise coming from my room.

During the first hours of the night these enemies came about me like a wind and I could do nothing to help myself. As much as I could I restrained the natural fear that I had at first, and I let them do whatever they could and whatever God allowed them. With his help I was victorious and they went away shamed and confused.

Chapter 36
Porter: Charity to the Poor

WHEN I had lived in the monastery of St. Francis about six months an order of our Father Provincial came to the Father Guardian that I was to leave the kitchen and take charge of the door and of the refectory. Also I was to have the care of a young Friar who had just finished the novitiate; he was to be the cook and I would instruct him in everything pertaining to that work.

I gladly accepted this obedience though I knew I was not suited as a porter, since I was too young. This office requires a man of mature age and of great prudence and piety, because of the various daily occurrences that involve persons of all circumstances. Because I liked retirement very much I naturally felt some repugnance in having to deal with seculars, especially since anything can happen, for the weakness of our lower nature lives on in us with its natural affections. We are like infants that greatly desire the things that please them most because as yet they have not sufficient ability to reach out for the peaceful state of holy indifference. That is why, when something that delights their eyes is taken away, they begin to cry pitifully and will not stop until their parents give it to them again.

This natural part of man, friendly towards one's own comfort, tries to lead us even in that which seems—so we think—better for serving God in peace of soul and without any disturbance. But our Lord, who greatly loves virtue and is the tireless friend of the cross, knows well that as we grow detached from love of the world and of sin we come to lose ourselves and to be indifferent about this peace and lack of disturbance, though they seem good.

The sacrifice the good Lord wants of us is to die to

ourselves. And because this is a very difficult step to take for our human nature, which feels the burden to the extreme in becoming used to it, our Lord prepares us little by little, not only through illuminations and acts of virtue but by the very passing of time. So if at times we see faults committed on this point by the spiritually young, we should not be scandalized when they think they are doing well and advancing in perfection just because they stay in one office or particular place of their choice. They have not yet grasped the meaning of holy indifference which despoils us of all our affections.

So I started the duty of porter, an office that calls no less for charity than does the kitchen. In whatever pertained to the Friars I took every pain, not thinking any time wasted or any work useless if I could satisfy them according to our state of holy poverty. I judged that in them I was serving God and that he was very pleased as long as it was under obedience.

His Lordship Cardinal Francis Barberini[1] had assigned seventy loaves of bread a week to the monastery as an alms. Now some of the Friars before me had not taken it out of scrupulosity;[2] I took it every time and never let it go by since it was a great help to the Friars.

At times our Tertiaries[3] were sent from one monastery to another to fill the needs of each place. I noticed that besides being weary from their journey they were occasionally bespattered with mud and wet from the rain. I received them cordially and made a fire where they could warm themselves. Then I brought hot water and washed their feet, treating them as I would the Friars themselves. I had a holy envy of them since they were serving His Divine Majesty with great

---

[1] Cardinal Francis Barberini (senior), raised to the cardinalate in 1623, was Protector of the Friars Minor from 1633 to 1678.

[2] It looked as though they lacked confidence in divine Providence, for this was a stable and secure revenue.

[3] Converts from the world who wear the religious habit and profess the Rule, not of the First, but of the Third Order of St. Francis.

humility and rejection of the world, and had chosen the lowest state in religion. For this I loved them very much.

The charity that I showed the poor who came to the door every day took the concrete form of cooked vegetables whenever there was not enough soup left over. When they came I had them kneel down, make the sign of the cross and recite an *Our Father* and *Hail Mary*; then I gave them something to eat.

Whenever I went into the city to beg alms I came upon poor people along the way and even more needy ones in their homes, and I helped them with the little our Lord provided for me.

I had spent a year in the monastery of St. Francis when plans were made to build a new monastery for the Poor Clares of the reform of Sister Mary Frances Farnese.[4] While this monastery was being built the nuns came to live at St. Francis and we went to live at their house of St. Andrew.[5] This was about 3 December 1640, at the order of Cardinal Francis Barberini.

This change left only a few of us at St. Andrew and very few provisions were needed. It gave me a better chance to be charitable toward the needy poor who came for food. But the devil wanted to hinder me in this good work. He stirred up some of the Friars to complain to the Father Guardian that I was over generous with the poor and that I gave them too much for our state of poverty; it was just not good in any way. The Father Guardian listened to these complaints and then one morning he held a chapter of faults in the refectory on this very question, to quiet the disturbance. He reproved me for my indiscretion and told me that it was not becoming

---

[4] The Venerable Frances Farnese (*d.* 1651) of Jesus and Mary founded four monasteries of Poor Clares, at Farnese, Albano, Palestrina, and Rome; she gave them very austere constitutions in conformity with the primitive observance.

[5] The Institute of the Child Jesus.

poor Friars who lived by alms to be so free in giving things away; besides, it was being taken away from other poor persons.

Since only a few Friars were staying at St. Andrew, as I mentioned, the quest for alms in the city alone brought more than was needed; that is why we did not have to go into other places to beg, as we formerly had to. Still, some of the Friars began murmuring on this very point. They zealously maintained it was not good to give up the quest in those places, for the benefactors would thus lose a lot of merit. They registered their displeasure at this with the Father Guardian who in turn became very displeased. The next morning he held another chapter of faults in the refectory and gave me a good scolding and a penance. Then I was told to take the discipline. He gave me an order that after I had eaten, my penance was to go out immediately to some of the Castelli round about and beg alms. Another Friar was to be my companion, one to whom our Lord had given a way with benefactors; it was easy for him to arouse their charity.

After I had eaten I set about this obedience at once. Night overtook us when we came to Zagarolo and the Conventual Fathers kindly put us up for the night. The following morning we continued the quest for alms and though there were many generous people in those parts, our Lord permitted us to obtain very little bread; as it also turned out in other places.

On our way back home my companion began expressing his amazement that we had collected so few alms. I took the chance to say a few words about this and pointed out that when we lived at St. Francis the Friars were quite a few in number and we were charitable to the poor; yet our Lord provided for our needs there for he inspired benefactors to be generous. "Now that we are at St. Andrew and are only a few, he provides only as much as we need, in measure with the poverty we have promised!"

Now though the city was generous to us we never could obtain enough olive oil there. The need arose to go a distance looking for some. The Father Guardian sent me with a companion to places where olive oil was generally made, such as Sezze and Sonnino. We took a large Roman flask with us—it was heavy—and some smaller containers. From having lifted heavy objects I already had a hernia and so the first day, with that heavy weight on my shoulders, I became unable to walk and the journey was made very difficult.

I had a great devotion to Blessed Salvator of Horta[6] of our Order, who in life and death was distinguished for his miracles. Because of my need I knelt down on the ground and affectionately commended myself to him, beseeching him to intercede for me with our Lord in the matter of my health so that I could carry out this obedience. After I had prayed this way with faith we continued our trip. I walked only a short distance when I realized I was well again. When we had carried out the obedience we went back to our monastery.

Since the Provincial Chapter was to be held at Easter—it was then the middle of Lent—the Father Visitator sent me as a substitute to the monastery of St. John Baptist of Piglio.

---

[6] Lay-brother canonized by Pope Pius XI in 1938.

CHAPTER 37
TRANSFER TO CARPINETO

URING Easter Week our Provincial Chapter was held and Father Bernardine of Siena was elected the Minister Provincial.[1] At the same time I was sent as sacristan to the monastery of Carpineto[2] where the house of theology was located. It was flourishing at that time and many learned men went forth from it.

When the Friars learned that I had been chosen as sacristan some of them advised me against going there. They knew my limitations and the trials one suffers in that work, and out of charity more than any other reason they counselled me to let my Superior know about my inability; this could be done lawfully, they said, since St. Bonaventure and other Doctors teach that in such cases we should manifest our needs to the superiors so that they may console us in the Lord.

I could not see that in this case I had enough reason for having recourse to my superiors. When we do not know how to do something we have to obey and try to learn it. As the proverb has it: No one is born master of a trade.

I realized that everything they told me, though apparently very reasonable, was really a trick of the devil to have me give up right thinking on holy obedience, something a religious should not abandon in spite of all human contradictions. In the spiritual life we must not seek ourselves but simply God in whatever he has arranged.

---

[1] He was an outstanding professor and preacher, Minister Provincial, and several times Commissary of different provinces. He died at St. Francis a Ripa, 12 January 1658.

[2] The monastery of St. Peter the Apostle in Carpineto Romano was founded in 1610. In the period when St. Charles lived there, and afterwards, it flourished as an important centre of studies.

So it happens that even though they have grown old in the spiritual life, many gain no particular profit because they follow human prudence and leave behind what is better, namely, allowing themselves to be led by God, the true and safe way.

Notice, then, the great damage that can be caused by not being well advised at times and by not having a guide to lead us along the right path of perfection, especially in what pertains to holy obedience; on it religious progress depends. Sometimes under the cloak of devotion and charity, false piety prevails in having us abandon the path we originally set out on and go back to the one which we had renounced for the love of God, that is, our own will.

When we begin to abandon right thinking a special grace of God is needed to come back to it, because then nothing satisfies us; there is always something lacking to our taste and so a person never reaches any perfection since true holiness cannot be had where one's own will is found. For that reason we have to be very watchful and courageous when the tasks that are given us seem like mountains. It is then we must run to our Lord with faith; he can bring these mountains down and make them seem like the most pleasant plains of spiritual delight.

When the new Guardian came I told him of my resolve to go where holy obedience ordered me, and he immediately agreed to give me a companion when I asked for one. He arranged for two priests to accompany me on the Feast of Saints Philip and James. That is how I left the monastery of St. John Baptist of Piglio for that of St. Peter of Carpineto.

Because the trip was rather long and it was late when we left, we went that night to a place called Castellacio. The next morning we completed the journey. At the monastery of St. Peter of Carpineto we were welcomed with the customary marks of charity by the Father Vicar and all the other Friars. The Father Guardian had gone to Naples and had not yet returned. In his absence the Father Vicar had me take charge of the sacristy, serve Masses and do everything that would be necessary; and when the Guardian returned he would settle everything. The Fathers taught me what I did not know about the sacristy; first one helped me, then another. The things that seemed difficult they made appear very easy. This is the mark of true charity.

Chapter 38
Strict Spiritual Director

HE spiritual director I had from the very start in this holy place was the Father Vicar of the monastery. He was a person of great austerity and rigour. In age it could have been said he was old rather than young. He wanted to govern the Friars with the same rigorous austerity he demanded of himself, just as we read about St. Bernard when he first started his Order. Consequently, the poor religious lived under a strain, without spontaneity. Still, they suffered it all willingly for the love of God, and everyone forgave him, for they knew he did not have much experience in governing. They went on hoping in God that in time there would be relief, with the return of the Father Guardian. The penances and mortifications this Father Vicar gave the clerics and lay-brothers never came to an end.

Under the discipline of this Father the Lord wanted to try the little patience I had. One of the clerics became ill as a result of the ordinary penances of our way of life. I went to see him, to help him in his needs as St. Francis commanded in the Rule; I begged him to be patient and to bear his sickness for the love of God.

This act on my part was, I believe, very displeasing to our common enemy because, from what followed, it seems he put into the Father Vicar's mind the idea that the sick cleric had not accepted with good grace the penances he had given him! Also that I was in league with this cleric and had written to the Father Provincial about him, the Vicar. This appeared like a dream to the two of us. Father Vicar began exerting his power to give me more than ordinary penances. Almost every morning in the refectory he held a long chapter of faults on me, mortifying me, to the great sorrow of all the Friars. They were saddened at the fault they believed I had committed but more so at seeing me constantly under penance. With a lot of charity they often exhorted me in the Lord to be patient because sometimes these trials are from God to make us saints, perfect in virtue.

Because I had never given attention to a true mortification of the interior man by any special means, and because of the counterweight of the lively nature that was mine, my whole being revolted at what was being done. Revenge stirred up an indescribable conflict within me, especially when certain words touched me in more sensitive places. Such is the misery of man!

But what seemed hardest for me to accept was that he treated me in confession with the very same rigour. Usually we enjoy some solace here at opening up our heart. But I persevered as well as I could. I strengthened myself with the thought of our Lord's sufferings and the reward of the glory to come; I constantly commended myself to the most glorious Virgin through whose intercession I was a religious; and when the period of the day allowed I often went into the garden and chanted the Magnificat with a buoyant spirit and heartfelt joy.

Since things became worse with time, some of the good Fathers who perhaps thought I could not go on bearing this strictness, charitably advised me to write to the Provincial Superior and ask to be transferred to another monastery where I could observe the Rule with greater peace of mind.

I began examining the matter and I recalled that my good father had not taught me to act that way. What he did teach me was that I should really be obedient, and no matter how difficult something might be I should not fail to carry it out as long as it was not against the law of God. So I thanked my confreres for their thoughtfulness and quieted their misgivings with a few words.

When the Superior scolded me for my faults I made special efforts to meditate on the mystery of the Passion of Christ, the better to bear whatever was said to me and to accept without any reservation the penance that had been imposed. When I was scolded I tried to keep my head properly bowed and my face neither too joyful nor too sad, so that I would not have the Superior think I was making sport of him by looking too happy, nor that I was not gladly accepting his admonitions by looking too sad.

But even though I went to the refectory prepared with the thought of the sufferings of Christ, one morning when the Superior was holding a chapter of faults about me I seemed to feel especially annoyed at what he said. My feelings were so hurt and given such a terrible blow that they lifted me almost completely out of my usual way of reacting. A dreadful temptation was trying to lift me from the floor, where I was kneeling very low, to go and lay hands on him! making me forget that he was my Superior, that he was correcting me in the place of God and of my father, St. Francis. I would surely have done this if His Divine Majesty had not come to help me with his grace, by restraining my diabolical rage. I quickly came to my senses; I called on the name of Jesus with the most powerful sign of the cross, while I recalled how much our Lord had suffered for me in his most bitter Passion and how terrible was the evil I wanted to commit.

No one should be scandalized at hearing this for I am simply telling what is part and parcel of man. We should rather wonder at the kindness of God who is so anxious to help us. The thought of our Lord stirred up in my heart such compunction that I would easily have suffered any great torment; any kind of martyrdom would have seemed nothing. For when His Divine Majesty makes us equal to it, it is impossible to describe the acts of virtue we can perform, but when he leaves us to our own nature then it is impossible to find an evil so great that we would not commit it. So I am no longer amazed when I hear what others have experienced, especially if they are really good persons. Those to whom our

Lord has given the grace of governing should proceed with great prudence and always be charitable in word and action, so as not to give their subjects any excuse for being downcast.

The Superior was furious at seeing me make the sign of the cross. He misinterpreted the action, no doubt thinking that I was being disrespectful. With even greater indignation he kept up the chapter of faults, saying that he was not a devil as I thought he was, whom one puts to flight with the sign of the cross, but that he was a religious of St. Francis. There were other words easily said by a man in the heat of anger. And the more he said the greater my compunction grew. I realized that because of my sins I really merited all he was doing to me.

When he had finished correcting me he allowed me to sit at table. I rose from the floor and was moved to go to kiss his feet. But this was pouring oil on the fire because he then grew even more angry.

His rigour toward me lasted for three months. Our Lord saw that I was weak and unable to go on suffering this. He willed to put an end to my trouble when the Father Provincial came on his visitation. He assured the Father Vicar that I had not written a letter against him, as he had been given to believe.

From then on he was more humane to me and showed that he wished me well. Two years afterwards on my return from Urbino and the holy House of Loreto, I called at the monastery where he was the Guardian. He could not have been more cordial and he tried to keep me there almost a week. He often confided in me with deep feeling that he had persecuted me unjustly. Perhaps our Lord permitted this to ground us both in virtue, to have each ask pardon of the other sincerely and to show us how to love one another with a special love and charity.

Chapter 39
New Confessor-Office of Sacristan

HE Guardian, Father Maximus of Marrubio, came back from Naples. His return meant a great and consoling hope to everyone of living with greater peace of mind in the future.

They told him about me and what had happened. He had me come to see him, spoke in a very friendly way with me and in every manner showed that he was a kind and most charitable father. He offered to take care of my every bodily and spiritual need. Knowing that the five years had passed during which the young Friars admit their defects every morning at culpa, he had me come to the refectory the following morning for this exercise. When all the Friars were assembled at table he lifted this obligation from me. Then he ordered me to take charge of the sacristy as had been decided by the Father at the chapter, and that I might do this more willingly and for the love of God he gave me the merit of obedience.

He wanted to give me a Father confessor whom he liked. This was Father Archangelus of Varalla to whom he gave special orders to guide me along the path of spirituality. The solace at having such a spiritual father was so great that I seemed as it were to rise from death to life. I think this was because I really lacked virtue; I did not have that precious pearl of saintly balance that remains satisfied under any condition and lets the fickleness of our lower nature complain unheeded. When we have this balance, passing trifles do not detain us in our advance to holiness; in fact, they help the soul go lightly from virtue to virtue up the holy mountain of God to reach the ineffable enjoyment of him.

But since I was still a child not very accustomed to eating the hard bread of trials, I received a special consolation of body and soul from having this Father as my guide. He had a gift from our Lord of leading souls to perfection in a gentle and smooth way.

What is more important, he was very practical and at the same time sufficiently learned, two good qualities in a spiritual director. He wanted me to practise resignation and to restrain that imprudent zeal of mine. Beginners have the tendency to kill themselves with penances, as though they were the end and not the means. However, he made me perform penances when they seemed right to him and not when I thought of them. Especially when some vigils of great feasts came along he had me keep silence with the Friars, for he claimed that a person who likes to talk a lot will find it difficult not to give up the spiritual life.

It seemed that at last our Lord had allowed me to find what I had desired for so long a time. But because he wanted me to walk the way of the cross, so necessary for me if I was to bring death to my former nature, this wonderful benefit did not last long. This Father was sent to the monastery of Montefortino[1] and in his place I had Father Leo of Ariccia who was teaching theology there at that time.

As I said before, the Father Guardian gave me the duty of sacristan. My Master was Father Peter Paul of Sezze, a student priest. He was to instruct me in everything that concerned the sacristy, such as sweeping the church, preparing the altars and making hosts for Mass and Holy Communion.

At the start it was very hard for me since I knew nothing about these things, but with the help of God and the charity of Father Peter Paul I learned everything to the great satisfaction and consolation of all the Friars, and especially of my own soul which rejoiced in our Lord's mercy. This always happens when we put our hope in God and distrust our own

---

[1] The monastery of St. Mary of Jesus in Montefortino, now Artena (Rome) was founded in 1629. In 1917 a college for aspirants to the Franciscan mission was annexed to it.

ability. He takes special care of us and permits us to advance in all things.

That is why this advice given to the brothers in the Order will be very useful: allow yourselves to be carried by His Divine Majesty. If we do this our conscience will never be confused and disquieted, for to follow the footsteps of God in our superiors is a sweet and peaceful yoke that strengthens and comforts the soul.

Chapter 40
Desire for Martyrdom

I HAD been in the Franciscan Order about eighteen years when His Divine Majesty allowed me to enjoy the divine consolation that comes from desiring martyrdom. The consolation is so great that I am unable to describe it. This holy gift had its start, at least partially, when I was still a layman at Sezze. I had gone to visit the church of St. Mary of Grace which belongs to the Franciscans and there I saw a painting of the twenty-three Franciscan martyrs of Japan which showed them nailed to crosses and pierced by lances. When I looked at them they made me intensely eager for martyrdom and I hoped to gain its crown when I became a religious.

When the year of novitiate was over and I was stationed at Morlupo, Father Anthony of Virgoletta came to stay there for a while. He had obtained permission to go to Japan[1] where he died, and after his death our Lord granted some favours through his intercession. He had wanted me to go with him as his companion and I was very eager to do so, but I was too young and could not grow a beard, which the religious had to wear in that land.

The second time I had a chance to be a missionary came from one of our Fathers who was going to Albania. I was then at St. Mary of Grace in Ponticelli and the same reason kept my superiors from sending me.

The third and last opportunity of going among the infidels came when I was at the monastery of St. Peter in Carpineto.

---

[1] Father Anthony of Virgoletta (Massa Carrara) was an outstanding missionary. He did not evangelize Japan, as the Saint writes mistakenly, but Ethiopia where he was the first Prefect Apostolic after the Holy See had entrusted this mission to the Franciscans. He died a saintly death in 1641 and worked miracles after his death.

About a year before, when I was at Palestrina, a Father from Bergamo, who belonged to our Roman province, and I agreed to go somewhere in Portugal, if I am not mistaken, where the Friars were doing wonderful work. With the hope of helping those souls we made ready for this holy adventure. It was settled that there would be four of us, two priests and two brothers. The other brother was Anthony of Venice, an expert in this kind of work for he had been on the missions several times.

But since the judgments of God are inscrutable he arranged something other than what I had in mind to do. On the vigil of the Feast of the Nativity of our Lady, September 8th, a fever surprised me. There was no evident reason for it. Without knowing my condition the Superior sent me out on the quest that day to a section called Maenza, about seven miles away from Carpineto. I gladly went, hoping the fever would leave because of the obedience, for it had turned out that way several times before; but when I reached Maenza it got worse. That night I was very sick, and the next day also. It exhausted me to go asking for alms, but I did so and then returned to the monastery. The doctor was called immediately; he saw that I was very sick and ordered that if I was to recover I had to be taken to Rome as soon as possible.

In the morning Father Guardian said Mass for the two of us and then he put me on a donkey. Two brothers were sent with me, with orders to take me to Rome. That morning we got as far as the monastery of Montefortino. The fever was so bad that during the night I thought I would surrender my soul to God. I had them call a priest to hear my confession and I made what amounted to a general confession of my sins. The priest who heard my confession was Father Theodulus of San Vito.

Once in Rome my companions took me to St. Francis a Ripa. In that monastery there is an infirmary where the sick are affectionately attended to by other Friars. It is easy to imagine what I suffered. The infirmarians in Rome took care of me and gave me the medicines the doctor had ordered.

My sickness grew worse and at the same time a fierce inner struggle started that gave me a lot to think about and kept me unusually disturbed. It seemed that I had never been a religious, that I had never done any good and that I did not know where I would go if I died! Very earnestly I commended myself to our Lord and begged him without ceasing, to forgive me there and then, and to permit me some time to do penance for my sins. If His Divine Majesty granted me this favour I promised I would do great things.

While I was being very much bothered this way, one of the infirmarians came to say that it would be good if I went to confession. I would gladly do so, I told him. So they called in Father Angelus Maria of Rome in whose hands I had made my profession after the novitiate. The good Father came and very charitably heard my confession. During it I told him how I had decided to go among the infidels, and of the letter I had with me to Cardinal Anthony Barberini. When I finished my confession he gave me a penance, and as for going among the infidels he put my mind to rest on that; he ordered me not to think about it any more since it was not the will of God. He asked me to give him the letter and when he had it he requested permission to burn it.

With the strength of the sacrament of penance I was very much at peace and resigned to God's will, as I commended myself again and again to Blessed Salvator. I had a vision of him. He appeared great in stature, venerable in countenance, with a coarse and patched habit, all joyful and happy in light. The vision lasted only a short time and when I returned to my senses I was cured. I kept getting better every day and finally they discharged me from the infirmary. Now I knew clearly that it was not the will of God for me to die a martyr, but to embrace the martyrdom of holy obedience.

Chapter 41
Spirit of Fornication

THOUGH I had hoped to enjoy some little peace after I had regained my health and was being helped very much by the Father Guardian in spiritual matters, our Lord—who does not want us to be idle in his house but always practising virtue and advancing in his love—had other plans for me after the little cross of my sickness. He allowed another cross to come in the form of a frightful and horrible temptation to fornication. This is a torment that reaches down into one's very being, taking away honour and reputation in what seems an unjust persecution by men. As Christ our Lord says in the Gospel, our persecutors cannot really touch our soul. To have a cruel and pitiless tyrant, however, who leaves us interiorly crushed and doubtful of God's friendship against our will, after causing us a living death, this is as it were a punishment similar to that of the damned who are deprived of the vision of God!

Our Lord allowed the spirit of fornication to war on me in a new way. It put in my imagination the figure of a woman with whom I had spoken years before on the occasion of begging alms, that great service of our Lord. In all the time that I came in contact with her I can truthfully say that I never looked at her face. For on those occasions when I spoke to her I took care to stay recollected, I raised my mind to God and protested to him that I would not consent to any evil the enemy would put before me, as I said from one of the Psalms: "Preserve my soul, O Lord, from all evil".[1] In fact, whenever I went out I used to say with the prophet David: "Turn away my eyes that they may not behold vanity: quicken me in thy

---

[1] This quotation is actually made up of parts of two verses from the Psalms: 85. 2 and 120. 7.

way".[2]

Since our Lord wanted me to show charity to my fellow men, I was free, when I conversed with them, of the sort of uncleanness that can stain the soul, and all my senses were in peace. Still I never considered myself safe in this regard.

Because of the great confidence they had in me and out of their marvellous respect for the Franciscan habit, many persons were led to do penance for their sins—especially a count who for most of his life had served at the court of a princess. When I told him that every hour of his life, though it was late, was a favour from God, he left the court, was clothed secretly in the habit of the Third Order of St. Francis at our monastery of St. Francis a Ripa and went into seclusion to do penance.

For five years the temptation to lust lasted as a kind of martyrdom. At night when I tried to rest, all hell turned on me although I threw the water of devout thoughts on it by imagining that I was within the sacred wounds of our Lord or in the presence of God and of my Guardian Angel. I was like a slave, tied and unable to defend myself, free only in the act of my will which did its best to keep united with His Divine Majesty and far removed from the sensual movements of the flesh. With lips and heart I called on the name of Jesus and Mary, telling them I was willing to die a thousand times and suffer any kind of martyrdom rather than offend the law of God.

O Lord, forgive me if in this I disturb the chaste ears of your servants who read this and who have a pure and clean heart, not sullied as mine is. Even here I simply wanted to please your Divine Majesty and comfort those who are afflicted by a martyrdom of this type.

I think this accursed demon was given me by God as a chastisement and that he gave him all power over my person, except my will, for when those rushing attacks had passed I

---

[2] Psalm 118. 37.

was very afflicted and doubtful with a fear that I had offended God.

Besides running to God for help I tried hard to do my part through penances with the permission of my spiritual director. I put on a hair-shirt made of animal skins but I was forced to give it up because it made me too warm if I wore it for any length of time. I made a kind of vest of good-sized chains and wore it for eight to ten years. Every night I took the discipline and only rarely did I sleep. When I did sleep, it was on a table. I drank water only and ate meat rarely. As a special devotion I began to make all seven Lents that our holy Father St. Francis made.

These and other penances helped only a little. To think of wanting to chase off temptations by force of arms is vanity and madness, for this is done only by the favour of divine grace.[3] When the time our Lord had set for freeing me had come, he caused the hellish image to disappear as if it had never been.

Still the tempter did not stop warring against me with other more horrible imaginations and thoughts, for the trunk of this baleful tree went right on growing in my flesh, sending out roots of different temptations which would have frightened a spiritual giant and an experienced anchorite.

Blessed be the Lord who is served in this way by humbling my pride and keeping my head bowed all the time that I lived in religion. When people ran after me and took pieces of my habit and cape, and called me a saint, I said to myself: "If they only knew me as Jesus Christ who sees my wretchedness knows me, they would pick up stones and kill me with them!"

---

[3] Though different forms of penance are helpful in combating temptations, the first place must always be given to divine grace which we are to ask for without ceasing in humble prayer.

Chapter 42
Appearance of the Devil in the Form of Our Saviour

SINCE he desired to get inside the fortress of my soul and put everything in confusion, the deceiver used a very subtle strategy. One night he attacked me very dreadfully with the obscene image I spoke of previously, and because it was very unusual I was left more than ordinarily afflicted and doubtful as to whether I had consented to it. Fearing that I had, I went to church in the morning with the other Friars and began to pray in the chapel of our Father St. Francis. When I was right in the middle of my prayer I saw the image of the Saviour appearing before me in a cloud. He was dressed as he is usually pictured, but his face was troubled and threatening. He was showing great indignation and he made signs of disapproval as if I had offended him seriously. He did not speak but he conveyed all that he wanted to say by look alone. This vision lasted only a short time and when it disappeared a great obscurity and a dark cloud of sadness began to come over me.

Because I considered myself guilty due to the scruple and doubt in which I had remained during the temptation, I did not think that this was the enemy of God but really Jesus Christ who showed how very much displeased he was with me for the misdeed I thought I had committed.

The trial I went through is indescribable for I lacked all spiritual aid, and the temptation increased. I went to my confessor, told him of the misery I was going through and the awful affliction that was mine, but I did not mention the vision of the evil spirit.

I cannot well remember how I happened to do this, yet I know I did wrong, for it was a very important matter on which I should not have been silent.

Although my confessor was very learned our Lord did not permit me to obtain much solace from him. Actually he used him to put a heavier cross on me, for very scholastically and philosophically he showed how wrong I was, nor did he excuse me from mortal sin. I was confused and had no answer. I shut myself in my room and wept inconsolably over this misfortune.

I say that the chastity of the unmarried is a great benefit but also a great danger since keeping it is something that God gives, and it exposes one to a constant martyrdom. Blessed is he to whom our Lord grants this grace since the degree of glory that he will give him in his eternal dwelling will be no less great!

I kept thinking that the infernal enemy was stronger at seeing me commit this great fault, believe his false apparition and not speak of it to my father confessor. He began increasing his attacks and went ahead to strike me with the temptation of despair. Subtly he led me to believe that I was damned and there was no way out of it. In everything I did I heard a voice saying to me: "It does not help you to be so upset for you are damned!"

These words resounded in my soul and stirred up a sea of sadness in me. My poor soul was as if buried in hell and at times tried by such interior afflictions that I not only experienced unbelievable struggles but was provoked to anger and impatience. I could not bear even the least criticism and when I saw how these imperfections were overcoming me I sometimes begged the Friars to try not to annoy me or to ask any favour, but to do it themselves and pray to our Lord for me!

As much as I could I tried to be cheerful but I could not keep hidden what was in my heart. It escaped me, and when it did it caused some of the Friars to wonder. Perhaps they believed that there are no afflictions of soul for persons who serve God; perhaps they believed they are always joyful and peaceful and sensibly united to God, and do not feel the heavy cross they are carrying. It is true that none of this happens to ordinary persons who are walking the common way of the spiritual life.

Though I kept hearing that I was damned I did not for that reason give up devoutly doing the work in the monastery that was my assignment. Even if I were damned I counted it a great favour to spend myself for the love of God in his vineyard before dying. I said many times: "O my Lord, if an angel should come from you and say that I have been sentenced to damnation I would want to love and serve you all the more; give me, then, the fervour to do so!"

With these ejaculations I at times felt some relief and solace of heart, but it was only a little for the sadness rose again and became what it had been. Besides, it produced other temptations, such as blasphemy against God and the saints, infidelity, and others.

His Divine Majesty willed that this falsehood be uncovered and that I have some alleviation, so he permitted Father Archangelus of Varalla to arrive at our monastery of Carpineto. As I have said, he had been my confessor. In confession I told him all that had occurred since he went away, beginning with the impure and unusual temptations that were followed by the vision of the Saviour. I told him what was going on in my soul and the internal struggle I was suffering. He understood immediately and with his calm reasoning quieted me.

First he began to discuss the shameful temptations and told me that I should not be so disturbed over these; I was not the first one to whom they had happened, but even the great servants of God and saints of the Church, like St. Jerome and St. Catherine of Siena, had experienced them. Also, penances cannot remove them for they have become entrenched in our very bones. He told me that from the signs which accompanied the apparition I could have gathered that it was an evil, not a good apparition, for though good ones may cause fright, yet they stir one to further sorrow for sin. The sinner rises to a better life and does not despair, since His Divine Majesty wants to grant him everlasting life, not eternal death. "So take care", he said, "not to fall into these same mistakes in the future. Pay no more attention to these and to the other temptations you mentioned than an elephant does to a fly!"

He gave me his blessing and left me very consoled.

Chapter 43
Exercise of Carrying a Cross

THOUGH I was oppressed by various great temptations I never desisted from the usual amount of time spent in prayer; in fact, under God's inspiration, I added a most helpful *exercise*, that *of the cross*. For it I made a cross of two plain and rather large pieces of wood; and every day, if nothing came to prevent me, I first recollected myself briefly and then I put this cross on my shoulder and walked around my room with a rope hanging from my neck, my habit without the cord, body bent over, as if I were carrying a heavy weight. I was trying to imitate our Lord in this devotion. I begged him for pardon for my sins and grace to change my life; and with this exercise I felt in my soul the sentiments of his love along with other good effects.

Though I was constantly nailed to the cross of my weaknesses our Lord did not fail to help my soul and to give it ever further advancement. I think that at this time I was leaving the sleep of the faculties that I experienced when the ecstasies first began. My soul was more aware of entering within itself in God and of being separated bit by bit from the bodily senses as it received a greater knowledge of God through faith.

Oh, what great favours we lose by not corresponding to divine inspirations and not having the purity and cleanliness of soul required for receiving these favours!

At times when this light came to my soul I was suddenly lifted about a foot from the ground and my soul took along with it the weight of the body, making it leap as it were. Often when I was on a journey or visiting churches, all of a sudden this would catch me and I was lifted up and down five or six times so that for quite a while I was out of myself, so to speak.

When this happened in public I felt great shame and confusion. Anyone who does not know of these things easily diagnoses insanity, as happened once in Rome in a group of priests. While my priest companion was talking with one of the Fathers in the library I stayed by myself praying, and this spirit came over me. The priest saw this and he asked my companion if I was crazy or out of my senses. When he told me this as we were going back to St. Peter in Montorio it gave us something to laugh about along the way.

It was something for which to praise His Divine Majesty because at times these raptures caused me to sing out loud and to make up hymns. They made me preach about God with great fervour of spirit as happened to me in church after Matins when the other Friars had left. They were a great advantage to my soul.

Since I knew that because of excessive penance my head was becoming weaker and I could not give the holy exercise of prayer the continued attention it requires—not to mention that I frequently felt sick—I lessened somewhat the rigour of the penances and I made up my mind to lead a more moderate life so that I could better attend to both the active and the contemplative life.

Chapter 44
Epidemic Around Carptneto

OR about two years if I am not mistaken, when Father Bonagrazia was Guardian of the monastery of St. Peter of Carpineto, a plague settled on the land and many died from it. When they saw the danger in which they were, the people came to the Friars because they were short of priests and were concerned about the spiritual welfare of those who were dying.

Our Father Guardian was a person of great charity; he was very moved at their troubles and gladly offered to give them all the aid possible. He decided to send out four Friars every day, two priests with companions—and more if he could. I was one of those he sent as long as the plague lasted. We did not hesitate to go where we were called. Just as soon as someone in the contaminated area fell sick with the fever and its flow of blood, the sacraments were given him. Death was not long in coming.

Since twelve or so died every day a terrible fear and terror arose among the people. Nothing more could be done but to bring the holy sacraments to the poor sufferers and to take the dead to the churches in carts. In every street we heard people weeping. In one place they were mourning over a dead father; in another, over a dead mother; in still another, parents bemoaned the loss of their children. The bells tolled in every parish. This brought anguish to the very soul and caused greater fear than the pestilence itself, especially to those who were sick. To remedy this I went to the Vicar General and obtained the favour of having the tolling of the bells stopped.

Our work of charity went on for the three months during which this epidemic lasted. Though it began in May and lasted till August our Lord gave me the strength not to fall ill myself from the evil odour that came from the places where the poor sick people lay. The Friars of the monastery sincerely loved me and told me to take care of myself. They doubted that I would live through this; to me, dying for love of our Lord while helping my neighbour seemed a wonderfully great favour to receive from his hand.

Now, as I saw that some of the poor died more from want than from the epidemic, I made this known to the civil authorities so that they could find a remedy. As much as I was able I tried to beg eggs and bread; I went to the homes of the well-to-do for them. With permission of the Father Guardian I took some vegetables because they happened to be quite abundant during this time of need, and I also put a little bread with them. In this way I saved a poor boy who became very attached to us.

I spoke to the Father Guardian about how needy the poor were and the little food there was for them. He was very sorry for them and remembered that the people of the region had charitably given the Friars some grain to help support them. He delegated me to take it and have bread made to be dispensed to the poor. Accordingly I made out a note in his name and took it to one of the officials in charge of welfare in the city.

I went to his home and found him sick and dying; he could no longer speak. When I saw this I was astounded and did not know what to say now that I was unable to carry out my plan. From the depths of my heart I commended myself to our Lord and then approached the dying person with great confidence. I pleadingly called on him to sign the note in the name of Jesus and for the love of God. When he heard the most sweet name of Jesus the sick man, though he was stretched out in his death agony, suddenly sat up to the amazement of everyone there and said that he would more than gladly do what I wanted. He got himself to write his signature and then he gave the note to me. After that he begged me to recommend him to our Lord in his last hour, and to the prayers of all the Friars. When he finished talking he lay down again and in a few moments left this life for the next.

One night I was with a dying youth who was in the prime of life. He was very near death and deeply distressed. He tried to sit up in bed to ask this question: "If someone has offended God all during his life, will he find mercy with His Divine Majesty?" When I heard him talking this way I judged that the devil was tempting him to despair. My answer was that God has said in Sacred Scripture that every time a sinner is sorry for having offended him, he will pardon him. "If Judas had asked forgiveness for his sins no matter how great, Christ our Lord would have pardoned him as he pardoned St. Cyprian who had been a magician and soothsayer. He also pardoned St. Mary Magdalen and St. Mary of Egypt who were public prostitutes, and he has pardoned an infinite number of sinners. So you too should be confident that God will forgive your sins since it was for sinners he came into this world to suffer and die!"

"Well, if this is true," the young man said, "I also want to hope that God in his great mercy has forgiven my sins." Then I settled him down on the bed again and a short while after that he breathed his last calmly in the Lord.

When the month of June and a good part of July had passed the plague was still at its height. Now, in our church of St. Peter there was a picture of St. Ann through which God began to grant favours; it was becoming known to these people who till then had shown no devotion to this great saint. They carried votive candles to her as a mark of favours granted. Among them was a lady by the name of Antonia Canali, a very devout person and a great benefactor of the Friars. Eighteen years had gone by in her marriage without a child being born to her. She commended herself to our prayers and I encouraged her to have devotion to St. Ann, for she would grant her this longed-for favour. She had faith in what

I said and soon gave birth to a daughter. This caused an awakening of devotion to this wonderful saint in many hearts; especially in this time of so many deaths great numbers had recourse to her intercession.

Some devout persons grouped together to have a picture made for the feast day of St. Ann, hoping that through her intercession deliverance from the pestilence would come on that day. Everything was done with the permission of our Father Guardian since they wanted to put the picture in our church, and I was engaged to carry out the plan. Offerings came in and they were quickly sent to Rome with a letter to one of our Fathers at St. Francis a Ripa to make every effort to have the picture made.

A Tertiary of our monastery who had been sent to Rome for this purpose came back on the Feast of St. James the Apostle. He had the picture with him and some statues of St. Ann. I went to the captain of the soldiers, Signor Angelus of Senica, the most influential person of the region, to request him to honour the occasion by sending his drummers with some riflemen. He promised to do everything I asked him.

In the chapel of our Lady an altar was prepared where the picture was to rest and where Mass would be sung on the morning of the feast. In the meantime with the help of Father John of Rome I made a large number of rather small banners from cardboard and attached them to short poles. On each was written the name of Jesus, of Mary, of St. Ann and of Blessed Salvator; and on one of them, the largest, was a picture of St. Ann with the seven Madonnas of St. Luke. These banners really meant a lot to the sick; they considered it a favour to have one.

The procession started. The picture of St. Ann was carried by two priests, and the chanters intoned the hymn *Ave, Maris Stella*. As the procession entered the garden of our monastery a large number of children stood there arranged in beautiful order and all of them cried out as they lifted up the little banners I had given them: "Viva Sant' Anna! Viva Sant' Anna!"

The riflemen stood near the door of the monastery. As we came out they began to fire volleys. The drums rolled and the bells rang out. This and everything that followed gladdened the hearts of those poor people. Then the picture of the Saint was turned toward the city and kept in that position for a while. Meanwhile all knelt on the ground and with great compunction of heart and tears begged help in their need.

According to what was told me later, at that very moment a large number of the sick sat up in bed and began to regain their health. The disappearance of the epidemic started through the intercession of this great saint.

The next morning, the day of the Feast, Mass was sung with the same happiness as the day before and almost everyone received Holy Communion. Father Peregrinus of Lucca, who was then the Vicar, preached the sermon in honour of glorious St. Ann, mother of the Mother of God, and urged everyone to have devotion to her.

Chapter 45
Devotion to St. Salvator of Horta

NCE devotion to St. Ann was established in our monastery church at Carpineto the Father Guardian wanted devotion to Blessed Salvator of Horta in Spain to be introduced also, for he was famous for his miracles.

He told me what he had in mind and asked me to have a picture made. I went into the church and spoke with great familiarity as I knelt on the floor: "Blessed Salvator, my brother, help me if you want the picture, because I cannot get it made. These people are poor, so you find the way."

A few days passed when the only child of the captain of the soldiers, Signor Porta, became sick. When he saw the danger his child was in he quickly sent someone to the monastery to request the Father Guardian to have the Friars pray, and to do him the favour of sending me to his home.

The evening *Ave Maria* was ringing when the Friars came looking for me. They told me what the Superior wanted me to do. Before leaving the monastery I went to the church and knelt down to say before the statue of Blessed Salvator: "Blessed Salvator, now is the time if you want the picture!"

Without further ado I went out as Father Guardian had ordered me. When I reached the home of the sick child the captain with his brother and a few others met me and very tearfully said that little Charles was quite seriously sick. With the greatest longing imaginable they pleaded with me to beg our Lord for his health. I asked them if they had devotion to Blessed Salvator. As one man they replied that if Blessed Salvator granted this favour they would gratefully have a picture of him made and exposed in our church of St. Peter. "If that is so," I told them, "our Lord will cure him."

I took the relic of Blessed Salvator, made the sign of the

cross with it in water and then gave the water to the little fellow to drink, as I invoked the name of Jesus, Mary, Ann and Blessed Salvator. I had three sweet ring-shaped biscuits with me; I blessed them. The lad ate them, the fever left and in a short time he was entirely well again. The gentlemen did not fail to carry out the promise of having the picture made.

Another wonderful case happened in the region of Montorio. I want to tell about it here though it took place when I belonged to the monastery of St. Mary of Grace in Ponticelli. The Guardian had given me an obedience to accompany a priest to Montorio where he was going to hear confessions in preparation for a feast day. While the priest was hearing the confessions someone came in a great hurry about a poor man who was dying.

We went to him as fast as you can imagine and there was the sick man in his last agony, unable to make his confession. I was very disturbed that he would die without making his confession. I urged him to ask pardon of God for his sins and have recourse to the intercession of the Blessed Virgin; also to beg the aid of his Guardian Angel. Meanwhile the Father confessor went back to the church. I recalled the many miracles God had worked through Blessed Salvator and that he had endowed with great power over fever some little written notes in honour of the Blessed.[1] I put one of these on the man's sleeve and requested everyone present to say an *Our Father* and *Hail Mary* as we begged the servant of God for the health of this sick man. He was no longer giving any signs of life, but after our prayers he left the bed and to the utter amazement of everyone dressed himself as he praised God and told all as he stood there of the visions of the devils and of some of the saints he had had. He wanted to know my name. I said that it did not matter but that he should go to our

---

[1] These are cards on which is written a prayer in honour of St. Salvator asking for the cessation of fever. They are similar to the so-called *Brief* of St. Anthony of Padua.

monastery to thank the most holy Mother of God, go to confession there, take care not to sin any more, and be devoted to Blessed Salvator.

There was another occurrence similar to the above, at our monastery of Carpineto during the epidemic I spoke of previously. A woman who was long widowed fell mortally sick. She used to give me oil for the lamp of our Lady. Now the time had come when, having received the sacraments, nothing else could be expected except her burial. Actually arrangements had been made to purchase the candles for her funeral. When I heard this I began thinking that if this woman died there would be no one to carry on her charity. A very fervent spirit came over me; I went to the altar of the Madonna in the church and without realizing the little humility and the great presumption that was mine I prayed: "O most holy Madonna, if this poor old woman dies there will be no one in this region to give you oil any longer; so if we want to keep your lamp burning you have to cure her". The most holy Virgin interceded with her Son for the health of this woman. She became well again and to continue her devotion as before sent the Friars the candles that had been bought for her funeral.

After the epidemic died out among the people it finally came into the monastery itself. Eight or nine of the Friars fell sick and because this was a contagious illness they could not be taken to Rome to the infirmary there. One of the Friars died, Brother Gregory of Biscia, a religious of great zeal for work and holiness of life.

It was a wonderful chance for me to be charitable. I served the sick because His Divine Majesty gave me the grace, though my nature abhorred this type of work. I did it with such love and devotion that on the days I was going to Holy Communion with the rest of the Friars I considered it a marvellous preparation for approaching the eucharistic table to be able to give some very small service to the sick brethren.

When I actually came to give it I was all joyful and content, for I knew that God appreciates the love we show our neighbour more than a whole morning spent praying in church.

From the love I had for the sick there was born in my soul a great thirst to serve and spend myself for them all my life; but our Lord did not allow it, perhaps because I was not worthy.

CHAPTER 46
FIRST ATTEMPT AT WRITING

IN this monastery I began to write some devotional articles such as were the *Meditations on the Passion of our Lord* and some others, all of which I destroyed at the command of my confessor.

What mainly started me on something so beneficial for the welfare of souls as writing, was that one of the students of theology who was shortly to finish his studies and take up preaching entreated me to compose a sermon for him on the Passion of Jesus Christ, something very sad and doleful. I excused myself by saying that I did not know how to write well. Excuses were of no avail since he urged me to do my best and he would correct it. With the blessing of my father confessor and after much prayer I wrote the sermon simply as I had meditated on the sufferings of Christ in prayer. When I had finished it I thought it would be well to make a summary of the sermon with chapter headings and points as a help for my meditation; which I did.

I believe this greatly displeased the devil for sometimes he bothered me unusually while I was writing a particular heading. But though our Lord told me some of these things in the kind of ecstasies I was having at that time I still related everything to my father confessor who was then Father Primus of Castelnuovo and, in his absence, to Father John of Rome, both professors of sacred theology. Father Primus told me to write. So I began, but not with much order for our Lord did not wish to let me know everything at one time; he wanted me to be humbled by forgetting some things.

I started meeting with some opposition from the Friars over this writing which I began out of obedience to my confessor; not because I in any way neglected my daily work, for what I did in the line of writing and have done till now was accomplished for the most part at night when the Friars were sleeping and during the day in periods of silence, or when I had nothing else to do. The writing then served to prevent idleness.

The Minister Provincial was visiting the province at that time. He did not come, however, in person to visit our monastery, but sent another Father who was told to find out all about what I had written. After speaking to me in the personal visitation he called me to the refectory where all had gathered and ordered me not to do any more writing. I gladly followed that order.

When the Visitator departed the Father Guardian also felt he had to carry out his duty of keeping the young Friars mortified; so one morning he called me to the refectory and held his own chapter of faults as the Visitator had done, declaring that it was not fitting for lay-brothers to write, and that the Church had no need of my books since it had plenty of very learned men.

I accepted this mortification for the love of God; this was only a little taste of what was to come. There was very much to suffer from our Lord's having put me to a task which belongs to men of great spiritual wisdom and not to a poor ignorant person like myself, who came into religion for no other reason than to work in the kitchen, wash the pots and pans, and sweep the church, not to turn out books, and who, to get books written, was forced to pass the censures of learned men and needed the special help of God so as not to fall into error on some point.

We certainly believe that nothing happens without the particular permission of God so that his works will be purified in us, as gold is refined in the crucible. Still, even iron should be valued when the smithy can do with it what he wants after it has been put in the fire and the rust has been removed on the anvil. Our nature is so intractable that it cannot accommodate itself to contradictions because of the opposition that rises from our imperfection, which in turn comes from our ill-will. Consequently, as I understand it, it is almost a necessity for our Lord—even while we are doing good—to keep us under the mallet of adversities and strike us with the hard blows of tribulations.

Chapter 47
Transfer to Rome

I HAD endured many frightful and terrible temptations from the devil, from my senses and from persons while at the monastery in Carpineto; at this point a new Provincial Chapter took place. Father Joseph of Rome of the Rivaldi family was elected the Minister Provincial in the middle of March 1646, in the time of Pope Innocent X.

I abhorred going to live in Rome because I knew how uneasy and restless the people there were; it had been noticeable on different occasions. But since God has arranged with infinite wisdom the things we cannot escape, once the chapter was held the news was brought to our monastery that the superiors had assigned me to the Roman community. I still did not know to which of the two monasteries I was assigned, whether it was St. Francis a Ripa, the principal one, or St. Peter in Montorio.

Led more by fear than by spiritual considerations I ran to church before the statue of St. Ann and very earnestly prayed that our Lord would be pleased—if of course it was his will—to have me sent to St. Peter in Montorio. It seemed to me that place was more remote and just made for peace of soul, not realizing that I was showing a great imperfection in this. Really, the most secure and the most perfect thing is simply to leave God to handle the matter because he knows how to give us fervour even in the middle of a public square among a crowd of people, if we are truly obedient!

A few days passed and the order came from the Superior indicating which Friars were to stay in Carpineto and which were to leave. I was to go to Rome to the monastery of St.

Peter in Montorio[1] to assist the Father sacristan there.

I left Carpineto in the company of three other Friars who were going to Rome. Besides walking through snow for three days we had a lot of rain, hail and wind, but we suffered all this joyfully for the love of Jesus, out of obedience.

I reached Rome on the glorious feast of St. Joseph, 19 March 1646, being thirty-three years old and ten years in religion. I showed my obedience to the Superior at St. Francis a Ripa and with his blessing went to the monastery of St. Peter in Montorio. There I was received by all the Fathers with special joy, especially by the Guardian, Father Maximus of Marrubio, under whom I had been during my first year at Carpineto and for whom I had a singular affection. He gave me the office of assistant to the Father sacristan as had been determined in the Provincial Chapter, and ordered me to obey him in everything. At the same time he told the Father sacristan to teach me all I had to know and to exercise me in the usual mortifications expected of young Friars.

The Father sacristan was by nature very strict and austere. It was with this spirit he showed me what I had to do and he allowed no fault to pass without scolding me. It was a great struggle for me to form myself according to his wishes and to follow his way of acting. Frequently he had me take apart and remake things when they did not suit him. I think he now enjoys in heaven the reward of his efforts.

Our Lord knew well what he was doing in having me associated through the medium of holy obedience with such a strict person; it was to make my impetuous nature die bit by bit through this mortification, and now that I saw things clearly from experience I was careful not to ask the blessed

---

[1] Built near the place where tradition says St. Peter was crucified, this monastery was given by Pope Sixtus IV to the Franciscan, Blessed Amadeus the Portuguese, in 1472. From 1626 till its suppression by the Italian Government in 1870 a flourishing College of the Foreign Missions was seated here.

God for what pertained more to my will than to his good pleasure, and in every event to give myself to him without wishing to go either here or there but wherever it pleased him. No matter in which of these two monasteries I would be stationed, or in others under similar circumstances, I knew that though I was weak by nature His Majesty would fit my shoulders to the work of carrying it all with patient resignation and of suffering the ceaseless complaints of my lower nature, for he had done so at other times.

Chapter 48
Freedom from Two Serious Trials

MONG the things I very anxiously took care to do when I arrived at the monastery of St. Peter in Montorio was to seek a father confessor to whom I could entrust the affairs of my soul—one who was not only a man of prayer but also learned.

This means very much in the matter of doubts and other difficult temptations that can arise. It is a wonderful advantage from our Lord if he sees fit to have us meet a person of these two outstanding qualities, goodness of life and learning; for with the first, one can advance along the spiritual path through practice; with the other, all difficulties can be smoothed out, while with an understanding of the Scriptures we avoid the errors and deceits of Satan who frequently enough transforms himself into an angel of light. This cannot be done with a confessor who is unlearned and not very devout; though in any case, when no other arrangement can be made, our Lord will step in with a special grace and give us the light and help that we need. In such circumstances he would never allow the confessor to hold us back when he sees that we are ready to serve him.

When I left the monastery of Carpineto my father confessor there, Father Primus, told me that at Rome I should take Father Bernardine of Siena as my confessor since he was a very learned and good preacher, at that time professor of apologetics at St. Peter in Montorio; he also mentioned another less learned Father. After thinking it over well I chose the more learned, Father Bernardine of Siena.

I believe that taking this Father as my confessor was the will of God because of the temptations and doubts that were passing through my mind, especially about the Immaculate Conception of our Lady. I could not persuade myself that she had been conceived without original sin, though I believe this was so.

I often discussed this matter with him while he gave me suitable, well-founded doctrinal reasons why it was true. I also went to listen to the sermons on the Feast of the Immaculate Conception, especially when he preached, because he cited many authorities from among the Fathers and the Supreme Pontiffs.

Though these sermons and the discussions I had with other learned persons gave me great solace I was not completely at rest; and if I impelled my mind simply to believe it without any doubts I still remained bothered by them for four or five years. The time came when it pleased His Majesty to take away all hesitation. One day—I do not know how it happened—I realized I was completely changed interiorly; I became like a person taught to believe without hesitation that the Virgin Mary in her conception did not in any way contract original sin, because she was preserved from it by Almighty God who was able to do this and who had chosen her from all eternity as his Mother.

Another even worse temptation that came almost at the same time was that of revenge. This resulted from the terrible misfortune with which my uncle met, the canon from whom I had received so many favours. He had been murdered and his body found all disfigured forty or fifty days afterwards in a wood two miles out of the city. It was held that two persons committed this frightful crime, two whom he had corrected and told to lead Christian lives.

Though I was rather disturbed at this I left everything in God's hands and immediately went to church before the main altar where I knelt low before the most Blessed Sacrament. There I pardoned from my heart those who had committed this crime while I made an act of love of God and prayed our Lord for the soul of the deceased.

I quickly wrote a letter to all my brothers to do the same

for the love of Jesus Christ, assuring them that in doing this they would not only be performing an act very pleasing to His Divine Majesty but would also know if they really loved me.

But because we are human and blood is thicker than water, I looked into the fact more as the days went by and it made a greater impression on me. My perverse nature aroused me to revenge and to picture those brothers of mine as little better than cowards since they had not used weapons against the lives of those who had taken that of their uncle.

While I was being battered by this terrible temptation I ceaselessly called on the blessed God. I made acts of love and protested that I preferred to die before committing such an evil or being its cause, as there was no lack of those who were helping to stir up the fire.

Our Lord wanted me to put into execution all that I had promised him in prayer about pardoning my enemies. It happened that I went to Sezze as a consolation to one of my married sisters who was seriously ill. What I proposed to do first on reaching the monastery there, was to visit the family of the ones who had reportedly committed the crime and who had run away. I was able to do this with the help of another sister of mine, Mary Valenza. She had joined the Third Order of St. Francis and now was a Poor Clare nun in the monastery at Sezze.[1] She came to visit me and we discussed what we would have to do if we were to go into the city without being seen and without our brothers' hearing about it.

When we reached St. Andrew's gate it suddenly began to rain heavily. Consequently the people who had been out of doors had all gone inside and we went our way safely. All along the way we spoke of God before coming to the home of the first of the two men who had committed the crime, as it

---

[1] Mary Valenza became a nun in the monastery of St. Clare in Sezze and took the name of Sister Mary Frances of Jesus; she died on 9 March 1709. This monastery of St. Clare was built towards the end of the sixteenth century.

was claimed.

When the good woman of the house saw us approaching she herself came out to meet us and asked us to come in. With the love God at that moment gave us we greeted each other and promised for the love of our Lord to remain the very same friends as before; and as a token of this I gave her some small objects of devotion that we religious of St. Francis usually carry with us.

One detail stands out in this meeting. While we were all standing there talking one of the little boys came to kiss my hand. As he did this I felt my blood boiling. To conquer myself I raised my thoughts to God, took out a rosary of our Lord[2] and gave it to him. At the very same instant I was freed of this awful assault. We left the house quickly and went to visit the wife of the other man; she was being kept a prisoner on parole in a private home. We consoled her and urged her to have patience, as we wanted justice to be done. But because she was poor, this sister of mine secretly took care of her needs all the time she was kept in custody.

Then I went to see my brothers and exhorted them to offer peace as often as it was asked of them, reminding them that they were Christians and therefore had to imitate Jesus Christ who so willingly pardoned his enemies.

---

[2] The author of this rosary was Blessed Michael of Florence, a Camaldolese, about the year 1516. It consists of the recitation of thirty-three *Our Fathers* in honour of the number of years our Lord lived on earth.

Chapter 49
Considerations on Discerning the Spirit of God and Avoiding a False Spirit

AT this time a woman who had the name of being very holy often came to see me at the monastery. She had ecstasies and revelations and though she was uneducated she sometimes explained the Gospels in a remarkable way.

In her visions, so she told me, she often saw Jesus as he was scourged at the pillar, covered with blood from the many stripes, crowned with thorns, a cross on his shoulders, all for the sins of the world. She also claimed that she saw into the souls of others and could tell in what state they were, and that some of our religious left the monastery pure and innocent, only to return quite changed.

I was amazed at these visions. But she gave me something to think about when she said that certain religious whom she named had committed various sins, because not only did I know them as ordinary good persons, I was sure they were very good. They esteemed virtue and were in turn esteemed by the world. But the merciful God who is eternal wisdom does not permit the deceits of the devil to remain hidden and to have assistance.

One day this woman came to visit me and because she wanted to travel a short distance outside Rome she asked me for the mantle I was wearing; she wanted to wear it herself as she was a Franciscan Tertiary. I told her that according to the rule which we professed, we religious were not the owners of the habit we wore and so I would sin if I gave her the mantle without the permission of my Superior. She became very upset at being told this and scolded me for having so little charity. Because she was poor I was not being considerate, she exclaimed, and then she began speaking badly of the above-mentioned religious.

Now I knew the poor woman was deceived by the devil and that this spirit was not of God. I spoke the first words of the Apostles' Creed: "I believe in God, the Father Almighty!" and at this she left, completely distraught, and went round to people who knew me, muttering that I was a good-for-nothing.

Through his deceitful visions and revelations the devil led this poor woman to pride, detraction of good persons, disobedience towards those in authority, and wanting to have her own way, yet all the while she sought praise from everyone. When a devout servant of God who was also a Tertiary of St. Francis heard of this deceit she began to take care of the woman very solicitously, hoping to find a remedy for the evil. In the meantime she kept in touch with me about everything that was happening. Many times she tried to arrange a talk between myself and the unfortunate person but this was impossible because the latter avoided me as the plague.

While I was returning once from Rome, it pleased God to have me meet this sadly deceived woman as she was praying at the spot where St. Peter the Apostle was crucified.[1] I greeted her kindly and after we talked a little I asked her if she wanted anything. She said that she would be glad to have a little wine to drink. I wasted no time in going for it and brought it to her in a terracotta cup of the kind the Friars use for drinking.[2] As soon as she took the cup into her hands she was raised from the ground and went into what seemed an ecstasy. The Friar with me was astounded.

Our Lord gave me the light to recognize that this was not

---

[1] An allusion to the tradition according to which St. Peter was not crucified on the Vatican, but on the Janiculum Hill where a small church by Bramante was built.

[2] This was a cup with two handles.

a true ecstasy but the work of the devil, as was evident from the woman's face. Our Lord does not work these favours for anyone who lives in such a headstrong way outside obedience, though he does not cease making their soul experience remorse of conscience so that they will leave their error and be themselves.

When I saw her lifted up with arms extended it occurred to me that I should command her to quit this ecstasy and so I said: "Since I am not a priest I have not the authority to command you. But as a Christian redeemed by the Blood of Jesus Christ and as a religious, therefore as one who is over you, a woman, I command you in the name of Almighty God that you willingly desist from this ecstasy." She obeyed immediately. I asked her why she had stopped being obedient. Her answer was a bold one. She had no further obligation, she said, than to obey Jesus Christ. She had a bronze crucifix with her and as she held it she spoke of having taken our Lord for the spouse of her soul; she would never be separated from him since he was her one good. My answer was that it was a very holy matter to obey God in all that he commanded us; still we also have to subject ourselves to our superiors who are responsible for our souls because God himself willed this. In converting St. Paul Jesus Christ gives us an example of this for, after that, he sent him to Ananias who had been told what was to be done.

The woman, or the devil in her, answered: "It is true that we must obey our superiors and we should do this when their lives are holy and perfect; but when this is not so then we are not obliged to obey them, because, if I see that they are not holy and perfect, I do not recognize them as my superiors."

My answer to that was: Since His Divine Majesty has given us superiors and directors of souls, to be obedient to them, we are not to wonder at their imperfect lives but simply carry out the obligations they place on us as our Lord himself taught us in the Gospel: "The scribes and the Pharisees have sat on the chair of Moses. All things therefore whatsoever they shall say to you, observe and do; but according to their works do ye not."[3]

She used the same Gospel for her rebuttal and argued so loftily and learnedly that I feared very much I would not be able to answer her. When I saw that, I raised my mind to God and begged him for the grace not to be beaten at argument by a woman, so that the devil would not become bold.

Our Lord had me answer that it is clear and cannot be denied that all our perfection consists in obedience. Jesus Christ our Lord gave us the example when he became obedient even to death.[4] All other reasoning yields to this.

When the spirit of pride that cannot listen to words about the humility of Christ heard this answer he lifted the woman's arm and with bold words made a furious motion to strike me on the face. Now I was all the more certain of the deceit involved here and I asked commandingly: "Who are you, O evil beast?" The devil kept silent; he saw that he was discovered and did not say a word. The woman was all confusion and shame. I gave her a long exhortation, especially on being obedient and not yielding to the devil.

Another case, just as notable, happened to me at the monastery of St. Peter in Carpineto, which I think I should write about at this time. The Father Guardian had sent me to beg for oil in the places close by. I came to a place where I was known and stopped a while at the home of some people I knew very well. Quite a group of people gathered because of their love for the Franciscan habit. A woman approached me to speak of the favours our Lord had granted her. I listened gladly. Among the matters she confided to me one was that Christ crucified often appeared to her.

Now I knew this woman very well and because I was

---

[3] Matt. 23: 2-3.

[4] Phil. 2: 8.

aware that up to this time she had not attended to her spiritual life and to the mortification of her senses, and also that her prayer was not of the high degree to qualify her for such apparitions, I told her what I thought, namely, the one whom she said was Jesus Christ in the form of the Crucified was none other than Satan.

The woman acted as though I had uttered a blasphemy or some terrible defamation when she heard this. She could not be persuaded that this was the devil, for many times the apparition had shown her the wounds and she had kissed them. I did not say anything further because time did not permit it; I only replied that she should be on her guard.

A year after that it chanced that I went back to the same place. As I was going through the city to return to the monastery I saw this same woman coming after me, all upset and nervous. She very tearfully begged me to make the sign of the cross over her; she feared she was possessed. I pitied her and since it was late in the day I told her that it would not be good to do that in public for it could cause talk. She should please come to the monastery in the morning. She came with another woman, a confidante, who understood her well and spoke to me of every deception the devil had practised on her. He appeared to her not only in the form of the Crucified but of angels and even of saints, especially in the likeness of St. Anselm and St. Philip Neri who advised her that she had given enough alms and had done enough good for religious. In her heart they put great desires for loving God and for visiting holy places to which they transported her in spirit as happened once when a longing to see the treasury of St. Mark in Venice came over her.

During this same period an extraordinary desire possessed her of sensing in her soul and body the pains experienced by our holy Father St. Francis when the sacred stigmata were impressed on him; suddenly she felt pierced by a sweet pain in her hands, feet and heart, that carried her out of herself.

These demons in angelic and saintly forms planted in her the desire to perform miracles by making the sign of the cross over sick people with a piece of wood they brought her, from where I do not recall.

If I were to recount everything else that befell her there would be no end to it. A large book could be filled. I will tell only what the devil finally did to accomplish his purpose, which was to make her offend God. She was a widow and the devil put the thought in her heart of marrying a certain man. These false angels and saints appeared beforehand to tell her that she should marry him because this was God's will; and what they would do for her if she did, only God knows. But the marriage did not take place because her parents held out against it and our Lord came to her help.

After the woman had told me all that the devil had done she asked me if there was any hope left for her salvation. She was kneeling on the ground, crying bitterly. I made the sign of the cross over her, saying an Ave, *Pater and Credo*, as I told her comfortingly to have a strong hope and faith in the mercy of God who would pardon her sins and bring her back to his fatherly embrace. I added that the remedy for being cured and freed from the devil's deceits would be a general confession of her sins. Then I advised her for the future to live more prudently under the guidance and counsel of a spiritual father, for the devil shows himself not as he really is but under the appearance of God. She left me, consoled and thankful to our Lord. The remainder of her life was praiseworthy.[5]

---

[5] These events show how prudently one needs to act so as not to be deceived. They will also be of benefit to spiritual directors.

Chapter 50
Printing of a Small Book of Meditations

LESSED be our Lord forever who wants us very much to imitate him and to carry the cross of tribulation as long as we are pilgrims in this life, that with it we may enter into his kingdom. I realize that in this I have a great obligation of gratitude to him, for mortifications came to me like waves of the sea and when one passed I could see another coming, though I was barely able to keep my head above water. Trials never ceased, for each superior wanted to be satisfied about the sincerity of his subject. Blessed be our holy Order, always very cautious so as not to make a mistake!

I think that as he used these means our Lord derived much pleasure from seeing me fight; he allowed me so many trying occasions as to be amazing.

On leaving the monastery of St. Peter in Carpineto for Rome I had a little book with me containing some meditations I had written on our Lord's most holy Passion. Whenever I went on the quest to nearby places I would take it with me and before retiring in the evening I would read one of the mysteries to all present and they were moved to compassion. It not only served to enkindle devotion in hearts but also to disperse the worldly thoughts that always hide within themselves the danger of offending God.

When I finally managed to have this little book written in a good hand—my handwriting was poor—it was seen by some devout persons, particularly by a gentleman whom I knew very well and who wanted to have it printed.

This made me fear very much that I was not going to escape without some misfortune. So I told this gentleman and the others to do nothing without the permission of the Father

General who then was Father John of Naples.[1] I do not know if it was through simplicity or the permission of God that this man did just the opposite of what I had told him. He went directly to the Master of the Sacred Palace,[2] who read my composition, passed it, and gave permission to have it printed.

After this was settled at the Sacred Palace, the man who had the book brought it to the Father General. When he saw what had happened without his knowledge he gave way to a great rage and, since he had all authority, threatened to have this poor man sent to jail. Then he turned to the Friars around him, demanding to know who this Brother Charles of Sezze was from the monastery of St. Peter in Montorio and giving orders that I be put in prison.

As luck would have it my Guardian, Father Maximus of Marrubio, was there at the time. When he heard my name he told the Father General that this Brother Charles belonged to his monastery and he begged him for the love of our Lord not to send me to prison, for he knew how to correct me in a way that would satisfy his Paternity. The Father General became somewhat calm when he heard this and ordered the Father Guardian to hold a chapter of faults in the refectory and impose penances on me.

When the Father Guardian came back to St. Peter in Montorio he called me from the sacristy when all the Friars were in the refectory without in any way advising me as to what had happened. I went, and on my knees admitted the fault of being negligent and not very mortified. Then he began holding a long chapter of faults, scolding me for having

---

[1] Elected General of the Order 3 June 1645, and governed till his death 26 September 1648.

[2] The Sacred Apostolic Palace is the home of the Holy Father in Vatican City. The title of Master of the Sacred Apostolic Palace is given to the priest who is the Pope's personal theologian. He belongs to the Pontifical Family and lives in the Vatican. Formerly one of his many duties was to read manuscripts; he either gave or denied permission for them to be printed. [*Translator.*]

presumed to send books to the printer, something that so many learned men in this monastery had not done, and here I, a lay-brother, had presumed to do so. Publicly he gave me a penance; when the meal was over I was to go before the Blessed Sacrament and say five *Our Fathers* and *Hail Marys* in thanksgiving, and then he placed me under obedience not to write any more and to take from my room the pen and ink and everything necessary for writing.

The night before I was given this command something of great import had occurred. Some days previously one of our religious by the name of Brother Bonaventure of Cori died at St. Francis a Ripa. His life had been a very exemplary one; he had shown signs of sanctity in his most exact obedience, patience, charitableness and exalted prayer, and he had received the gift of miracles and the spirit of prophecy from our Lord.

The news of his death reached far and wide, especially the city of Urbino. The Friars there kept asking me to write a short sketch of his life and send it to them with some objects he had used.

There was little for me to write on the various circumstances of his death. While I was in church that night I felt interiorly a great impulse to go and write a complete life of this servant of God, rich in the poverty that was his greatest treasure. This impulse was so great that I had to leave the church and begin writing. I did this with many tears, for after receiving the Sacraments Brother Bonaventure had exhorted the Friars to the observance and the love of the Rule; then he folded his hands, raised his eyes to heaven in prayer and very calmly gave back his blessed soul to his Creator.

When grace after meals had been said I went straight to church to carry out the imposed penance while a whole cloud of different thoughts followed me; for though I accepted the entire mortification for the love of our Lord and though my feelings which had smarted were at rest, now all was changed by a breath of wind from the devil who raised such a sea of temptations in me that I became completely upset. The temptation regarding my reputation was the most violent; this has great power with the devils to lead us to despair. And because some religious of other Orders had been there that morning a great apprehension seized me that my fall would become known to other monasteries and that I would be disgraced.

As I came to the altar of the most Blessed Sacrament and recited the five *Our Fathers* and *Hail Marys*, thanking His Divine Majesty for all that had happened, I asked him from my heart to help me in this serious need. Though I was unworthy our Lord mercifully heard my prayer and I understood him to say to me interiorly as from the tabernacle: "My son, these things that you are meeting will not keep you from entering paradise but will make it easier!" That is what our Lord said! This is the place to reflect that all the saints became more glorious by being dishonoured and persecuted, because whatever our feelings hold in abomination pleases God most, when we suffer it for love of him.

Like a flash the temptations fled at these words of our Lord. A complete tranquillity of soul was mine on being enveloped with his power as with a dew. I thanked him affectionately for having deigned to console me with the sweetness of his words and for having put my enemies to flight.

Chapter 51
Desire to Possess the Love of God

THROUGH my religious exercises I kept advancing. Still, I was not free of the weighty troubles that held my poor soul to a constant battle, though it was at peace with God. Because our Lord wanted to enrich me with fresh favours, he caused me even to desire afflictions, that my soul might more intensely resist its enemies and persevere in his love. More than ever before, from that moment on I began to experience a great longing to possess the love of God. This desire was like that of the holy spouse in the *Canticle of Canticles* when she heard her beloved knocking on the door of her heart and went out of the house to look for him throughout the city, the streets and squares, asking everyone she met if he had seen the beloved of her soul.[1]

The result of this anxiety of soul to have the Divine Majesty give me his most divine love, was that I was very frequently impelled to request it of him. In burning words I said: "O my Jesus, give me your love. Lord, though I do not deserve it, do not deny me it!" And I just could not seem to utter any other words but these. Then I would turn to the most holy Virgin: "O Mary, Mother of God, beg for me from your Son his holy love!"

This sentiment of mine lasted for almost two or three months and to such a degree that I could not quiet it. But since the love of God springs from mortification and self-conquest our Lord arranged things in a way that could not be attributed to anything but his divine wisdom.

Father Daniel of Dongo, who on the death of Father John

---

[1] Cant. 3 and 5.

of Naples succeeded him as General of the Order, became seriously ill here at the monastery of St. Peter in Montorio. During his illness he had me come twice a day, morning and evening, to sign him with the relic of Blessed Salvator because of his devotion to this saint. In the same reliquary there was also a relic of St. Lidano. I urged him to recommend himself to this saint also with the hope that health would be requested for him.

He had become much worse and was almost dead when one day as I was in my room during the period of silence there came over me a sudden strong impulse of soul to recommend him with particular devotion to glorious St. Lidano, with confidence that a favour would be obtained. And for the favour that would be given I resolved that every time my superiors would allow it I would visit his body in the principal church at Sezze. The Father became better quickly and when he was quite cured I told him of the obligation I had of making this pilgrimage and put myself in his hands as regards it. He was pleased to permit me to carry this out. So when one of our Fathers had to go to a monastery near where St. Lidano is buried I accompanied him.

The arrangement made by the Father General was that at the monastery where my companion was going to stay, an obedience enabling me to complete my journey should be given by the Guardian there and another companion assigned to me.

We left Rome in the direction of Frascati. The Guardian there gave me an obedience and a companion as the Father General had ordered, and I went to visit the body of the saint in Sezze.

When I had satisfied my devotion I returned to Frascati. The Father with whom I had come there had returned to Rome and had notified the Father Provincial of my going to Sezze, without telling him that I had been sent there by the Superior General. I thought it must sound very bad, my going there without an obedience from him. When I returned to the monastery of St. Francis in Rome I found some of the Fathers fearing greatly that I would be punished as an apostate.[2]

I was not dismayed though naturally I felt afraid; I sought courage by recommending myself to God and then I went to submit the occurrence to the Minister Provincial. He charitably corrected me for having gone to Sezze without his permission. He wanted to know exactly how it was I had gone there, for being very prudent and learned he did not want to fly into a fury. I told him the whole story: how I did this with permission in the service of the Father General and how I had forgotten to notify him, the Father Provincial. When he understood this he told me to rise from my knees, embraced me and sent me back to St. Peter in Montorio without giving me a penance.

I went to see the Father General who was very happy at my return and at the favour our Lord had granted him through the intercession of glorious St. Lidano. I asked for his blessing without telling him anything of what had happened with the Friars, and I went to see my Father Guardian, Father Barnabas of Palermo, a very meek person. He was still upset since he blamed me for a fault he believed I had been guilty of; and as a penance he ordered me to stay out of the sacristy until further notice. Walking behind the donkey I was to accompany the Friar who went out to look for wood. I gladly embraced this obedience without desiring to justify myself or speak to the Father General, because I considered it more important to obey and be mortified than to make my innocence known.

I regarded it as a great favour to be assigned as a

---

[2] An *apostate*, that is, from the Franciscan Order. If anything, the Saint should have used the term *fugitive*. But it is evident that in this case he was neither an apostate nor a fugitive from the Order since he had gone to Sezze with the regular permission of the Superior General. Without thinking, he had omitted the formality of notifying his Provincial Superior of the permission obtained.

companion of this faithful servant of God, because of his devotion and the familiarity between us. We very often talked over things together, for his was great goodness of life and observance of the holy Rule, especially of poverty. He had some sort of spirit of prophecy, as I well know since I had discussed it with him. His name was Brother Simple of Sant'Elia, which is a village near Rieti. The facts corresponded with his name for our Lord had given him an outstanding simplicity joined with prudence. May God be praised! I think he is now happy in paradise. His soul left the prison of this world in the first year of the epidemic of 1655,[3] about the seventy-third year of his life.

When he heard that I was to go with him as a companion the good old man felt the same joy as I. In the name of the most high God we started for Rome to beg charity in wood, doing it all in a deep quiet and union with God.

The tempter who never sleeps availed himself of the occasion. He knew I had been very humiliated by my Superior so he started a fierce struggle in me. Before me he put the points of elementary uprightness, of honour and of reputation with the Friars and with other people; as I thought of them they had such an effect that the disturbance I felt was extremely great. But it was conquered with the help of divine grace and the virtue of obedience, while the desire for the love of God never left me. The longer I waited the more vehement these desires of my soul became, and like a thirsty stag that looks for springs of water to slake its thirst, so I sought God the fountain of living waters, of which those who drink will not die for ever. In my longing I often said to my holy Spouse: "My Jesus, give me your love!"

When I went to Rome to beg and happened to pass before a church I knelt down before the door as I led the donkey, turned toward the most Blessed Sacrament and begged our

---

[3] A contagion that made many victims in Rome and its environs about 1656, during the reign of Pope Alexander VII.

Lord to give me his love.

For many days I persevered affectionately in this practice. One day I was begging in Capo le Case[4] and I came to a church named after glorious St. Joseph, to which is attached a monastery of Carmelite nuns.[5] My companion told me to stop there and have the donkey cared for in the vicinity while he went round seeking alms.

I knelt down to pray, for Mass had begun at the high altar. I begged our Lord who resides invisibly in the holy tabernacle that he would deign to give me his most divine love, through the intercession of the glorious St. Joseph; I continued in this prayer right up to the consecration. When the priest lifted the consecrated Host, with the eyes of my soul I saw streaming from it a ray of light that came and struck my heart. It happened so quickly that I would not know how much time it took. Now the effect that it had on my heart was as of something done to iron, and it took place exactly as what we see happen to a piece of metal when it is put in the forge. It is completely turned into fire and then when it is placed red-hot into a container of water it makes a sizzling sound. Blessed be St. Joseph! Through his intercession I had been pierced by the hand of our Lord with the dart of his love.

I do not know how to form a mental picture of the pain I felt, so as to be able to describe it, nor how I lived. It was so spiritual and penetrating that without God's help it would have been impossible to bear it with human strength alone. But though the pain was great it was tempered by an excessive sweetness that penetrated the very depths of my soul and transformed it through so much love that it seemed

---

[4] A district of Rome with this name.

[5] A monastery of the reform of St. Teresa, the first in Rome in order of time, founded in 1597. In remembrance of the wonderful event to be described, this community annually celebrates the feast of St. Charles, though the nuns have moved to a new monastery also dedicated to St. Joseph.

it would have to leave the body, placed as it was between the two extremes of pain and sweetness. It would have been a great pleasure to die at that moment, since dying from love brings no pain. Not being able to die caused a loving affliction at the absence of the beloved whom my soul wanted to enjoy in the secure state of glory.

For many days I did nothing but say: "Blessed be God! Blessed be God!" And so great was the love I felt in my heart that I could not really understand it myself. For the great sweetness I could have kissed the ground, the plants and rocks; I could have borne any torment, any tribulation, any martyrdom whatsoever that all the saints have suffered, together with the pains that are experienced in purgatory and hell. All of these would have seemed little in comparison to the great love I experienced. The waters of all rivers combined could not have extinguished it!

I think it was the month of October 1648 when our Lord deigned in his generosity to grant me this favour. Blessed be the Lord God for ever! Blessed be glorious St. Joseph, spouse of the Virgin most holy! And blessed be mortifications since by them one receives so great a benefit from the bountiful hand of God.

The time during which I sensibly felt my heart pierced was about three years and all the while I was so weak that very often I put my hand over the wound to lessen the pain somewhat, since it continued like a living fire. A very hot flame of the love of God burned there and like a divine teacher kept instructing my soul, urging it on to the perfection of unitive love, purifying it all the more from its natural imperfections by the ardent influence of its grace so as to dispose it to receive the divine influx; and through the sovereign light that shines in it, giving a much higher awareness of the divine knowledge it possesses, and a readiness to incessant love.

Because of the ardour of this divine affection I sometimes

experienced such intense palpitations of the heart that in their vehemence they seemed to want to break through the prison of the body, and cause the soul to leave it in the excess of its love. Since my natural powers failed me I kept repeating those loving words: "Blessed be God! Blessed be God! Jesus, my love! Jesus, my love! Help me, for I am dying of love!"

This was a special experience of God in my heart through a most pure knowledge of him. It takes place in the soul through the action of God himself; it is not limited to times or periods but comes when he wills it and to whom he wills it. That which a person seeks to do of himself so as to be disposed to receive this,[6] is to be in the state of grace and practise the virtues along with the two kinds of mortification, interior and exterior, by which we die to ourselves and come to live the life of God. He is the true way lighting our path; he is the truth teaching without deceit; he is the life giving us spiritual existence as he leads us to himself, eternal life.

I do not know how to describe the love I felt. You, King David, Francis, Philip, Teresa, Catherine of Siena, and all you other saints who have experienced it, tell us something about it with your heavenly tongues! I only know how to say with the holy spouse: "Stay me up with flowers, compass me about with apples, for I languish with love!",[7] since my soul is liquefied in feeling the living flames and hearing the voice of my Beloved who speaks a language divine.

Out of this divine love grew pulsating desires to do great things for the love of that Jesus who worked the magnificence of his grace in my heart. I wished I could have performed every great penance to humble this feeling at the feet of everyone and by mortification to bring it to a perpetual obedience to reason; I wished I could have exercised all the virtues perfectly and not omit doing anything for Christ so as

---

[6] The most pure knowledge of infused contemplation.

[7] Cant. 2: 5.

to correspond to this abyss of love.

Though the favours granted by His Divine Majesty are great, still they are given only for a time and our passions have the chance to war against us and keep us in constant training. It is true that in virtue of the grace our Lord then gives us, we remain strong in our resistance to the attack of these different evil appetites through which our will is moved to desire evil, but it would be a great mistake to suppose that those to whom our Lord has granted these gifts no longer feel the usual natural aversions to which we are subject or that they make us safe, so to speak. Life here below is not secure; it is a warfare, as holy Job tells us.[8]

That is why the counsel the Holy Spirit gives will be very helpful to us, namely, that when we experience floods of heavenly grace emptying into us, then we are to prepare our soul for temptation.[9]

---

[8] Job 7: 1.

[9] Ecclus (Sirach) 2: 1.

Chapter 52
Appearance of St. Teresa;
The Three Ways of Meditation

HOUGH by divine permission I was assured by my director Father William that my prayer was of an infused supernatural kind, His Divine Majesty wished to give me greater certainty by bringing to my notice the thoughts on the love of God of that great teacher of spirituality, St. Teresa, and allowing me to see her.

On the occasion when I was requested by some of the religious in the monastery of St. Sixtus in Magnanapoli to speak on spiritual matters with one of the nuns there, they wanted to give me all the writings of their holy Mother Teresa, arranged in several volumes. As I had never seen them before and did not know what they contained I did not make much of the offer and politely excused myself, saying that I was not used to having many books except some little thing on meditation, and so I thanked them. But they begged me so much that, in order not to upset them, I contented myself with taking the smallest of the books, the one containing the *Thoughts on the Love of God*, the *Meditations on the Lord's Prayer*, the *Exclamations* and the *Seraphic Canticle*.

On reading it I found that it treated in large measure of the union of love that takes place in the soul on the path of holiness. It spoke also of those heavenly sentiments or awarenesses of God that inflame with love and work various marvellous effects for one's spiritual profit. The content was indescribable and no other delightful thing in this world, I am sure, could compare with it.

A special devotion to St. Teresa formed in my heart and I maintain that our Lord—as he kept me busy writing on prayer[1]—had given me this saint as my teacher. This turned out to be true on more than one occasion.

When I was with the other Friars at prayer in the church of St. Peter in Montorio before the most Blessed Sacrament of the Altar, all of a sudden my mind opened and with its eye I saw, so to speak, a ray of most resplendent glory. By divine revelation I understood that in that ray was the glorious soul of the saint, Mother Teresa. That light penetrated right to the depths of my soul which became illumined by the brightness of glory and stirred by so great an impulse that I thought it wanted to leave my body and go with the saint to praise its Creator.

This all happened in a moment like a flash of lightning; my soul was fully satisfied and through a language that is divine—without any words being spoken but simply with the sight given by intellectual knowledge—I understood more than if long hours had been spent in thought.

Oh, how good are these visions of the saints when they are really from God! Though they are not seen speaking in these visions, still they leave sacred truths impressed on the soul and it seems that they break up all that is evil in us while they put there what is good, the virtues.

On the persuasion of a devout person I was commanded by my confessor, Father Anthony of Aquila, to write something pertaining to prayer[1] and contemplation, to serve as an instruction for others. Though I had practised prayer and contemplation for many years, still I had not acquired the knowledge to express myself clearly on it. To know how to distinguish the degrees of prayer and the way in which the soul with its faculties advances in it, is a special gift from God. Since this more divine than human matter is so exalted I asked to be excused, for humanly speaking it was necessary to know theology well and to have practised it a lot, as I told the

---

[1] Actually the writings of St. Charles that have been published, *Treatise on the Three Ways, Interior Journey, Sacred Septenaries*, etc., treat mainly, if not exclusively, of prayer.

Father; and since I had not studied it and did not understand its terminology very well, nor the way to use it properly in writing, the whole thing would be too difficult. Because, however, one does not resist the divine will, I embraced this work compelled by obedience.

Since our Lord was to be the principal author of this writing he was pleased to favour holy obedience by infusing into my soul light from heaven as I needed it. One day while I was praying I suddenly saw my mind being opened and my soul filled with a divine and most resplendent light that poured into me a special wisdom and knowledge about supernatural matters. The knowledge I then had of these cannot be expressed.

I began to arrange the material in orderly fashion and learned how to express myself on the matter of the favours our Lord went on communicating to me. The style I used was not rhetorical but simple and accommodated to my intellectual capacity. In that way I divided the states of contemplation into two parts and dealt with them according to the manner in which His Divine Majesty dictated them to me and as I had experienced them in prayer. When this writing on the contemplative life was finished I showed it to my father confessor. After looking over it and thinking about it he judged that it was only for the perfect whom the Lord had drawn to great heights of prayer; there was nothing there for beginners to work at and so for them I was to write what the blessed God would inspire me to write.

As I listened to this second obedience I became very confused because I did not know where I was going to start. I had recourse to prayer and begged our Lord for two whole nights to help me to be able to carry out the obedience. As I persevered in prayer the third night I recalled the farmer who wanted to sow seed in his field. When he found the ground unploughed he realized that it would first require much work to cultivate it, for first the weeds had to be removed and the land tilled; only then could he sow seed there. When the seed begins to grow he has to watch it carefully and protect it from thorns and weeds so that they do not smother it, if he is to bring it to maturity. Once the grain is ripe he will reap it and put it in the granary. Really this metaphor is from heaven, from the Father of lights, and though it is a humble example both in the subject and in the person whom it represents, actually it is exalted in the sacred notion expressed spiritually.

I also understood that this metaphor was like a theme on which I was to write concerning the path beginners take as they flee from the world and I saw that it would very well fit the three ways of meditation, namely, the purgative, *illuminative and unitive.*

Once I had this lesson in prayer from our good Lord I began to arrange the material and tell beginners how they must walk the three ways. I continued with the other chapters also, according as our Lord favoured me with his help, and when I was not able to continue with some of them I went before the altar of our Lady of the Pietà and begged her to give me her help, after I had said some prayers and served holy Mass. I had hardly asked her when she deigned to hear me and opened up my mind; and what had seemed difficult I then accomplished with the greatest facility.

Chapter 53
Assignment to the Monastery of St. Francis a Ripa

TWICE till now I have been given the office of sacristan at the monastery of St. Francis a Ripa. The first time was in 1650, the Jubilee Year of Pope Innocent X.

The work entailed was very heavy as our religious came from all parts of the world to gain the sacred indulgences. Among the great servants of God who came—not to speak of saintly priests—was a Brother Anthony of Bari, of the Province of St. Nicholas of Bari. One morning as he was praying in the very middle of the church of St. Francis he was raised into the air about a foot and remained there quite a long period. He was very old, wasted from penances and possessing the spirit of prophecy and the gift of miracles. Another was Brother Alexander of Agnone. Many times I went with him to visit the churches that year; in all I made twenty-eight such visits, barefoot, and through these works our Lord gave me many graces.

Now that I had come back to St. Peter Montorio and as I thought over the great amount of labour I had borne in the sacristy at St. Francis, it seemed it would be very hard for me to be sent back there again and not die. This very strange thought built up an extreme melancholy in my heart as if, so to speak, I had been created by God never to die but to live like another Mathusala who stayed on earth nine hundred years!

So as to entice my will and put it under God's will in this confusion and rebellion of my nature, I kept reminding myself that I was a child of obedience and that suffering and dying through obedience was the same as dying a martyr. Thinking this over well brought me some relief of soul but it did not last very long; the fear returned as before and I think I went through the misery of three years! It grew worse as the Provincial Chapter approached and I was at Sant'Oreste as a companion of Father Thomas of Rome who had been sent as the extraordinary confessor to the nuns at the monastery of the Holy Cross there.

In the meantime the chapter was held and no one sent us any news about it either by letter or by word of mouth. But a strange thing happened to me—I do not know if it was the doing of God or the devil—and it was that there was impressed on my mind the special certainty that the chapter had already been held and that I was going to be in the sacristy at St. Francis a Ripa with the sacristan I first had in St. Peter Montorio, the Father who taught the young Friars so strictly.

I discussed this revelation with Father Thomas along with the repugnance I felt in belonging to the community at St. Francis, and he urged me to be patient till the reports were published.

But the pressure put on me by my nature was for this reason tremendous as I reflected on the double reason for having to be in contact with the unattractive personality of the above-mentioned sacristan: I would be living with him in the same monastery and at the same time be under orders to him. His strictness I abhorred extremely.

I paid little attention to this blind feeling but earnestly made fervent acts of love of God, and during this storm of passion lifted my hands and eyes to heaven as I said: "When this happens or if someone tells me that I have been transferred to the community of St. Francis a Ripa I will kneel down, kiss the earth many times, and say: The will of God be done! I thank God with all the affection of my heart."

When Father Thomas had finished with these good religious and I had prepared myself for whatever was to come, we set off for Rome. As we neared the monastery of St. Francis two Friars came out and told us the news of what had taken place at the chapter. The new Provincial was Father Angelus of Bergamo, and I was to belong to the community at St. Francis as companion to the Father sacristan already mentioned! On hearing this I went down on my knees and kissed the earth, while I said over and over: "The will of God be done!" I made myself ready to embrace holy obedience courageously and to die for it every time it would be necessary.

With this good resolve I went into the monastery and after the ceremony of washing of feet I paid my obedience to the Superior and went into the sacristy. The Father sacristan was already there. When we saw each other we embraced spontaneously, as a father does when he sees his son; as a son, when he sees his father.

Oh, the wonders of God in obedience! I saw that the Father was completely changed in his ways; his great strictness had turned into love. The defects of which I was guilty—deserving full punishment—he corrected with the same love, leaving me amazed at seeing the remarkable change that had come over him!

Though the work in the sacristy brought great fatigue with it, His Divine Majesty gave me such strength that I went about the tasks as though always lifted up in spirit. The result was that I never felt pressed or irked; really, the work enlivened me to dispose my soul more for union with God. Like smoke before the wind I dispelled all rebellion and fear, turning bitterness into joy and sadness into gladness. So great was the gladness I felt in my heart that it seemed I was going to God transformed. Then it was that I wrote the chapter on "Gladness of heart" as found in the third part of the book The Three Ways of Meditation. This gladness springs from holy obedience as the fruit proper to this heroic virtue.

We should not grieve that at times we have to embrace the

things that appear to us as very high mountains, for our Lord protects us with his grace and makes their accomplishment very easy and smooth, as he did with the Israelites who passed through the Red Sea with dry feet.

This gladness of God in my heart lasted all the time that I stayed at St. Francis.

Chapter 54
Daily Holy Communion

IN the period during which holy obedience made me a member of the monastery of St. Francis my confessor was Father Joseph of Rome who, as I said before, was elected Minister Provincial in the year 1646. Though he was a very learned person he was also greatly inclined to devotion—it is a grace from God to meet with confessors who have both these good qualities—and this gave me confidence to talk with him about the affairs of my soul.

For some years now I had begun to sense on tongue and lips at receiving Holy Communion such a heavenly sweetness that I cannot describe it. Added to this sweetness which made me wet my lips, a divine fire was enkindled on my tongue which broke into spiritual flame and warmed my spirit as it held my soul in the grip of a limitless love for this indescribable mystery.

At different times I had spoken with my spiritual directors about this favour His Divine Majesty was giving me. They listened to me but did nothing about it; perhaps they were following the method of other confessors who, when something like this is told them, close their ears so as to sound the intention of their penitents and then send them away without discussing it or without fully examining the matter in the effects it produces.

Now this is how I reacted to my confessors when something special happened to me such as this. If they listened to me, well and good; if they did not, that was well and good too. Either way, I was satisfied at having done my part even though they gave me no explanation of what was occurring.

But after I spoke to the above-mentioned confessor he told

me without hesitation that I should be very happy because the sweetness of taste I was experiencing was from God and that before long it would enter my heart; consequently I should be very grateful to God and stay humble.

After I had been transferred to St. Peter in Montorio it was not long before the spiritual fire that was setting my tongue aflame entered my heart, causing such a great longing to receive our Lord in the Sacrament of the Altar that this desire became stronger each day.

The very unusual excess I felt toward the most Blessed Sacrament, and the thirst I could not quench, I discussed with my father confessor, Father Anthony of Aquila, and asked him what he thought about my receiving Holy Communion daily. He did not give me a reply at once but left the question unanswered; and as for me I did not think it was right to do it without the permission of my confessor.

I let some days pass. When I saw that this hankering did not diminish but grew, I recommended myself to our Lord and asked him to tell me what he wanted. With this in mind, one day I went to the altar of the most Blessed Sacrament and said to our Lord: "If it is your will that I receive Communion every morning I will go to my confessor right away and he will tell me". And that is what I did. I went straight to him and as soon as I had gone to confession I simply asked him if he would be willing to allow me to receive every morning. Yes, he said, he would permit me to do that. With his blessing I have never failed to receive Holy Communion daily when there was nothing to prevent me, even though at times I did so with much coldness and when I was not well prepared. The graces I received from our Lord are innumerable.

Chapter 55
Cure of Illness Through the Intercession of the Blessed Virgin and St. Ann

T this time I fell seriously sick with a fever and to make me well again I was taken to our infirmary of St. Francis. Another very ill lay-brother was also there. In the world we had been friends and besides the confidences we had shared, there was also a great spiritual bond. This brother was critically ill and there was little hope that he would live much longer. From his waist down he was no longer able to move his limbs, nor could he move his arms. His mouth was distorted and he could barely speak.

The head infirmarian, a very charitable Friar, put us both in the same room so as to be company for each other. As I saw my fever getting worse I prayed very earnestly for a return of health and I consoled myself by devout discussions with the other sick Brother. Through the intercession of the Virgin Mary, the feast of whose Nativity was approaching, I hoped to be well again.

When the vigil of this feast had come the fever was at its peak around the hour when Vespers were to be sung. Within me, however, all was serenely tranquil; through his favouring grace our Lord deigned to grant me a marvellous exaltation of soul and this lasted till the Friars went to chant Vespers.

As the *Magnificat* was being sung, all of a sudden I saw before me Father Angelus del Pas who had died in St. Peter of Montorio with a reputation for great holiness and is buried there near the main altar. He paused a moment looking at me with heavenly eyes and majestic face; then he disappeared without speaking.

I did not make anything of this first apparition, but only a short time passed before he appeared again and stood only a few feet distant from me, dressed in the holy habit, his face joyful and beautiful as an angel. When I saw him this second time my soul was aroused and I felt a very great compunction as I looked at him. With sentiments of humility I burst out: "O servant of God, I do not deserve that you should appear to me, for I have done nothing to merit it. The only thing I did, for it was my duty, was to keep the stone over your burial place free of dust." When I stopped speaking he disappeared, leaving me consoled in soul and body.

Hardly had Father Angelus vanished when I saw coming even closer the most Blessed Virgin with glorious St. Ann; both reached the infant Jesus out to me as they looked at me joyfully and pleasantly—a thing that made me forget every affliction. At this vision I went out of myself as though rapt in spirit and could not speak at all, but rejoiced extremely in the deepest silence at this divine presence of Jesus, Mary and Ann. The holy Virgin had the form of a most beautiful young woman, her face the colour of wheat, as also were her hands with which she held up and offered me the infant Jesus. St. Ann was of about sixty years of age, her face venerable and olive-coloured; her right hand was on the shoulder of the Child whose feet were bare and who seemed to be about a year old. His divine beauty, grace and the colour of his most holy flesh with all the other features cannot be described. His gaze shed clouds of grace and his very movement ravished my soul and inflamed my heart with his heavenly love!

At this vision the thing that I understood interiorly was that both of us would be cured of our sickness. By a special impulse from our Lord I turned to my companion to say: "Brother, we are cured!" After I said that the sick Brother became much worse; the Father infirmarian gave up all hope. Seeing the great danger he was in I began to doubt a bit, humanly. Still I could not persuade myself that he really was going to die. As I hung between hope and fear, the change for the better came, and with the help of God through the intercession of the Virgin Mary and St. Ann he recovered his health completely with time.

As for me, my fever left me immediately after the vision, and with the return of my health I fell back as before into my usual imperfections. When I realized that I had carried out few or none of the resolutions formed while I was sick, our Lord made me understand by an inner illumination that if ever I were sick I should not again ask for my health in an unconditional way but leave it to the divine will without any thought as to life or death.

Chapter 56
Revelations and Visions:
The Holy Ghost Is His Teacher

As His Divine Majesty kept illuminating my soul I began to receive from his most bountiful hand some special knowledge and locutions that are a touch of the spirit of prophecy and bring with them revelations of what the future holds either for oneself or for others.

At times, before I had to visit someone, either at the very moment of starting out, or during my prayers, or as I received Holy Communion, I heard in my soul a heavenly locution in distinct and formal words as if the divine Teacher had briefly instructed me on all I would have to say and on everything that would happen to me, as well as on the answers to questions, especially when people became curious.

I would easily have become confused if our Lord had not first revealed everything to me and then caused it to come to mind again at the moment it was needed. Whenever our Lord saw fit to give me this favour, it was very easy for me to speak with people and give them the advice they required.

Here I want to tell what happened to me as I went out to beg alms. A young man followed me for two miles for he wanted to get my advice in settling his affairs and choosing a vocation in life. All that distance I did not know what to say to him on these matters and if I did say something it required a great effort, for I had become like a person who is stunned and stupid. Now after some days had passed the young man came to visit me at St. Peter Montorio. With the assistance of the spirit of our Lord I easily settled everything he had discussed with me. He had to tell me then that I left him very discouraged the first time; he had wondered very much at my not being able to give him one word of help, and now—praise be to God!—he was leaving very consoled.

For the comfort of my soul and through the same bright heavenly light, it pleased His Divine Majesty to let me see some good souls still confined to the prison of the body. I saw how they shone with the brightness of the divine rays issuing from the grace with which they were firmly united to God. They looked like the sun on a clear day when it has reached its noonday heat and light.

When I reached St. Paul's during my visit to the seven churches, one of the Benedictine Fathers, a very learned person whom I knew, was coming out to say Mass. A few years previously he had dedicated himself entirely to the spiritual life. In his great humility he wished to place himself under my direction that I might instruct him in prayer. As time went on he made great progress and our Lord granted him many graces in prayer because of his humility.

While attending his Mass in the chapel of the most holy Crucifix, I saw his face aflame with a seraphic fire after the consecration and this lasted with special consolation to my soul till he had consumed the Body of our Lord in Holy Communion.

Another time I went to the Basilica of St. Peter to see one of the Father Penitentiaries of the Society of Jesus,[1] a very close friend of mine. Besides having given up much for Christ this holy religious was outstanding for his charitable assistance to the poor. I found him just as he was returning from saying Mass at the place where the body of the Apostle Peter is buried. His face was as resplendent as that of an angel.

At the monastery of St. Francis a Ripa I saw the same thing in one of our Friars, a Brother Justin, who has since gone to a

---

[1] At present the ordinary Penitentiaries at the Basilica of St. Peter are the Conventual Fathers, but up to 1773 the Jesuits had this office.

better life. He was an ecstatic religious of great virtue. One morning as he received Holy Communion and went off to make his thanksgiving in a side place where I happened to pass, I found him in ecstasy with hands joined and face lifted to heaven. His countenance was shining resplendently and just to look at him afforded me sweetness and devotion.

In spirit our Lord also permitted me to see two religious; one was a Discalced Carmelite nun and the other, also a woman, was a Franciscan Tertiary. It seems to me that during the time our souls spoke together we did not employ actual words such as these bodies of ours use, but that we conversed in some other rare manner. They made their thoughts clearly known to me by their faces alone, as I rejoiced in God and relished him who is infinitely good.

I think that using our voices would have been more of a hindrance to us than a help, as happened once when I went to the Roman College to visit a Jesuit Father. As the two of us were going into the porter's room we met a Father Peter Caravita. Father Peter and I greeted each other warmly and spoke together very well without using our voices as we knelt on the floor united in God for quite a space of time. From then on we were very close friends.

Once in Rome as I was talking to the Reverend Mother Prioress in the parlour of a Carmelite monastery, three religious of St. Frances of Rome came to the door. They had a young girl of about thirteen with them. She had saintly ways and was of a good family. Because she knew me, she greeted me. As we stood near each other, with the light of my mind I saw her soul exulting joyfully and very festively together with mine. After remaining in this state for quite a long time without saying a word we greeted each other in Jesus Christ and I exhorted her briefly to keep her innocence and purity.

Whenever I received these revelations I took from them certain points of instruction which they contained for me as regards knowing how to guard against evil and to profit from what is good. Apart from this I let them be, because I knew that to pay too much attention to them would have occasioned great damage, since our perfection does not consist in having visions and revelations but in loving God through the observance of the divine law, performing works of charity and suffering for love of him.²

---

² A very good and practical reflection because ordinarily these revelations are not to be sought, but if God gives them they are to be received with great humility and circumspection.

CHAPTER 57
UNDERSTANDING OF SACRED SCRIPTURE

UR Lord was also pleased to grant me a knowledge of Sacred Scripture not only that my soul might keep itself busy loving God through this means but also for the accomplishment of the task he had given me through my father confessor, the writing of books.

It is a very ordinary happening that when our Lord is pleased to open up the deepest meanings of Scripture to our soul, it is not only intellectually illumined but is also satiated with a divine substantial food that strengthens and consoles it, while bestowing a more spiritual state than before, a transformation in love. We can say truthfully that in Scripture there is found the very love of God which, like a pen or a tongue, speedily impresses on our souls the mystical meanings of the incomprehensible omnipotence, wisdom and goodness of God.

To understand how much help is needed in the matter of Sacred Scripture I shall tell how for a very long time I could not grasp the meaning of the words found in the first chapter of the Canticle of Canticles: "Thy breasts are better than wine, sweet smelling of the best ointments".[1]

One evening when I was writing the book Interior Journey, I knew I must speak of the divine breasts after I had explained the passage in the same Canticle of Canticles, "the voice of the turtle is heard in our land".[2] But though I grew weary trying to understand what they meant, I got nowhere for my understanding was darkened and I did not know where to turn.

It was late, and since I was fatigued from thinking I

---

[1] Cant. 1: 1-2.

[2] *Ibid.* 2: 12.

prepared to retire with this holy thought, as I asked our Lord to help me. When I awakened during the night for my devotions I could not find the rosary that was always attached to my cord. So I employed the means of recollecting myself mentally and while I was united with our Lord, a newly-born child, wrapped in swaddling-clothes, appeared mentally to me. Through a special light I understood the desired meaning of the words in the Canticle, namely, that to little children newly-born, milk, not wine, is suitable food for their nourishment and growth, and that wine is for young men and mature persons.

I also understood that those souls which give up their vain pleasures and turn sincerely to God while living in the world, are like infants in the spiritual life. That they may grow in this life perseveringly and detach themselves through love from sensual delights, our Lord acts with them as a nurse does with a child. In all their exercises he very generously gives them the spiritual milk of sensible devotion. To them their tears are sweet; their penances, pleasant; the subjection of their will, delightful; his love, entertaining. This is so because if, from the very start, he gave them hard bread, meaning the food of men grounded in virtue, the blows of frightful temptations and the trials of gloomy desolations and aridity, they might run the danger of turning back to their former ways. His Divine Majesty nourishes them with this food of infants, disposing them to suffer willingly through the pleasure of the divine taste; so much so that, if it were possible, they would consume their bodies even more with penance for the love of Christ and would gird themselves to suffer the most atrocious torments, as did the martyrs.

I shall recount what happened when I longed to know how I could clarify and apply to a contemplative soul those words of the Canticle in the sixth chapter, "There are three score queens, and four score concubines and young maidens without number. One is my dove, my perfect one is but one.

She is the only one of her mother, the chosen of her that bore her."³

I lived with this thought for two years. When I was in the infirmary of St. Francis a Ripa my soul was lifted up in a special way with the love of my Creator and with devotion to Mary his mother; I seemed to be completely transformed into the love of both, experiencing an unspeakable contentment, while everything in me was so clarified that my soul shone as the sun.

At that same instant I understood the meaning of the above words of Solomon. The sixty queens signify those souls who are most pleasing to His Majesty. They have reached the highest degree of perfection as had the holy Patriarchs and Prophets, the Apostles, Martyrs, Doctors, Founders of Orders and other Saints. These have merited to be the closest to God in his kingdom because of the great charity and love they had for him and their neighbour. The eighty concubines signify the other saints who reached a lesser perfection than the first. Just as in the Old Testament the concubines also were lawful wives of the king but did not take precedence over the queens, so these saints, though of lesser perfection and glory than the first, are like them also the chosen spouses of the heavenly King himself. They serve him, praise and bless him, and rejoice in that degree of glory of his boundless love.

By the young girls without number I understood all the other chosen saintly souls; and there are so many of them, all those who walk the way of the commandments of God in simplicity without obliging themselves to the evangelical counsels. And as this last degree is of lesser perfection than the preceding it embraces all other states and gathers together religious, seculars, children; because should one choose a perfect state but not walk in the perfection it requires, one does not merit the degree of holiness that another attains who has busied himself more diligently in a less perfect way of life.

---

³ Ibid., 6. 7-8.

"One is my dove.... She is the only one of her mother, the chosen of her that bore her."—By this dove I understood the Virgin Mary, daughter of the Eternal Father, spouse of the Holy Spirit, daughter and mother of Jesus Christ. She was of such innocence as never to contract the stain of sin; she was kept safe from the concupiscence of sensuality and was full of all graces and supernatural gifts. Her perfection alone far surpasses what all the saints of the three degrees, and the nine choirs of angels, together have acquired. In her humility and obedience she surpasses in merit the saints who have been, who are and who will be, for she possesses every gift and virtue in full perfection.

She is the "only one of her mother", which is the divine essence of the living God, who "from eternity" conceived her in his mind before creating all things; and "of her that bore her", namely, holy Mother the Church who continuously conceives, begets and nourishes children for heaven.

Till the following day I remained in this exaltation with the elect of Jesus Christ, the Virgin Mary our Mother, while I was transformed as if into another creature and placed outside everything created. I did not see the most holy Virgin in any material form, but with the eyes of the soul; and so, better than if I had seen her materially.

If the sight of her now while we are in darkness so delights and ravishes the soul, what must we think it will be like when we shall see her in paradise, completely enveloped in glory, near her most sweet Son, Jesus Christ, loved and caressed by the three divine Persons, honoured and revered by all those heavenly citizens?

Chapter 58
The Interior Journey

I COMPLETED the book *Three Ways of Meditation*, along with *Discourses on the Passion of Christ*; and so as to keep my mind occupied and distracted from temptations, not to mention that it was the will of God, my father confessor ordered me to write the book entitled Interior Journey which contains the explanation of the *Spiritual Songs* which I had composed and which were already published together with the *Three Ways of Meditation*.

I began preparing myself by praying to many of the servants of God and by recommending myself to our Lord, to the most glorious Virgin and to the saints. With special devotion I made a visit to holy Mother Teresa in the church of the Madonna della Scala[1] where there is a painting of this saint I liked very much; it gave me a feeling of familiarity as if it were alive. I thought I heard the saint say: "He who enlightened me with his grace will give you the light you need".

In explaining the afore-mentioned *Spiritual Songs*, this was the plan I followed; before commenting on a stanza I received Holy Communion for this reason and in all the Masses I served that morning I begged the blessed Lord to illumine me on what I had to write. When I was ready to write I first said the hymn, *Veni, Creator Spiritus*, with the Sequence, *Veni, Sancte Spiritus*, and the prayers that follow it. Then I raised my thoughts to God as I invoked the most Holy Virgin with all my beloved saints and said the verse of the psalm: "Lord, enlighten me with the light of your grace and keep me safe

---

[1] It still belongs to the Discalced Carmelite Fathers. The chapel of St. Joseph, redecorated towards the end of the seventeenth century, contains a picture of St. Teresa, but not the one St. Charles knew.

from error".² This done I took up the pen and began writing in the name of Jesus, as St. Paul instructs us.

It was almost the usual happening that when I began to write I became as one who has lost the use of reason, and this in spite of the fact that the material was there, for I had experienced it in prayer at different times. So great a fear took hold of me that I seemed to be in a deep sea without knowing how to get out of it; often I felt something within me that very bitterly reproved me for what I was trying to do, as though there were a dog gnawing at my very vitals and harassing me extremely.

At such times I would occasionally pick up some book to see if I could find light in explaining my idea, but that never helped. Then I had recourse to the book of the Crucified always there in front of me. The darkness would begin to scatter and the clear light come through. The dog fled and then came the teacher to instruct me, namely the Holy Spirit, giving me understanding of what was to be explained.

At other times I remained in this mental darkness. Then I began to pray as I knelt before our Lord in the most holy Sacrament of the Altar. While united to him my mind opened and, like a vista, all that I had to write was there in orderly fashion, with the passages of Sacred Scripture I wanted to use and a suitable explanation.

If at times I faltered in composing a paragraph or when some phrase escaped me, I lifted my mind to God and with my hands joined and my cord around my neck I said the *Pater*, *Ave Maria* and the *Credo*. I recommended my need to the saints, to those who when writing had depended very much on the most holy Virgin: the holy prophet David, St. Peter and St. Paul, the four Evangelists, St. Thomas Aquinas, the *subtle doctor* John Duns Scotus—to him I recommended myself in the manner our holy Mother Church allows us since he was an enlightened teacher of saintly life, very devoted to the Mother

---

² Psalm 26. 1. The Saint is quoting very freely. [*Translator.*]

of God—and finally to glorious St. Teresa who frequently communicated thoughts to me sensibly, like someone speaking in my ear.

It happened that when these motions were more vigorous I was urged by a very pleasant impulse that interiorly impelled me to think of our Lord and to adore him with special adoration. While turned to him hanging on the cross I made many profound bows and said with St. Thomas the Apostle: "My Lord and my God!"[3] And with St. Martha: "Thou art Christ, the Son of the living God, who art come into the world!"[4]

When the devil tempted me to vainglory because I had explained the sense of the Scripture passages and had handled the other material well, I said as I turned to our Lord: "My Lord, everything is yours, nothing is mine. You are everything and I am nothing! To you alone be honour and glory for all ages. Amen."

At other times I experienced a marvellous exaltation from the truths my intellect received and because of the love I conceived in understanding them. Just as I was at the moment, with pen in hand and my spirit in God, I waited for the ecstasy of so violent a love of God to pass.

Our Lord often had me remember people I knew while I was wrapped in that divine union during writing; either those who had recommended themselves to my prayers or others who were suffering persecution, or were afflicted by temptations or sickness. I would stop to recommend them to the blessed God and I did the same with the souls of the deceased, by whom I was frequently visited. With the light of my mind I saw them as a very bright light in which I could see that it was the soul of this or that person.

I will give some examples from my holy Order. First, about

---

[3] John 20. 28.

[4] John 11. 27.

a priest who had lived in the most exact observance of the Rule and hardly ever spoke. About eight days had passed after his death when one morning after Matins, as I was going back to my room to retire, he appeared to me as when he was living and said with a joyful countenance: "Now I am going to paradise!" When I heard this I called out: "Wait for me, Father! Wait for me, Father!" But he turned to me to say, "It is not your time yet. You have to wait a while longer."

Another deceased lay-brother who had already gone to heaven appeared to me. We had been close friends. While he was full of fun, he had great charity. This good religious appeared to me twice, telling me of the glory of the blessed; and though I did not understand what he told me because of the lofty nature of these matters, still my soul was held in a special enjoyment of God. The first time he appeared I asked him what things most pleased our Lord. He answered: "Purity of heart!" The second time I begged him to tell me how the blessed in paradise lived. At this he did not say a word; he simply extended his arms in the form of a cross with his eyes fixed on heaven and vanished. By that I understood that the blessed are entirely filled with God and rejoice in him with their whole being.

So great was the consolation I felt when deceased persons appeared to me this way, that for some time afterwards I was in ecstasy, all on fire with the love of God.

CHAPTER 59
SOME TRIALS AND GRACES FROM OUR LORD

RIBULATIONS are something that always has to accompany heavenly favours; but I say they should be turned to one's advantage more and more, so that the spiritual edifice will not be knocked to the ground by the winds of our proud nature, once it has been built up through so much work and sweat.

One morning as I was in the church at St. Peter Montorio serving holy Mass, I realized that our Lord was speaking to me interiorly as the priest elevated the sacred Host at the consecration, telling me that I was to suffer many hardships, as did Henry Suso of the Order of the great St. Dominic.[1] Some time passed and then I encountered two so distressing conflicts that it seemed heaven itself had turned against me. One came from outside, from the world; the other from within, and it touched me to the quick. I would not have believed it, though I had often thought it could happen.

The storm that was to come and envelop me from the outside, our Lord allowed me to see in its entirety before it struck. I tried as hard as I could to prevent it, but my efforts were of no avail. Blessed be the Lord! It all came from him and for no other reason but zeal for the welfare of my soul since he cannot have any evil purpose. For several good reasons I will not say anything else about it. Out of zeal for the honour of God I did what I could so that no scandal should result, for all hell was turned against me. Several servants of God who are still led by the right kind of zeal said that I was doing evil after they had listened to the reports that were brought to them; as they would not have understood the facts but were

---

[1] Henry Suso (died 1365) was an outstanding mystical author. His most widely read work was the *Horologium Sapientiae*.

going only on what was told them.

This affliction lasted for three years and I had no help except from God—this was never lacking—and from my father confessor to whom I reported all that had happened and whose counsel I followed in every detail. Though I felt this tribulation in my flesh in a way that at times took away my natural powers, I did not give up my usual devotions; in fact, I had recourse to prayer with greater solicitude as I pleaded for divine help.

While I was in the very thick of this battle the second storm came upon me. Though it did not last very long it really caused me great distress in every way during the time it was interwoven with the first one. How strange it is! When tribulations start raining down on the servants of God, one would think that heaven's cataracts have burst forth, for like a flood they come down to drown them.[2]

Our Lord permitted me to commit I do not know what faults, and in order to satisfy his conscience the Superior began to give me penances in public at meals. All this happened when I least expected it and was hoping for something to console me.

Blessed be the most high God who so rules his servants in this life as to keep them humble, and yet does not fail to give them fortitude to suffer without despair. For it is to despair that the devil then greatly urges us; the result he wants is that a person will give up regular discipline and become a prey to his senses when he sees that he cannot find peace, at least at times, among people who are so holy. Really these cannonades are so frightful that occasionally they make even the greatest champions of God's cause tremble. They leave the mind darkened, the reason overwhelmed and the lower instincts in continual rebellion. The only thing that seems to

---

[2] One need only think of the story of Job, so rich in its practical instruction on the wise and loving plans of God for trying his chosen ones by every sort of affliction.

remain, though hidden, is the fear of God which keeps a person from actually doing what human malice is dictating.

In the midst of this conflict the blessed God willed to console me with the certainty of the salvation of two of my brothers, who shortly before that had died truly Christian deaths during the plague.[3] The elder one was John Baptist; the younger, John. Both were good men. When they saw the terrible mortality around them—a very reliable report came my way that where they lived about four thousand five hundred persons died—they fearlessly exposed themselves to great danger by working hard in helping the unfortunate people, assisting the priests in bringing the sacraments to the sick, supplying the poor with goods to such an extent as even to give up what they had in their own homes, grain, wine and other necessities.

When the contagion struck him, John Baptist received the sacraments. By acts of love of God and sorrow for his sins he calmly disposed himself to die willingly for the love of our Lord. Towards the end he constantly recited vocal prayers with our sister who was with him every moment; she was then a Tertiary of St. Francis and now is a Poor Clare nun in the monastery of Sezze, Sister Mary Frances of Jesus. He said the *Miserere* especially. Realizing that his soul was about to leave his body he said the prayer *Mary, Mother of Grace*, as he thanked God for this his will. He blessed my sister and turning his eyes heavenward gave his soul into the hands of its creator with a countenance full of joy.

The other brother, John, younger than the first, had received among other gifts from our Lord that of charity. Though he was just a person of ordinary means, one of his acts of almsgiving was that he supported a poor man of good background by giving him a certain amount of money every day. This man lived with his sister, a poor young woman whom he had lifted from sin and kept from it for the last three

---

[3] In the year 1636.

years of his life. He supported her and made her keep the respect that belonged to her, as she served our Lord devoutly.

That year this good brother of mine harvested more than two hundred bushels of wheat; he deprived himself of them to help the poor who were needy. He used to say: "It would never please God were I to watch my brothers die"—that is the way he spoke of his neighbours—"and not want to help them!"

Exhausted from this kind of holy work the plague struck him too, and so badly as to bring him to death's door. With outstanding devotion he received the sacraments, thanking our Lord for granting him the favour of dying while assisting his neighbours. Before his soul left the body he was as though in ecstasy for three hours. When he returned to his senses he told us he had seen the most Blessed Virgin and that she had shown him the glory of paradise. Though he was a simple, uneducated person he spoke for some time of the glory of the blessed, to the wonder of those about him. He said he had within himself what he had experienced and the sweetness that he felt could not be put in words. With such an excellent guarantee, this very happy soul went from the body to enjoy its Lord.

After I had recovered from the conflict I mentioned previously, I was sent to the monastery of St. Bonaventure in Frascati as a companion to one of the priests. One morning while serving this priest's Mass I saw the glory that my two brothers were enjoying in the next life, as the sacred Host was elevated. I remained there as in ecstasy, full of unspeakable interior joy.

CHAPTER 60
RELATION OF OBEDIENCE AND CHARITY TO PRAYER

NE night while I was at common prayer before the most Blessed Sacrament with the Friars in the church at St. Peter Montorio, I was overcome by a great elevation of spirit there in the chapel of the Conversion of St. Paul.

Without knowing how or by whom I seemed to be put at that moment in a certain place, which divine inspiration gave me to understand signified the Probatica pool as described by St. John. It had five porches where many sick people lay waiting for the water to be stirred by an angel who descended on it at a certain time. In this multitude there was a man who had lain there sick for thirty-eight years. When Jesus approached he asked the man if he wanted to be cured. The sick person answered: "Sir, I have no man, when the water is troubled, to put me into the pond. For while I am coming, another goeth down before me."[1] Our Lord healed him, telling him to take up his pallet and walk.

As I found myself in spirit at that spot I understood within me that I was like the man who had been sick thirty-eight years. The man's sickness was worse than that of any other person waiting there because he had not the strength to manage to get into the bath by himself before the others; besides, his poverty was so extreme that he had nothing to give someone to assist him. There he had to stay, the poor man, very sad and afflicted, waiting for divine help since he had completely given up human aid.

Many times I had taken and read this gospel without

---

[1] John 5: 7. The account of the cure of the paralytic begins with verse 2.

reflecting on it. But when our Lord desired that I understand it under the light he gave me, I then realized full well the depth of the mysteries that lay hidden there and I began to experience them in substance. I found myself so changed and realized I was so weak that I seemed to have no spiritual health left, while I sensed that my poverty of soul was greater than any other poor beggar in the house of God. My poverty was like Adam's after he had broken the commandment of God, for then he knew that he was naked and so he covered himself with the leaves of a tree. No sooner did our Lord show his mercy to me in putting me in that condition than aridity reappeared, to a degree even more terrible than it had ever been.

To add to this desolation the passions reasserted themselves even more strongly than before. Like a horse without a bridle each one tried to run whither its disordered desire urged it. I had all I could do to repress them and had to keep the sword in hand all the time. The tendency to irritation became so ungovernable that it made me almost powerless to bear the demands of the body with all its instability, as well as annoyances from those about me. At times I fell into acts of impatience. The many imperfections I committed sometimes made my fellow religious wonder, all the more since they had formed a certain opinion of me. Perhaps they believed, as I had been told by a very learned Father, that people who have reached a high degree of the love of God are not subject to these weaknesses, and that the lower senses no longer bring to the soul what is contrary and harmful to it, but only what will suggest heavenly and divine things.

I went to Sacred Scripture and the examples of the saints to recall there in prayer that what the Father had said was true: our Lord has granted this special privilege to some saints. But, generally speaking, we see that though their sanctity was great, some had been left subject by our Lord to certain natural imperfections. This was for their greater welfare, for at the same time he gave them the strength to be able to curb these.

Satan began more than usual to batter me with impulses so wicked that very often I experienced a powerful urge to leave the monastery and do what I had never done before. The strong hand of our Lord was sufficient for me because it reinforced my spirit.

No one should wonder at seeing in men who are treading the way of perfection, vessels of flesh that are unclean and full of many imperfections. But each one should be contrite and ponder what man is in his nature: that of himself he is incapable of anything but evil, and that here the mercy of God shows how great it is by supporting him against a fall and the loss of divine grace.

What helped to make this temptation even more frightful was that I knew it came by the permission of God, as I will now relate.

A certain religious who was very learned and a really outstanding preacher hankered after ecclesiastical renown. Though he was close to God it did not concern him that he was losing his first fervour. Perhaps, however, he was carried away by some worthy goal or human affection. But in his foreknowledge God is aware of what can harm us or help us in the matter of our soul's salvation. Since he does not want us to come to a fall by being lifted up too much, he permitted the angel of Satan to strike this religious like another St. Paul. For a long time he was so awfully afflicted that he despaired of being saved.

Since he had great faith in my prayers he begged me in all humility to commend him to the blessed God and to our Father St. Francis. I prayed often to our Lord for his sake, pleading with him to have mercy on him. Through a revelation from heaven I learned what God's secret was in his regard but I did not tell him about it exactly as it was, though he would have understood me because of his learning. Among other things I told him that, so as to keep us humble, our Lord puts us under the power of such temptations and we cannot gain a victory along any other path, but are meant to persevere humbly in our vocation. I also told him that the blessed God—whose judgments are hidden—would be able to draw forth from this evil a great good, his salvation.

He continued to live in deep affliction and disturbance of soul. He was extremely displeased at what was offending God, though he would not deliberately have committed the slightest venial sin; in fact, he would have given himself up to a thousand deaths rather than offend his Creator. Seeing him as if despairing of his salvation I had the greatest sympathy for him and began to pray very insistently to our Lord to free him from this evident danger. To save his soul I told our Lord I would be satisfied to take upon myself that awful temptation.

I do not say for sure that this was why it did come upon me, but it was not long before I realized that within me the flame of that very temptation was raging, and so strongly that for about two years how much I suffered only God and my father confessor know. The danger to which I had exposed myself was great but the help that came from the mercy of God, who had allowed it, was greater. The flame of the temptation began to die down when news came that the good Father had passed from this life to the next.

From this suffering I gained greater insight into what man of himself is worth and how we need to think correctly of ourselves no matter how much we seem to have been favoured by God. For that reason during the awful struggles of that trial I sometimes turned to God and said: "See, O Lord, what great crimes I would commit if you left me free; this animal of my body can think of nothing except pursuing its own desires to the offence of the Divine Majesty, forgetting all your benefits and how much you have done for it!" And at other times: "Lord, I cannot watch one hour with you!" by which I meant, "I cannot remain recollected for a moment before Your Divine Majesty!"

Due to the good lessons that one learns from this purification and annihilation of spirit, it came about that I could not distinguish prayer from obedience and charity.[2] It left me wondering very much when I heard a certain learned and holy person saying that he did not want to busy himself in some things, even acts of charity towards his neighbour, for the simple reason that things like this confuse the mind and cause the spirit to wander—that spirit that is so delicate that once lost it is regained only with very great difficulty.

My answer was that the eminence of the spirit does not consist in staying attached to our own notions but in allowing it the liberty in which our Lord breathes; that true charity does not confuse the mind and expel the spirit, but strengthens, enlightens and convinces it of divine things, communicating to the soul the excellence of the true spirit which consists in charity itself; and that if it were as they claimed, then Jesus Christ our Lord would not have exercised charity with such perfection.

Though his was the highest and excelling contemplation, still he was never idle while he lived among us. And when it was needed, he left the holy work of contemplation to busy himself endlessly in the welfare of his fellow men, associating with and speaking to them without any exception, so as to win them all, accommodating his speech to his audience so that everyone would understand and receive the truth of his word, which is spirit and life.

The Virgin Mary, his mother, and the holy apostles, did the same. Though they were persons of very exalted prayer,

---

[2] Inasmuch as the manual work was prescribed under obedience the Saint performed it, as he did all his practices of piety, not only because he thus accomplished the will of God in conformity with what St. Augustine had said, "*Non cessat orare, qui non cessat bene vivere*" (He does not cease praying who does not cease doing good), but also because the work, far from distracting him, united him more closely to God.

through the Holy Spirit whom they had received, they were never still; they went abroad through different countries, preaching and sowing the seed of the holy gospel in hearts, planting the Catholic faith and becoming martyrs for its sake.

Let us discuss those desires which seem perfectly suited to being directed by us to our spiritual advantage, and let us say that it is really an imperfection for a religious—when he finds himself in a place that is not to his taste, or has to carry out a duty that is very wearying and brings a lot of distractions along with it—to be led to look for places of greater solitude and less activity for one or the other reason like this, since it seems to him that he is not preserving sensible sweetness in prayer. Now though these reasons in themselves are holy and good, still, great imperfection can come from them when they deviate from the pure meaning of holy obedience. Obedience wants us to lose ourselves and in God to possess it along with the other virtues; it wants us so to put ourselves in God's care that we are like a dead person in the hands of our superiors,[3] that they may dispose of us in every way as the blessed God inspires them. We will not desire or wish anything but what he wants.

Most of the time the desires which we are discussing can be effects of our nature which, even in spiritual things, is looking out more for its comfort than the good pleasure of the Lord. In the midst of people and at the height of bustling activity he is able to transform us in his love, as we read about St. Bernard. Once while measuring out wheat along with other monks he sensed such a great devotion and taste for God during the work that he was driven by a special impetus to praise and thank His Divine Majesty.

The consolations and favours which servants of God receive, as with clean hearts they approach the most holy table to feed on the living Bread of Angels, are without

---

[3] This comparison is identical with the one used by the Seraphic Father St. Francis (Celano, *Vita*, pars 2a, c. 112).

number: for example, ecstasies, satiety of spirit, the feeling as though one is burning with a heavenly fire accompanied by a sweetness greater than honey or anything else that delights the palate; and other greater things hard to describe.

Even in prayer I was despoiled of this sensible, spiritual delight, and it happened too that in receiving the most Blessed Sacrament I was like the sick man at the Probatica pool.

At this time my principal preparation was purity of soul, and faith. By purity of soul I tried to be without any sin; in my every action I was careful not to offend God and that is why I guarded my bodily senses. When I felt that something wanted to lower me, such as temptations, I said to myself: "Remember, Brother Charles, that tomorrow morning you have to receive the One who will judge your every thought and work!"

I did not go to Holy Communion to experience delights and other spiritual consolations but to receive the true Son of God who had become man, with the most Blessed Trinity, as our holy Church teaches. I went to receive from him grace, virtue, fortitude and holy perseverance in his divine service. In this way I kept detaching myself from spiritual delights and uniting myself in affection with God alone in a purely spiritual way. For him alone I made the effort of receiving Holy Communion daily, and though sometimes I had determined to omit it—a determination that seemed to be worsened by the temptation that left me very sad from the previous night—I felt I could not follow out my resolve. So I went with great timidity and shame and was amazed at how the Lord of Majesty condescended to come to dwell in so miserable a vessel as I was. But then he who was all mercy bestowed on me even greater graces. He drew me to himself as a magnet draws iron.

This partly shows the greatness of the mercy of God and of his infinite wisdom in detaching us from what he had once given us, since he knows that it could harm us because of our excessive affection for it. Yet he does not fail to love us and to give us a love for him that is still more noble and pure.

CHAPTER 61
MORTIFICATION OF THE BODILY SENSES

ET us begin, if you will, to discuss bodily feelings more clearly, concerning what we suffer in our flesh, for in my case this also our Lord wanted humbled and subjected to the spirit; he desired that I resign myself to his divine will. To accomplish this he saw fit to use a trifle; he sent me a certain redness of the eyes. The doctors judged that it came from an obstruction of the liver which they said was inflamed.[1]

But I now think that God's thoughts were different; from this he wanted me to draw profit for my soul. For though I constantly received graces from our Lord, some lesser passions still reigned in my heart in hidden fashion and on a few occasions became so lively that they made me slip, even though I was very aware of them and made acts of the virtues, especially when I received Holy Communion.

Many times I was justly mortified with public penances by one of my superiors. He really did this out of zeal to lighten his conscience concerning my soul's salvation, hoping to change me.

But when at times one of these hidden passions arose, it was with such force that my mind was darkened, my very being was stirred and I thought I was beside myself. The blind impulse did not allow me to listen to what was the truth and charity, but tried to make me listen to a lie, namely, that what my Superior was doing was incited more by passion than by zeal for the honour of God. This was very false; it was the

---

[1] The doctors diagnosed the Saint's sickness as a reactive form of liver obstruction. Some of his confreres, either jokingly or maliciously, as we can gather from what follows, interpreted it as a form of gonorrhea which he had contracted while assisting the sick woman of whom he speaks a little further on.

work of the devil trying to have me believe this.

That is why I often had to kneel before my confessor, since the aversion for him lasted for about two or three days. I do not regret telling of my shortcomings, hoping by so doing to obtain a zest for God and to help those who read this. They should not become discouraged when attacked by similar passions and temptations, but run to our Lord. They have to reflect that if the favours God gives us are great, the counterparts are no less great; we cannot become the great saints we want to be without difficulty.

From the untamed animality of our nature His Divine Majesty draws an endless stream of good, knowing as he does the ways to use it in healing our wounds. During the sickness that made my eyes red, such was the mortification and repugnance I felt, that there are no words to tell about it, especially at the beginning. Some told me, either derisively or jokingly, that it was a very evil thing unbecoming Christians, but especially religious who take a vow of chastity. They almost had me believing that God had sent this as a punishment because of the natural repugnance I felt in being charitable to a poor woman on one occasion when we were visiting the sick. At another time, I felt a similar distaste at having to kiss the hand of a priest of the Order of St. Dominic, a great servant of God, who was dying. His name was Father Gregory dal Vallo and he was a consumptive. But I entered into myself and thought as I lifted my mind to God: "It is better to be without a mouth than that charity suffer."

On these occasions I saw how far away I was from the resolutions I was making during prayer, when His Divine Majesty with generous hand gives us graces and favours so that we may offer ourselves very readily to any great suffering.

My fickleness, however, was such that to rid myself of a like sickness I would not have left anything undone so long as it was not against God or my soul. Miserable one that I was!

Mortification of the Bodily Senses

To be disturbed about my well-being and not understand the divine secret! Every day I was encouraging the sick to suffer, exhorting the troubled to be patient and here I was unable to bear the smallest pain; something that at times confounded me!

The doctor who at that time was kindly visiting the sick Friars in our infirmary at St. Francis saw my condition. He had me take purges for fifteen days. This did not help me at all. It resulted in such sluggishness that I could barely sweep the church and do my other house-work.

When he saw that this remedy was of no help to me, our Father infirmarian advised me with the approval of the doctor to go to Nocera in Umbria for the water-cure, stating that I would surely get well. But because it was the month of July my superiors did not think it advisable for me to be travelling on foot in such hot weather. They thought it would be better if I took the cure in Rome.

The following year they sent me to Nocera, in the company of my father confessor, Father Anthony of Aquila. We first stopped at Assisi to visit the body of our Father St. Francis. We stayed there eight days, in the little monastery that once held the stable where the Saint was born.[2] So I had many opportunities of going into the church to visit the holy Patriarch of the poor. The zest and spiritual fragrance that at times came to me was so great that I could not bear it. I can really say that within me there was a heavenly paradise where the soul rejoiced in God exceedingly through the intercession of this glorious Saint.

This is the place where I want to tell of two holy events. One day while I was praying contritely and fervently in the

---

[2] This monastery is called Chiesa Nuova after the church which was erected over the house in which St. Francis had lived.—It should be noted that, according to modern authorities, the possibility of there being any historical truth in the legendary story of St. Francis' birth in a stable is extremely remote. [*Translator.*]

church of the Saint, asking our Lord to fire my heart with love of him and of my Father St. Francis, I felt our Lord saying the following words that inflamed my soul and made it melt with devotion in an unusual way: "I will transfix him in such a manner that he will not be able to flee from me any longer!" The exaltation of spirit, the sweetness of these words of our Lord was great, with the result that not only was I completely on fire with love but was fully consoled interiorly.

The other happening is that while I was at Nocera taking the water-cure, the day came for the Portiuncula indulgence—the first of August,[3] when a great number of people gather. My father confessor and I spoke of our going there[4] together, because it was only about ten miles away. We had begun our trip when I was overcome by unusual sickness; I grew so weak that I had to make the journey by donkey.

Reaching Assisi and finding myself much worse the next morning I resigned my condition to our Lord and prayed that, if this was to be the hour for leaving the prison of this body, he should be for ever blessed, but that he should give me the chance of gaining the indulgence.

The time came for us to go there. Strengthened by the spirit of God and having the blessing of the Father Guardian of that place, I went into the church of St. Francis. All our

---

[3] It begins on 1 August at noon, but continues during the entire next day.

[4] That is, Assisi. In that age the Portiuncula indulgence could be gained only by visiting the church of our Lady of the Angels in Assisi. St. Francis had requested, and obtained, from Pope Honorius III the great benefit of a plenary indulgence for anyone who would visit this little chapel with a contrite heart and confess his sins—a request and a concession unheard of till this time. The Portiuncula indulgence has now been extended to Franciscan churches throughout the world, and to parish churches and oratories that have been so privileged by the bishop of the diocese. The conditions required for this plenary indulgence are: Confession and Holy Communion, and at every visit to the privileged church (since it can be gained many times within the day and a half) six *Our Fathers, Hail Marys and Glory bes* for the intentions of the Holy Father. [*Translator.*]

religious had gathered there and we went in solemn procession to the church of our Lady of the Angels, a distance of about two miles.

The procession started off with such great devotion that one cannot describe it. I was so absorbed in God that as I walked along I forgot myself and gained such spiritual vigour as to reach the holy spot with little fatigue. On entering the Basilica our Lord bestowed such an uplift of spirit on me that by the same spirit I seemed to be transported to the little chapel within the basilica, the original church itself where the indulgence is gained. There, in that holy place, I felt an extraordinary sorrow for my sins, a sorrow that brought a flood of tears from my eyes, but more so from my heart.

In that very sacred sanctuary called our Lady of the Angels— where, besides this great indulgence, our Holy Father St. Francis received very many other favours from our Lord and from the most Blessed Virgin when he started his Order—the Friars Minor are in charge.[5]

Because it was late in the day I wanted to stay in the monastery there out of devotion. I went to the refectory with the other Friars; with great faith I took some of the blessed bread from the table, dipped it in a little wine and ate it with special devotion. All of a sudden my health returned; my weakness, along with the lack of appetite, left me. I thanked our Lord and the most Holy Virgin with our Father Francis for the favour I had received and I spent a good part of that night in thanksgiving.

---

[5] They are still there as the jealous guardians of that holy place, so dear to every son of St. Francis, and certainly one of the most holy of sanctuaries.

CHAPTER 62
STAY AT NOCERA FOR THE CURE

EAVING Assisi the first time, my father confessor and I continued on our way to Nocera. During our stay there, lodging was given us by Don John Baptist Olivieri, who was then the pastor of the principal church.

While there I was not idle, for besides writing letters for Don John Baptist I went visiting the sick in his company. They called for me because of the devotion they had for the Franciscan habit.

I spoke with some devout persons, especially with a great servant of God who confided the secrets of her soul to me at the direction of her confessor. I found out two things about her spiritual life: one, that with what are called substantial words our Lord was interiorly instructing her in the observance of the divine law and means to be used in avoiding evil; secondly, that she was gifted by the Divine Majesty with a special conformity to his divine will, and this not only in her soul but also exteriorly, for our Lord did not fail to keep her disciplined.

A short while before I had reached Nocera, a fifteen-year-old boy, and also a baby girl, had died. This boy was to have inherited the entire fortune of a very wealthy family. Though her grief was great and felt also by her husband and the entire household, since they had put all their hopes in this lad, still the good, virtuous mother was not at all interiorly shaken, but in this, as in every other matter, she wanted only the will of God. She was such a friend to suffering that sometimes in her letters, especially when afflicted by any lengthy illness, she used to write that she would have regarded herself as the happiest woman in the world, and would have thanked God by singing the Te Deum, if to those in her home she had become so abominable as to have been thrown out and made to live in a stable along with the animals.

I began taking the water-cure when the sun entered Leo in the month of July 1662. Although the season was very bad due to constant rains, the treatment helped me a great deal in my whole body, and in my eyes. Especially my head seemed to have been made over new.

As I continued to use the waters my health increased. On the feast of the glorious St. Ann I received the most Holy Body of our Lord, and the same trouble in my face returned. From this I understood that it was the will of God, but like a weak and frail person I began to sense some rebellion in my lower nature. But since I knew this was happening with the permission of His Divine Majesty, I took counsel within myself, did violence to my senses and began begging our Lord that, if it was his will, he should lift the distress I was experiencing and grant me true conformity to him; and that if he did not want to give me this, but leave me a slave to my lower nature, suffering without any relief, I would be satisfied with this too. Only he should grant me every grace not to offend him.[1]

During the treatment my anxiety about being cured grew beyond bounds. I cannot really judge if this was something diabolical to make me lose confidence in God, or if it was the effect of nature, or something permitted by our Lord to make me know myself well and to take entirely out of my heart the passions already mentioned, which from time to time afflicted and disquieted me interiorly.

Seeing that the illness still continued in spite of the powerful remedy, I humbled myself contritely before our Lord; not as before, but in a much more lively way from the depths of my heart as I pardoned everyone who at the

---

[1] True love of God, consequently true virtue, can exist in one's soul in spite of intense natural repugnance felt at times, as long as an attempt is made to repress it. In fact, at such times virtue is all the more meritorious.

instigation of the devil had offended me or had any evil intention against me. I saw them in a good light and it was a pleasure when I could perform some service for them that is customary among religious.

With this little means of sickness, little but remarkably effective along with divine strength, His Divine Majesty was pleased to cure my soul and give me victory over the ugly passions that often dominated me and which I had been unable to destroy through many virtuous acts and exercises; this simply verifies what the Holy Spirit says in Sacred Scripture, that the blessed God knows how to bring forth great good for our salvation from the evils he allows to come upon us.[2]

Humbled in this way but with great gain for my soul, I discontinued the water treatment. We left Nocera on the 14th of August on our way to Aquila, the region of my father confessor. We first went to Norcia because in that town there was a sick person much devoted to me, a very influential woman. Since she knew I had been in Nocera, I obtained an obedience from the Father General to go to see her.

After carrying out this obedience of charity I left Norcia and reached Aquila the day before the Feast of St. Peter Celestine, the 28th of August. We stayed there practically all the month of September. I had little contact with persons there except with the Fathers of the Oratory of St. Philip Neri who are a wonderful spiritual help in that city. At the head of this Congregation was Father John Baptist Magnanti, an outstanding servant of God. There was the closest friendship between us. We had known one another for fifteen years from the time we visited the churches of Rome together. We met again with great consolation to each other and discussed spiritual matters.

The month of October was approaching when my father

---

[2] "To them that love God all things work together unto good" (Romans 8. 28).

confessor and I decided to leave Aquila to return to Rome for the feast of our Father St. Francis; but our plan was ruined when for three days without interruption the pains settled in my right side, something that I was used to suffering. Then with the help of God we left. I set out for Rome with great joy.

But the blessed God had matters turn out differently. Either because of the strain of the journey—I was still not quite myself—or else through divine providence, it happened that hardly had we reached Rome when my whole face became inflamed and such bad cataracts affected my eyes that I thought I would go blind. They had to bleed me and put poultices on my temples. Then I had recourse to my remedy of prayers, deciding to carry out a certain devotion. Next morning after Holy Communion I made the sign of the cross three times, called on the name of Jesus, and then put some saliva on the inflamed part of my face. But nothing helped. Besides, sensuality was waging a very cruel war on me, even more than before, and though I wore myself out at it I could not conquer my senses and subject them to the divine will. If sometimes they became quiet it was not long before they once again turned to torment me. Oh, the foolishness of man! As if we were God, not subject to human imperfection! This affliction was intensified when different people would say something to me; as when a good servant of God said after I had come back from Nocera: "Do what you want, but our Lord wills that you wear this mask!"

Once while kneeling before the most Blessed Sacrament, I was more than usually assailed by my affliction. Nature began to complain, for it had become quite impatient. From the tabernacle our Lord, who knows and sees everything within us, spoke to me interiorly: "Do you think you can be without a cross? And I?" From these words I understood well that though I had committed so many sins during my whole life, I could not get used to bearing a little mortification. Yet he who was innocent suffered so much for me! Our Lord's words caused me special compunction such as would come over a child who in no way wants to offend his father deliberately and who has been scolded by him for some defect.

From then on I very strongly determined, with the help of His Divine Majesty, to take everything from the loving hand of our Lord. If he wanted me to be blind I would be satisfied with that, with the help of his grace; and if giving me conformity to his will, of a kind that I could feel, did not seem best to him, I was content not to have it, for in that way he would be served and my sensitive nature would to that extent remain mortified and crushed. So when anyone said to me after that: "Brother Charles, how red you are!" or, "How inflamed your face is!" I no longer felt the same distress but answered very spiritedly: "Our Lord in his mercy has made me red and handsome! He has inflamed me with his divine love!"

May he then be blessed for ever! I am much obliged to him for this, knowing full well the great good that he has done me here. I can say with the saintly King David: "It is good for me that thou hast humbled me!"[3]

---

[3] Ps. 118. 71. The victory over his natural repugnance is really total, the triumph of grace is complete. According to the teaching of the Seraphic St. Francis, this is truly perfect joy.

CHAPTER 63
FINAL DEGREE OF PRAYER:
STATE OF THE LOVE OF GOD

FOR some years I had remained in a purification of a kind extremely painful, more so than any other. I was now forty-nine years old and had been in religion twenty-seven years. After so many conflicts experienced in different ways in the life of the soul the most high God was pleased to lead me into the state of his sweet and calm love, the highest degree of prayer. This consists in the pure observance of the divine law. If the Christian lays the foundation of a devout and holy life with this law, he will come to enjoy its fruit through a special heavenly favour after he has reached this degree of prayer. Its fruit is spiritual happiness, granted in this life only in the pure love of God. There the soul—to put it in a few words—despoiled of all affections loves only God its Creator. It is no longer attracted by sensible devotion and consolation but by the pure observance of the divine law, in conformity with what Jesus Christ says: "He that hath my commandments and keepeth them, he it is that loveth me. And he that loveth me shall be loved of my Father; and I will love him and will manifest myself to him."[1]

As I lived in this nudity of spirit in which all shadows and empty and useless figures had vanished from the house of my soul, God alone dwelling there in his Godhead and no other object remaining but he, I received light and strength to stay in his love and to persevere in the spiritual path, as also the ability to suffer gladly that which is suffered in prayer when one does not feel the touch of God, for in an habitual way I was enjoying the taste of that same God. It is a habit in which

---

[1] John 14. 21.

God clothes the soul after a long training in suffering, with the result that it is easy to allow oneself to be carried by him.[2]

We can say that because of a true annihilation the soul in this degree of the love of God lives simply in God without any attachment to its own love, busying itself gladly in whatever he puts before it without making any distinction among these things. It is indifferent whether it be dejected or exalted; whether it have a greater or a lesser perfection; whether it be inclined to spiritual or to temporal concerns. In its failures it is peacefully and resignedly consoled since it realizes that these natural imperfections are the remains of the sin of Adam and are really so many gifts of the Lord, for very often they are the occasion of humiliation.

In short, the soul lives with liberty of spirit, seeing God in all things, pursuing in them the divine will to which it ever aspires. When an occasion comes for being outside the monastery on business or works of charity, such a person quietly carries out his obedience. No matter what he has to do, he does it without paying any attention to the contrary remonstrances of lower nature—which complains at having to give up the common exercises, or at the annoyance it sometimes feels, or because it thinks there would be more profit in doing one thing rather than another—but with simplicity and pure faith it obeys, and is not upset at having to go from one occupation to another.[3]

I want to say that if His Divine Majesty recalls one, after occupying him through obedience with people or with any other occupation, then he should go to prayer with his usual calmness without letting anything of what has passed disturb

---

[2] This evidences what high perfection his soul had reached. Note well the expression "to allow oneself to he carried by him", often used by the Saint and which might be regarded as the programmatic theme of the interior life carried to its greatest perfection.

[3] In short, he gladly leaves God for God, according to a very expressive saving in great use with spiritual directors.

him, just as if he had not been occupied that day with anything else except prayer. Here one should prudently follow the safest path, which is the love of God in the fulfilment of the divine law. The blessed God does not command us to live dressed in hair-shirts and chains, or to chastise our flesh with scourges, but to love him above all things and our neighbour as ourselves.

Chapter 64
Elevations of Spirit and Interior Locutions

OUR Lord is truly great in his works, especially in the most holy Sacrament of the Eucharist where he gives favours to those of his servants who worthily prepare themselves as far as human ability allows, since he then acts in us as the food of our life. Miserable though I was and unworthy to approach this sacrament, from which I came away arid and dry, still our good Lord deigned at times to grant me some graces because he is a kind Father who loves us from the depths of his being. I want to speak here about some of these graces to complete the record on the generosity of his infinite mercy, and also to carry out holy obedience.

During the Mass I was serving on the feast of St. Augustine, at the moment of Holy Communion my spirit was carried away with a quickness that is indescribable, and I found myself as though submerged in the immense sea of the living God, in that invisible light which dims every other light.

A nun had been recommended to my prayers; she was a Carmelite at Rome, a great servant of God. While making her profession she had requested of God three graces: first, that he would give her holy perseverance in doing good in religion; second, that for his greater glory he would make her an outstanding saint; third, that he would grant her the favour of suffering so singularly as to obtain the crown of martyrdom. I think our Lord granted her this third favour, because interiorly and exteriorly she was suffering greatly.

While I was thus suspended in our Lord I recommended her to him and I heard our Lord saying—with such divine language, in a manner so pleasurable that it melts one with love, and so sublime that it transports the human spirit: "Both of you will be united in my love in eternity; and I will not fail in what I have promised you." Another time, on the feast of St. Martha, he told me: "I am permitting all these types of temptation in order to purify her as gold in the crucible, that she may remain in my love, for she is my chosen one." And on the feast of St. Peter Martyr he said: "I will protect her with my grace and she shall not perish for ever!"

Another time after the priest had finished the consecration of the Mass I was serving, I experienced a similar elevation of spirit which with the speed of lightning transformed me and united me to our Lord. In that union I felt myself urged by a special impulse to ask him for something for a woman who greatly desired it—and that was to have a baby boy now that she was pregnant—if His Divine Majesty would want to reward her for a benefit she had bestowed on my Order. I did this with the familiarity a child has as it lies in the embrace of its father, and as he had given me the chance in this rapture to ask it of him, so in his love he condescended to grant the favour. In time this woman gave birth to a boy.

Two sisters who were to become Carmelites in a monastery in Rome met with such opposition as to threaten to undo what they planned. Now since I had persuaded them to enter this lofty religious life I pressed their case very strongly with our Lord. It was while this was going on that I went to Subiaco to visit the holy cave there. Scarcely had I arrived when a letter from their mother caught up with me. It spoke of greater trouble, for the plan had been almost entirely ruined.

The following morning I received Holy Communion at the spot where glorious St. Benedict had performed such great penances. From our Lord himself I was given the certainty in my soul that these young women would really become religious of St. Teresa. "Do not doubt it", he said, "for already they have become spouses of the incarnate Word!" On my return to Rome the storm had died down and with great solemnity the two received the habit in a monastery where they have made great strides with God's grace.

Though the book Interior Journey was ready to be sent to the printer—a year had already passed since it had been approved by the Master of the Sacred Palace—the man who said he would pay the bill had for some reason delayed doing so up till that time. And so, like a person who is yet very carnal, I began to feel some unrest of soul that tried to make me break the rule which wants us to let ourselves be peacefully carried by God through incidents that will arise.

One morning after I had received Holy Communion I recommended the business of the book to God. His Divine Majesty who does not disdain our weakness and instability said to me: "I think of him who thinks of me, and I watch over the things I am doing". This short conversation with God brought me such sweetness that it filled my whole interior with a most substantial peace, turning everything into love. A few days later the book went to the printer.

One morning I was giving my attention to the preparation for Holy Communion as I served Mass and, because of the temptations I had suffered during the night, I kept thinking how this body of mine was a vessel full of filth and misery, and that so great a Lord had to come there! I began to say: "O Lord, look at what you are doing; coming to such a filthy and beastly body, very much inclined to evil!" The divine Word answered: "You do not know what beauty I have put in that body—your soul, an image and likeness of me so beautiful that the human tongue cannot describe it. Besides, I am its food by which it stays like that!" I kept a reverent silence and paid attention to preparing as humbly and devoutly as I could to receive so exalted a Majesty into the home of my soul. This taught me that no matter how miserable we may appear to ourselves by reason of some serious temptation, we are not to give up receiving the most Blessed Sacrament of the Altar, the true food of the soul and a beneficial medicine for the body.

On the fourth of August, when our holy Mother Church celebrates the feast of the glorious Patriarch St. Dominic, as the Body of our Lord remained invisible in the Sacred Host on the altar after the consecration of the Mass, surrounded by a multitude of angels, among other things for which I prayed was that he would lessen somewhat the stimulus of sensual concupiscence. Our Lord answered: "If I do this I will still cause every creature to tread on you." "In this, O Lord", I answered, "may your divine will be done!"

Some time before that, on the feast of glorious St. Joseph, Spouse of the most Blessed Virgin, I had been commanded by my father confessor to pray insistently at Holy Communion that through the intercession of this saint our Lord might wish to free me from so many impure temptations. I sensed our Lord saying what he had said to St. Paul: "My grace is sufficient for thee; for power is made perfect in infirmity".[1]

One morning while I was serving Mass, in the fervour of my spirit I began to think of Father Bartholomew of Salutio[2] and I started to ask our Lord as a favour from this servant of his, that he would be pleased to give me some of the love he had given him so that I could serve him better; but that if it were to his greater glory that I serve him with the coldness I presently found myself in, I would bless him for ever. From the Sacred Host I suddenly felt our Lord speak to me interiorly: "I will give you a share in his trials!" I answered: "May your divine will be done!" All at once the hand of the Lord came upon me with an overflowing of the spirit that reached into every part of my body, leaving me totally enkindled with his love.

When a few days had gone by I began to reflect on what our Lord had said to me and what the trials might be that were to come upon me. One day when I was not thinking

---

[1] 2 Cor. 12. 9.

[2] One of the most ardent preachers and spiritual writers of the seventeenth century. Died on 15 November 1617.

about it, as I returned to the monastery late, I found a messenger there from Sezze. He had been sent by my sister, Sister Mary Frances of Jesus, with quite a long letter. It told me that at Sezze a poor man of very good character had been murdered; the belief was that my brother and one of his cousins had done this. They had put my brother in prison and taken from him the little he owned. Though we suffered for a year and a half due to this I pass over it so as not to make this too long, but I had something here in which to exercise patience and charity toward others.

After I had received Holy Communion one morning I began to think of a servant of God who had many visions and revelations. I said to myself: "She is fortunate at having experienced our Lord that way!" The same Lord spoke to me immediately: "Am I not within you? Happiness consists in seeing and enjoying God!" From this I realized that substantial spirituality does not consist so much in having sensible experiences, such as visions and revelations, as in enjoying God within oneself through faith, in conformity with what Christ said in the Gospel: "Blessed are they that have not seen and have believed."[3]

When I was in Naples in 1662 in the monastery of St. Clare on the feast of St. Louis the Bishop,[4] August 19th, I thanked our Lord after Holy Communion for the many graces he had bestowed on this glorious saint who had merited them in giving up a kingdom to serve His Divine Majesty while wearing the rough and poor habit of St. Francis. Being a poor person, this is something I had not done. Our Lord comforted me as he said: "You also gave up a kingdom, your own will; and you should be consoled with this thought!" In a transport of spirit I replied by saying over and over: "I do not merit your love since I have done nothing; I have nothing for everything

---

[3] John 20. 29.

[4] St. Louis of Anjou, a Franciscan.

is yours. But if I had an infinite number of kingdoms I would give them up with Louis, just as I would give up one to come to you who are everything!"[5] These are a few of the results which God brings about as he speaks to our soul, inflaming us with fervent love, humility, detachment from desires of the world, and great regard for the divine law.

---

[5] This is the Dens meus et omnia (My God and my all) of the Seraphic Father St. Francis.

CHAPTER 65
FURTHER SPIRITUAL ELEVATIONS AND INTERIOR LOCUTIONS ENJOYED IN PRAYER

HEN I finished writing the book *Interior Journey* and had decided not to write anything else since it was very difficult for me, and besides I longed to live peacefully without wanting to be a further nuisance to the Friars, one night during my prayers in the chapel of St. Paul very near the main altar, I sensed our Lord near me, speaking and telling me to write the book called *Sacred Septenaries*. It is at this moment at the printers.[1] Our Lord told me briefly what it would contain and that it should have seven divisions for the seven days of the week, each division itself being sevenfold.

I could see that I would have an extremely difficult time with two of these groups, namely, the seven days of creation and the seven gifts of the Holy Spirit. As I realized this I said: "Lord, I will find the greatest difficulty with these two groups of seven." Our Lord answered: "Concerning these I will see that you have greater facility than in the others". He left me very contrite and resigned to the divine will.

Before starting to write I wished to get the opinion of my father confessor and of the Father Provincial who at that time was Father Barnabas of Palermo. Both gave me their blessing and commanded me to write the book. I was to rest assured that it was God's will.

I began writing on the last group of seven, the gifts of the Holy Spirit, and continued with very great ease because the same Holy Spirit illumined my mind. Then I wrote on the first group, and the same thing occurred. As I came to the fourth

---
[1] It was printed at Rome in 1666.

group which had to do with the seven journeys of Christ in his Passion, I thought this would be the easiest because I had meditated on it over so many years. It was just the opposite. An extraordinary mental block faced me. Each time I started a chapter I was like a senseless person. That is how our Lord humbled me at great cost for having relied too much on myself in the easy matters.

On the evening of the Feast of St. John the Evangelist I was to explain the last petition of the *Our Father*. First I prayed, recommending myself to the Father of lights. He deigned to comfort me. "Why are you afraid as long as I am with you?" My answer was: "Lord, I who am nothing am afraid to begin this part". O marvellous wonder of the power in God's word, and of his help to a soul! Just as soon as he spoke the darkness was dispelled, the fear fled and with a divine light I knew what I had to say about this last petition.

One night while praying with the other Friars in a chapel in St. Peter Montorio near the main altar, I experienced the bitterness that one feels at a time of spiritual dryness; and since my soul longed for the sensible enjoyment of its God I started to recite the verse of the Psalm, "As the hart panteth after the fountains of water; so my soul panteth after thee, O God!"[2] But as I saw that the aridity was growing more sensible and the absence of the Beloved greater, I began to recite in a conversational way a stanza from the canticle of St. Teresa:

> What life can any man enjoy
> when he remains apart from you?
>
> He can but suffer such a death
> than which there is no greater here.
>
> O piteous sufferer that I am!
>
> This my evil o'er which I weep:

---

[2] Psalm 41. 2.

I die because I do not die!³

In spirit I turned to our Lord to say: "O Lord, I want to love you!" Speaking in Latin he answered: "Keep my commandments for then you will love me fully".

One day as I was going to a monastery in Rome with the permission of Cardinal Ginetti,⁴ Vicar of Rome, to visit a sick nun, the Mother Abbess who was a great servant of God asked me to promise to intercede with our Lord for two favours: the return of the sick nun to health, and salvation for all the nuns living in that monastery. I promised her that I would do what I could. I visited the sick religious and prayed for her as I signed her with the relic of St. Ann. She regained her health from our Lord.

On returning to the monastery I began to pray for the spiritual health of all the nuns. Interiorly our Lord spoke to my soul and said that among those religious there were some hard-headed ones. Twice he left me after that remark and I was unable to know whether he had granted me the favour. I persevered in my petition, begging him a third time. Then His Divine Majesty deigned to grant the mercy of the salvation of all those religious, something that gave me immense joy.

From this occurrence I drew the lesson how displeasing to God is the arrogance and the disobedience of a religious towards a Superior, since our Lord was so hesitant in granting the salvation of those souls for love of whom he clothed himself in our flesh and underwent his passion and death!

In a city quite distant from Rome, where I was sent in obedience, a great crowd of people, especially of the nobility, had gathered because of the exposition there of the Blessed

---

[3] *Spiritual Works of St. Teresa*, Vol. 2, Venice 1739, p. 247.

[4] Marzio Ginetti (1585-1671), created cardinal by Urban VIII in 1626, was Bishop of Albano, then of Sabina and Porto, and Vicar of Rome under five popes.

Sacrament and the sermons that were being preached during an octave in the church attached to our monastery. When I saw the vanity of the women, how they came dressed very unbecomingly, I pitied them very much. With the eye of my soul I saw them as so many infernal monsters who vexed me extremely. I began praying very earnestly to God for their sakes, that with a ray of his light he would enable them to see the truth clearly. Interiorly I heard our Lord say to me: "These women hear my word and my doctrine every day", as if to point out that he desired his words in the Gospel to be a light that illumines. These people, however, were making little of it, valuing vanity more than the love of God.

Here I would like to tell of two cases I saw with my own eyes, to make us understand how displeasing vanity is to God.

One woman who had been educated in a convent was given to this vanity and, besides dressing immodestly, bathed every day in perfumed water. God punished her for this and for the bad example she was giving, by taking her husband away in death and sending on her a horrible sickness that covered with suppurating sores those members of her body through which she had been immodest. This even disfigured one of her eyes. Whereas she had formerly dressed so vainly and immodestly, she now had to clothe herself fully out of necessity.

The other case was of a woman whom I corrected charitably, asking her to dress properly, pointing out by some examples how much this displeased God, as well as that she was giving scandal. I promised I would pray for her if she did this. Seeing how obstinate her blindness made her I said with particular feeling that came from our Lord: "The time will come when you will have to dress properly!"

Because of a lawsuit not long after that, she lost all she possessed and became terribly sick. Since the courts had taken everything, even mattresses and clothing, she was reduced to using an abandoned straw bed, and for clothes she had to do with some dirty rags that had once been a sheet. When finally she sent for me I found her in the greatest misery. She was sorry for her sins and begged God to pardon her. Then she asked me out of charity to find her a blouse and a clean sheet, for the following day she was to receive Holy Communion.

I asked my companion what he thought about this. Because it was getting late and we were on the slope of Monte Cavallo, a great distance from our monastery of St. Peter in Montorio, he judged it would be better to go back home and not give the Superior reason to punish us for returning at night. I told him to have no fears about that. Every time we are ready to show charity our Lord will even permit the sun to stand still and not advance. O how wonderful is God! How much charity pleases him! We went to find a blouse, brought it to the woman and then returned to the monastery, and our Lord caused it to happen that we saw the sun in the very same position it had been when we left the sick person the first time. The next day I found sheets for her and another blouse, a modest one, with some other alms.

This is how God corrects and punishes sins of vanity in this life. It makes us think, too, of the next!

Chapter 66
Special Favours Received Through the Mystery of the Nativity

N the 22nd of August 1664, when I was at the monastery of St. Peter in Montorio I fell seriously ill with double malarial fever. To make me well I was put in the infirmary at St. Francis a Ripa. But the illness grew worse and it was accompanied by a frightful headache. Though I naturally felt a great repugnance to dying, still I began disposing myself for it as well as I could. In all this the hand of our Lord forestalled and transported me to himself so quickly and so graciously that wonderful things of God were revealed to me; the mind cannot grasp them and the tongue cannot describe them. In particular I heard within me the harmony of paradise that for its great sweetness almost took the soul from my body.

This lasted eight days and was like a pledge of the happiness the blessed enjoy. Though I longed for release from this prison because of the peace I was enjoying, our Lord still granted me such indifference that if my health could stand it I was not going to refuse the suffering, though I realized how much it would cost me; and if he thought it best to free me from the servitude of this flesh so as not to offend him further I asked that he would give me the grace of dying with a devotion like that of my Father St. Francis.

I still felt the misery and trial caused by the sickness. When the fever was at its worst my head ached so intensely that I did not know where to put it. Because of the headache I could not lie down; because of my weakness I could not sit up. To get relief I had to cry out at times. I turned to a painting at the other end of the room; it was our Lord on the cross, with his Mother and St. John. This was the room in winch Father Bartholomew of Salutio had died. I said: "O

Lord, O Jesus, help me because I cannot stand this any more! O Virgin Mary, O St. Ann, help me through your intercession!"

As I called out in this way to our Lord it seemed that he spoke to me from the cross and said: "Brother Charles, little one, you are lamenting a lot; look at me nailed to the cross! See my head, how it is crowned with thorns!" Sometimes I replied: "O Lord, this weak nature made of flesh which you gave me wants relief; forgive me for I do not know what I am doing!"

When I returned to the monastery of St. Peter in Montorio I had hardly begun to regain my strength when the furious demon of sensuality, like a lion loosed front his chains, tried to tear me apart spiritually; he made every effort to terrorize me with his roars so that in my fright I would give in to him. When I saw myself in this new conflict and recalled the peace I had enjoyed in that earthly paradise—that is what those few days of quiet were like, which our Lord had granted during my illness—I sighed: "O Lord, again I have gone back to battle! The struggle is great; help me!"

As the feast of my Father St. Francis approached, this demon of fierce sensuality attacked me with greater fury. For three days and nights he assaulted me continually, shooting different poisoned arrows to bring death to the soul in a body which for sheer weakness could barely stand on its feet. The third night the attack of the enemy was so intense that my wearied and sated nature began to rebel; it incited me to blaspheme the God who created me and to curse the day and hour of my birth. By abandoning myself to the divine will—the weapon servants of God use in battle—I bore this as well as I could in the higher faculties and made sure to keep my will firm, for I was determined to die a thousand times and to be buried in hell before offending so great a Lord from whom I had received benefits without number.

On the morning of the third day I went to confession so as

to receive Holy Communion during Mass that day. After the consecration all these temptations began to disappear. After I had received the most holy Body of our Lord, if I had all the tongues that are and will be I would not know how to tell of the compunction, the sorrow, and the consolation I felt within me. It seemed to me that a river of the heavenly dew of the Holy Spirit had gushed out in abundance over all my soul and that from this infusion of grace I had been transformed into God in another paradise filled with the songs of heavenly choirs.

I recalled the passage from St. Jerome in which he moaned and sighed in the desert, bitterly tempted day and night; and how after all those many afflictions he experienced a loving taste and longing while he looked up to heaven. Absorbed and caught up out of himself he thought he was among the angelic choirs and so he sang out joyfully: "Lord, we will run after thee to the odour of thy ointments!"[1] This is what the blessed Lord draws from temptations when we suffer them with patience.

In the year 1664 when I was putting up the Christmas crib and was almost finished, someone asked me what reward I thought I was going to receive for all that work. I said my reward would be whatever the blessed Lord would give me. After the Bambino had been placed in the crib that most holy night, I felt such divine love in my soul that I do not know if I ever had experienced any like it; and the weakness that at first seemed so bitter to me, now was changed into sweetness!

When the Bambino was to be carried in procession in the church of St. Peter Montorio, the day after Epiphany, 1663, there came over me an extraordinary elevation of spirit at that part of the function. While in it I besought our Lord to share the blessings he had bestowed on me with my fellow religious, and with all my brothers and sisters in Christ who profess our holy faith, begging him further in his goodness to

---

[1] Cant. 1.3.

grant me confirmation in grace so that I should never again offend him seriously.

Three times I heard our Lord say within me, speaking very clearly in Latin: "*Ego concedo tibi*; I grant you the favour you have asked!" Still, I did not give up living in very great fear, so as to guard myself from sin and the snares that are set for us in this life, and not abuse these great mercies of God, since we cannot be safe as long as we are not in the next life.

After I had received Holy Communion on the Thursday before the feast of the Epiphany, 3 January 1663, I felt a great desire to make a vow not to bear hatred for anyone, since several days previously I had fought an unusual battle with my passions which had excited me against my neighbour in this way. Sensing the great violence His Majesty was working in my soul and being conscious of my fickleness, I thought it over well and said to our Lord: "Every time Your Majesty allows these passions to rise against me, I will make the vow."

On the feast of Epiphany after Holy Communion, the violence was so great that I was unable to offer further resistance; so as far as human strength permitted I made the vow not to hate anyone voluntarily. Then that evening at the hour of Compline, when it was time to take the Bambino in procession from the crib, I begged him that, as he had urged me to make the vow, so he would grant me the grace never again to bear hatred for anyone and would repress what in this pertains so intimately to human nature. When I finished my prayer I understood our Lord saying interiorly to me: "I will bring it about that there will no longer be any hatred or disdain in your heart". At these words I was like one rapt in spirit in union with him. From then on I began with greater love than ever before to love everyone equally. In my soul I vividly grasped the truth that we are all children of one father who is God, and of one mother who is our holy Church; and in life eternal we will all live in one city, ruled by the same shepherd who is God, the source of all our good.

CHAPTER 67
STILL FURTHER SPIRITUAL ELEVATIONS DUE TO THE APPEARING OF SEVERAL SAINTS

INALLY we shall discuss some of the elevations, locutions and favours the great saints receive. As such close friends of God they want us to possess the good that is theirs and they do everything God commands them with the divine power he grants them. His Divine Majesty is pleased to have them aid us in our needs and he desires that we recommend ourselves to their intercession, as Holy Mother the Church teaches us.

On 9 March 1660, while praying before the painting of St. Teresa I asked her that, if our Lord was pleased to keep me on this earth, he would grant me the favour of never again offending him gravely as I had done in the past and of finishing the book entitled Sacred Septenaries which I actually started at his special command. As I stayed there quite absorbed in God I sensed the saint speaking to me in the depths of my soul: "What you have asked will be granted you."

On 28 July 1665, the feast of the martyrs Saints Nazarius, Celsus, and Victor Pope, our Lord appeared to me with St. Teresa. I begged a favour from His Divine Majesty for the religious of that saint who live in a monastery in Rome. It was their Mother Prioress who had recommended them to me with special insistence. Our Lord told me: "Let them stay united in my love for I will protect them for ever."

St. James of Alcala also appeared to me. He belongs to my Order of St. Francis and he urged me to pray to God for a woman who was very devoted to me; she wanted the child that was going to be born of her to be a son. I prayed for this many times and through the intercession of St. James our Lord deigned to grant this favour. At baptism the child was named Paul James, out of devotion to the Saint.

Not long before I became sick the last time, somewhat of an indisposition came over me as I was writing down in a book the account of my life and was just about bringing it to an end. It was a wearisome season since the sun was in Leo. Really I thought seriously I was going to become sick and die. The thought came to me to go to the church of St. Cecilia; there I prayed at her tomb with great affection and asked that, if it were for the greater glory of God, she would find the strength for me to finish the book. The saint spoke to me interiorly and said that I should be very sure that I would finish it, for our Lord had granted me this favour. A few days after that I became seriously ill and I was given up by the doctors; but then our Lord gave back my health, and thus was fulfilled everything the saint had revealed to me. Many things I do not now recall with certainty were made known to me through revelations.

When I came to the chapter about our Lord's prayer in the garden, as I was writing the *Discourses on the Passion of Christ*, such a mental dullness settled over me that I was all for leaving the work unfinished, so bound was I by human feebleness. Still I had recourse to prayer. While praying one night before the most Blessed Sacrament I recommended myself with special devotion to St. John the Evangelist, asking him to help me before our Lord. It pleased His Divine Majesty to have this saint come to me in a spiritual apparition. He spoke just these few words: "Do not leave me", and then disappeared. From this I understood that I should not have put aside his Gospel, the Gospel he had drunk from the fountain of the Divinity. I went back again to write and it all turned out easily.

Chapter 68
The Particular Virtues and Exercises the Saint Practised

MONG the virtues that I liked very much, one was holy obedience. Right up to this moment I have always allowed myself to be carried along in my vocation by this holy virtue, and with it I hope to finish as I began. I made special efforts not to deviate from it. I never looked for a particular place or room, or tried to wring a permission from my superior. I can truly say it was in this virtue that I found God in the peace of my soul.

When I happened to give advice to people on anything relating to this virtue I told them there was no need for me to give them any other counsel or for them to say any special prayers, but to obey promptly and simply, since our superiors are the interpreters of the divine will, fulfilled in us through obedience.

Other interior exercises which I practised were purity of soul and conformity to the divine will. As regards the first, I exercised continual diligence in watching over the five senses that are like doors of the soul. Through them enter enemies to sully our soul and the purity of our heart with various thoughts. I fled every occasion of sin; I never felt secure, but always feared my frailty.

I made a lot of this exercise as of something on which depends the truest and most intimate union of our soul with God and makes its works meritorious. When someone came and asked me to point out an exercise or devotion that would be more pleasing to God, I taught them this purity of soul. "Take the best care you can", I told them, "to keep your soul far from sin, for then you will please God since you will be united to him through grace. Also, while you are fighting against your vices, use the exercise of the love of God."¹

I likewise practised conformity to the divine will in those matters that go against our senses, taking care to quiet my intellect with Christian reason. Through this holy exercise I disposed my soul to find peace in the midst of the tumult and conflicts of this life. I knew I could not find it any other way. To keep myself aware of these good resolutions during manual work I said some ejaculations if I could not keep my mind recollected in God.

Under obedience I occasionally left the monastery. Because I knew how great the dangers are which can be met outside, I made the sign of the cross as I went out of the door and recited most of the Psalm which starts with the words, "Set before me for a law the way of thy justifications, O Lord: and I will always seek after it."²

I commended myself to the most Blessed Virgin who guarded me from all evil and favoured me in the work of obedience and piety in which I was engaged. To her I said some prayers like the *Sub tuum praesidium*, the *Dignare me laudare te*,³ and her Litany. I speak the truth that I received

---

[1] Purity of soul, or tenderness of conscience in avoiding the slightest sin and in carrying out the lightest obligation, is the foundation of true virtue and of genuine holiness. St. Thomas Aquinas says that this habitual disposition is the sign of perfect and heroic love of God.

[2] Psalm 118. 33.

[3] The *Sub tuum praesidium* is a prayer from the Roman Breviary: "We fly to thy patronage, O holy Mother of God; despise not thou our petitions in our necessities, but deliver us always from all dangers, O glorious and Blessed Virgin." At the hour of death a plenary indulgence can be gained by those who have said this prayer frequently in life, after having confessed their sins and received Holy Communion, or at least devoutly invoked the most holy name of Jesus with contrition for their sins. Cf. the Raccolta, 1952, pp. 234 and 235.

The *Dignare me laudare te* is also from the Roman Breviary. "Vouchsafe that I may praise thee, O Sacred Virgin. Give me strength against thine enemies." A plenary indulgence can be gained on the usual conditions, if this invocation is repeated daily for a month. Cf. the *Raccolta*, 1952, pp.

special assistance from the Virgin most holy in what I was then doing. She helped me in cases of great urgency.

I offered my obedience to our Lord in memory of the obedience he showed to his eternal Father.

It was a great pleasure for me to stay before the most holy Sacrament of the Altar and though I could not use my intellect in the consideration of so exalted a mystery,[4] I still in a definite way experienced the presence of God. In myself I reflected this way: if a rock which of its very nature is hard and cold becomes warm by being out in the sun, I hope that as I remain before our Lord in patient perseverance in spite of stone-like dryness, the time will come when he will look at me and will warm my heart by setting it on fire with his divine love, as he casts a ray of his light into my heart. This is what happened quickly. My spirit was raised to union with God; he revealed to me some of the secret needs of my fellow men while urging me to pray earnestly for them all, and to ask for three favours for myself after the observance of the divine law and the holy Rule. They were: light by which to know him, fear so as not to offend him, and love through which to love him.[5]

It seems to me that staying with us on the altar in the mystery of the Holy Eucharist our Lord wanted to empty out into our souls all the streams of his love and all the fountains of his grace. Since he is the shepherd of life eternal he gives himself as food to us, his sheep. There is no more that he can give us. It was my delight to frequent this most divine

---

209 and 210. [*Translator.*]

[4] The Saint is hinting at the difficulty he experienced at different times in his life in meditating according to the method commonly taught by spiritual directors, the use of the three faculties of the soul. In him this difficulty stemmed either from aridity or from his having been granted a higher degree of prayer (infused contemplation).

[5] These three graces are so fundamental and important as to contain every other grace and benefit.

Sacrament daily, for my soul was then feeding on its true food, to keep itself in union with him.

If in other spiritual exercises we work so as to catch some spirit of devotion, with the reception of our Lord's Body the soul is united to God sweetly and without labour in an exalted and divine way. In a union that is true and real, we are transformed into him. Drinking of the divine essence in that sea one takes into oneself all that one is ever able to receive, for in God all things are found.

Because of the intense hunger I had at times for this food of life, to satisfy myself I would have gone to Communion many times a morning if this had been allowed! Out of the respect I bore for this most Holy Sacrament I greatly revered priests as those who administer it to us.

I always leaned towards charity to the sick and to my neighbour; this was natural to me. I consoled them and when they were seriously sick I did not tell them right away about death but I gradually prepared them by saying they should always be prepared with the sacraments of the Church, for life and death were in the hands of our Lord. I told them that here on earth we always have the opportunity of good works and that the prayer of the sick person is his patience and his acceptance of the sickness for the love of Jesus Christ. This has great worth when it is motivated by the imitation of how much he suffered for us, and by penance for our sins.

When there were situations that could endanger someone's salvation, I offered to do something special as I did two or three times in the matter of child-birth. Once I offered our Lord to stay in purgatory thirty-three years, and another time seven, to gain graces for those concerned. For one person I would have remained there till the day of judgment.

For their greater advancement I advised religious, both men and women, to give all care and attention after the commandments of God to the pure observance of their rules and constitutions, for these are the principal means of advancing in perfection towards the conquest of the promised kingdom of heaven. Non-observance made me extremely sad and caused me intense grief because of the harm that comes to religion and the spiritual danger of those who live in it badly.

After I had cautioned young men and women who came to me for advice about a religious vocation to think carefully whether this calling was really from God, I urged them to apply for admission where the rule was observed, and I told them they would be placing their salvation in danger were they to go where it is not kept.

The poor prostitutes, for whom I had great compassion since they were in disfavour with God, slaves of sin and of the devil, I charitably exhorted not to stay in their evil ways. I recalled to them frightening examples and the eternity of punishment in the next life; besides, I told them that, as far as they could, they were not to give up good works, such as going to Mass every day, fasting on Saturdays out of devotion to our Lady, with the hope that some day our Lord would free them from so many miseries.

Mothers who had marriageable daughters I counselled to keep them safe so that they would not fall into the danger of offending God, because the perverse use many snares to catch these simple creatures.

In fine, I longed for the salvation of all persons and I would not have passed over doing anything for them since we are all children of one father who is God our Saviour, and of one mother who is our holy Mother the Church. I wish everyone had this desire for the sake of the union and the exercise of fraternal love, by which we are united in Christ as in our head, that we may one day reign with Him.[6] Amen.

---

[6] As in the case of every saint his heart also was full of the most ardent apostolic zeal for the salvation of souls and the spread of the kingdom of God.

Epilogue

EAR Father,[7] I have carried out the holy obedience you gave me. I have written as much as I could recall with certainty, in order that after the glory of God my fellow men may profit from it. Look at it carefully, correct it, and take away everything that does not seem good to you and cannot help souls. This is the only point you need attend to, for they have been redeemed with the most Precious Blood of Jesus Christ our Saviour. Living and dead I submit myself to the correction of our holy Mother the Church.

Glory be to God the Father, to God the Son, and to God the Holy Spirit, three Persons, one only God, united in one only divinity, who lives and reigns for ever and ever. Amen.

* * * * *

This work was begun in 1661 and completed on 15 August 1665, the day when our holy Mother the Church celebrates the feast of the Assumption into heaven of the most holy Mother of God. I was fifty-two years of age and thirty years in religion.[8] Praised be God.

---

[7] He is addressing his confessor, Father Anthony of Aquila, who had commanded the writing of this autobiography.

[8] In a special brochure the Saint described the visit he made in 1666, in the interests of Cardinal Cesare Facchinetti, to the shrines of Loreto, Assisi, and La Verna. This brought the account of his life up to the third year before his death.
In 1668 Pope Clement IX sent him to San Severino with several prelates on the occasion of the identification of the body of a holy woman, a servant of God, and then to Montefalco, there to try the spirit of a nun. The following year, 1669, Cardinal Facchinetti again summoned him to his diocese of Spoleto. From there he was to have gone to Venice according to the permission which the Princess Borghese had obtained from the Pope, but at Tolentino the critical condition of his health forced

him to turn back. He died at Rome, as he had very often clearly predicted, on 6 January 1670.

The process of his beatification was begun almost immediately. Clement XIV declared his virtues heroic on 18 June 1772, and on 1 October 1882, Leo XIII beatified him.

In 1946 the cause of his canonization was started. On 7 January 1958, Pope Pius XII approved the two miracles that are required, but due to his death in October of that year, his successor John XXIII delayed the canonization till the following year. It took place on 12 April 1959.

POSTSCRIPT
BY FR SEVERINO GORI, O.F.M.

N the first days of December 1669, Pope Clement IX lay seriously ill. He asked that Brother Charles come to visit him. The Brother was not very well either, but they brought him on a chair to the Vatican from St. Francis a Ripa.

"Holy Father, how are you?" asked the humble lay-brother. "As well as God wants me to be", answered the Pope, for he had no illusions about the seriousness of his illness.

Among those in the room was Cardinal Rospigliosi. Brother Charles requested His Eminence to bless the Supreme Pontiff with the relic he always carried with him. He handed it to the cardinal. But the Vicar of Jesus Christ desired instead to be blessed by the poor lay-brother with the relic. He obeyed. Then it was time to leave.

"Brother Charles, when shall we see each other again?" "Most Holy Father, on the feast of the Epiphany, at the feet of the Child Jesus."

Everyone present interpreted these words as meaning that the Supreme Pontiff would become well; instead, however, he died on the 9th of that same month.

Throughout Rome there was great discussion about this prophecy of Brother Charles which had not been fulfilled. On 31 December, the Brother was forced to bed because of serious pleurisy. All the known remedies were useless.

"This time you will not be praised for curing me", he told the doctor. To others he had even more clearly predicted his approaching death.

On 6 January 1670, the feast of the Epiphany, after having received on his knees the Sacrament he loved so ardently, consoled, too, by an apparition of our Lord accompanied by his Blessed Mother, angels and saints, the soul of Brother Charles of Sezze hastened to heaven, to the beatific vision. The prophecy of his meeting with Clement IX was fulfilled to the letter.

When his death became known, one might say that all Rome converged on St. Francis a Ripa to venerate the holy remains. To satisfy the devotion of all who desired a relic it was necessary to put a habit on his body nine times.

The general excitement went beyond bounds when it was learned that God was working a prodigy on the body of Brother Charles after his death. At the place of the wound of love (cf. Chapter 51) there began to appear a kind of nail formed from what appeared to be cartilage. As people watched, this nail grew from hour to hour and took the shape of a cross. A commission of doctors studied this phenomenon and judged it supernatural. This was one of the miracles recognized and approved by the Sacred Congregation of Rites for the beatification of Brother Charles in 1882. On that occasion the body, after various transfers, came to rest finally in the restored Chapel of St. Michael the Archangel in the church of St. Francis a Ripa.

St. Charles of Sezze unites and remarkably harmonizes human and supernatural elements in a remarkable attainment of the Franciscan ideal.

Though a humble peasant, yet gifted by nature with a simple and forceful character, rich in balance and initiative, he acquired with the help of supernatural favours such prudence and gentleness of ways that one would have thought him "the son of a prince", as Cardinal Donghi expressed himself to Father Angelus of Naro, a close friend of St. Charles.

In imitation of St. Francis and the two lay-brother saints of the Franciscan Order, Paschal Baylon and Salvator of Horta, he considered himself unworthy to become a priest. But God enriched him with such singular mystical gifts, joined to the heroic practice of the virtues, that he became an outstanding apostle through his humble and hidden life, no less than other lay-brothers who had distinguished themselves for their zeal in both the home and foreign missions.

In the springtime of holiness which at that time flourished among those who were the most faithful to the ideals of St. Francis (in the Roman Province alone there were seventy-five contemporaries of St. Charles who died with a reputation for heroic virtue) he shone with chastity and love. While some of his brethren were shedding their blood in defence of the faith of Jesus Christ, Brother Charles, "the martyr of obedience" gained a no less glorious victory.

To the Counter-Reformation through which Catholics of his day were living, this poor lay-brother brought the valuable weight of his great holiness and extraordinary writings. He became almost an idol of the Roman aristocracy, of the highest prelates of the Church, and of the Supreme Pontiffs themselves, including Cardinal Odescalchi, who became Blessed Innocent XI. By word and example he recalled to all the need of pursuing only that which is eternal.

Although St. Charles was quite unlettered, still through the ever increasing influence of the Holy Spirit he wrote books which, in number, size and content, make him one of the greatest mystical writers of the Church, ranking with St. John of the Cross and St. Teresa of Avila. In his own times this mystical doctrine, illustrated in this Autobiography and the booklets published on the occasion of his canonization, served as a powerful counterweight to fatal Quietism and Jansenism.

Besides, his doctrine was lived: "Seldom", wrote Inigo Giordani, "does one find such lofty thoughts expressed more humbly, and therefore brought within the grasp of everyone. One can say that they follow the essential lines of the great Carmelite and Dominican mystical theologies, filtered through a Franciscan humility and simplicity: the mysticism of a Bonaventure simplified by a cook of St. Francis."

APPENDIX I
CHRONOLOGY OF THE LIFE OF ST. CHARLES

1613	Birth and baptism.
1635	Reception of the Franciscan habit in the monastery of Nazzano; year of novitiate there.
1636	Profession of vows.
1636-37	Assignment to the monastery of St. Mary Seconda at Morlupo.
1637-38	Transfer to the monastery of St. Mary of Grace at Ponticelli (near Rieti).
1638-1640	Assignment to the monastery of St. Francis in Palestrina.
1640	Stay of about two months in the monastery of St. John Baptist in Piglio (near Frosinone).
1640-1642	Assignment to the monastery of St. Peter the Apostle in Carpineto (birthplace and home of Pope Leo XIII).
1642-1643	Stay of a few months in the hermitage of Castel Gandolfo.
1643-1646	Return to St. Peter the Apostle in Carpineto. There he began to write spiritual books.
1646-1650	Transfer to the monastery of St. Peter in Montorio at Rome. Attending Mass in the church of St. Joseph at Capo le Case while on the quest in the City, he received the wound of love from the Sacred Host (1648). He began writing the *Trattato delle tre vie* (1649).
1650	Assignment to the monastery of St. Francis a Ripa at Rome, where he completed the *Trattato*.
1651-1652	Return to St. Peter in Montorio where the Discorsi sulla Passione was written.
1653	Transfer to St. Francis a Ripa. There he began the *Cammino interno*.
1653-1667	Reassignment to St. Peter in Montorio. There he completed the *Cammino interno* (1658), wrote the *Settenari sacri* (1660-1662) and the *Grandezze delle divine misericordie* (autobiography, from 1661 to 1665), and began the *Esemplare del cristiano* (1666).
1667-1670	At St. Francis a Ripa he continued the *Esemplare del cristiano*.
1670	Died at St. Francis a Ripa. There was verified on his

	body the phenomenon of a large stigma.
1772	Pope Clement XIV approved his heroic virtues.
1882	Beatified by Pope Leo XIII.
1946	Cause of his canonization was taken up.
1958	Pope Pius XII approved the two necessary miracles.
1959	Canonization by Pope John XXIII, April 12.

APPENDIX II
WORKS WRITTEN BY ST. CHARLES OF SEZZE

1. ALREADY PUBLISHED

Trattalo delle tre vie della meditazione e stati della santa contemplazione, Rome, three editions, 1654, 1664, 1742.

After speaking of ordinary meditation suitable for anyone, he masterfully describes the various degrees of infused contemplation as he himself had experienced them.

Canti spirituali, Rome, 1654 and 1664.

Eighteen songs written on various themes and in different metres.

Cammino interno dell'anima, Rome, 1664.

A commentary on the Canti spirituali. Here he rises to the highest mysticism in a detailed and, at times, original manner.

Settenari sacri, Rome, 1666.

This is a course of meditations (two for each day) arranged in series of sevens, for seven weeks.

Esercizio devoto per la novena di Nostro Signore, Rome, 1666.

Considerations and prayers for the novena in preparation for the feast of Christmas.

Esercizio devoto per la novena della SS. Vergine Maria, Rome, 1666.

Considerations and prayers for the novena in preparation for the feast of the Nativity of the Blessed Virgin Mary, September 8.

APPENDIX II

2. NOT PUBLISHED

Le grandezze delle misericordie di Dio in un' anima aiutata dalla grazia divina.

This is his very interesting autobiography, of which the present volume is an abridgement and carries the subtitle *I Fioretti di Frate Carlo*. The critical edition is in preparation.

Esemplare del cristiano.

The life of our Lord Jesus Christ according to the Gospel accounts. This is the Saint's last work, the largest and the most important.

Discorsi sulla Passione di nostro Signore Gesù Cristo.

Many minor works.

Appendix III
Personages Who Had a Great Esteem for St. Charles and Sought His Help

POPES
Innocent X (Giovanni Battista Pamphili), 1644-1655
Alexander VII (Fabio Chigi), 1655-1667
Clement IX (Giulio Rospigliosi), 1667-1669

CARDINALS

Gianstefano Donghi (d. 1669)	Cesare Facchinetti (d. 1683)
Francesco Barberini (d. 1679)	Benedetto Odescalchi (later Pope
Celio Piccolomini (d. 1681)	Innocent XI; d. 1689)
Michelangelo Ricci (d. 1682)	Carlo Barberini (d. 1704)

NOBLE FAMILIES

Altemps	Ludovisi
Altieri	Muti-Papazzuri
Barberini	Orsini
Boncompagni	Paluzzi
Borghese	Pamphili
Caetani	Rospigliosi
Cibo	Salviati
Colonna	

APPENDIX IV
SAINTS CONTEMPORARY WITH ST. CHARLES

St. Francis Regis, 1597-1640
St. Peter Fourier, 1565-1640
St. Hyacintha Mariscotti, 1585-1640
St. Jane Frances de Chantal, 1572-1641
St. Andrew Bobola, 1591-1657
St. Vincent de Paul, 1581-1660
St. Louise de Marillac, 1591-1660
St. Joseph of Cupertino, 1603-1663
St. John Eudes, 1601-1680
St. Margaret Mary Alacoque, 1647-1690
St. Veronica Giuliani, 1660-1721
St. Pacificus of San Severino, 1653-1721
St. John Joseph of the Cross, 1654-1734

BIBLIOGRAPHY

Father Angelo Da Naro, *Memorie intorno a fra Carlo da Sezze*, a manuscript in the General Postulation of the Order of Friars Minor, Rome, catalogued J 5 12; Vita di fra Carlo di Sezze, three manuscript volumes in the General Postulation of the Order of Friars Minor, Rome, catalogued J 5 23; J 5 23bis; J 5 24.

Father Benedetto Mazzara Da Sulmona and Father Pietro Antonio da Venezia, *Leggendario Francescano*, twelve volumes, Venice, 1721-1722, vol. 1, 106-113.

Father Anton Maria Da Vicenza, *Vita del B. Carlo da Sezze*, Venice, 1881.

Father Jacques Heerinckx, O.F.M., *Les écrits du B. Charles de Sezze*, in the *Archivum Franciscanum Historicum*, vol. 28 (1935), pp. 324-334; vol. 29 (1936), pp. 55-78; Ariditas spiritualis secundum B. Carolum a Setia, in *Antonianum*, vol. 11 (1936), pp. 319-350; *Charles de Sezze* (Bienheureux) in the *Dictionnaire de Spiritualité*, Paris, 1953, II, 701a-703a.

Giovanni Battista Carissimo, *Il B. Carlo da Sezze e l'Eucaristia, in Numero unico del Congresso Interdiocesano Eucaristico di Terracina, Sezze e Priverno*, 1937.

Ippolito Rotoli, *Itinerario mistico del B. Carlo da Sezze*, Rome, 1943.

Father Severino Gori, O.F.M., *Il Beato Carlo da Sezze*, Rome, 1955; *Scintille Serafiche, raccolta di massime e pensieri del B. Carlo da Sezze*, Rome, 1957.

Father Vincenzo Venditti, *San Carlo da Sezze*, Turin, 1958.

Raphael Brown, *The Wounded Heart*, Franciscan Herald Press, Chicago, 1960.

Vita Minorum, a special number (March-April) on the occasion of the canonization of St. Charles, Venice, 1959, vol. 30.

www.ingramcontent.com/pod-product-compliance
Lightning Source LLC
Chambersburg PA
CBHW010824070526
44583CB00022B/2924